Alchemy of The Human Spirit
A guide to human transition into the New Age

Kryon
Book III

International Comments...

"I'm not sure why I'm writing or what I'm looking for, but a friend of mine told me I had to get your material... whatever the material is. I am the owner/manager of Iceland's only Metaphysical book and gift shop. I am also building a spiritual center outside Reykjavik."

G B
Reykjavik, Iceland

"AN OPEN LETTER TO ALL KRYON READERS: I want to thank you (and people of like mind) for your thoughts and prayers regarding this troubled part of the world. The political situation is still far from stable. Unfortunately matters with North Korea are far from resolved. I'm sure we all would benefit from your continued attentions. I hope you (Kryon group) continue to assist in whatever way you feel prompted to."

A P
South Korea

"Thank you for *Kryon The End Times*. I enjoyed it thoroughly! I am a practising Naturopath and Biomagnetic therapist (healing with magnets). I have found the negative (north pole) great in wiping out viruses! Looking forward to reading your next book."

D M H
Australia

"I was looking at books about Reiki, and didn't even think of the Kryon Writings, when all of a sudden I saw both books standing in the bookcase. There wasn't a doubt in my mind, and I had to buy those books. So I did. I started to read and I just couldn't stop. I had to cry several times while reading book one, something that almost never happens. It felt like I was reading about things I somehow already knew, and now somebody had written it down! I want to thank you for writing the books, they've enriched my life, and I'm looking forward to hearing from you. Needless to say I have changed a great deal since this all happened."

A C V
The Netherlands

International Comments...

"Somebody brought the Kryon books to Germany and somehow they landed in my hands. I had stopped reading books a while back, but the Kryon books gave me a key to USE the things humans were told by the Ken Carey books or by the knowledge of Rudolf Steiner and Tesla or the latest by Solara. The Kryon energy completes this series offered by the Universe by now telling us direct simple ways of using it. I love its clarity and joy."

K P
Frankfurt, Germany

"My life did change incredibly after the neutral implant. It was not at all a pleasant experience, but I got through it in a relatively short amount of time. We are totally delighted to share the Kryon teachings in our work groups. It is time to apply the knowledge we all carry within, and we need to be reminded of it."

A B
Nelson, New Zeland

"My name is D. P. I am a co-owner of a magazine called *The Piramid*. In the last issue of our magazine, which is the only futuristic New Age magazine in Croatia, I wrote about some new movements and devoted special attention to Kryon. In the meantime, I have gotten through Kryon I and Kryon II, and like them very, very much!"

D P
Croatia (see page 338)

"I would like to thank you for the outstanding and impacting knowledge you have been able to convey to us. The Kryon messages and your personal explanations are so clear, complete and consistent that I can't imagine any better way to guide those who are already on the path. My gratitude to Kryon and to you is enhanced by the fact of being myself a Jewish-Israeli businessman, deeply involved in spiritual development through personal and group work."

A D
Israel

alchemy *n.*

1. A medieval chemical philosophy having as its asserted aims the transmutation of base metals into gold, the discovery of the panacea, and the preparation of the elixir of longevity.
2. A seemingly magical power or process of transmuting.
   – **alchemical** or **alchemic** *adj.*

Alchemy of The Human Spirit
A guide to human transition into the New Age
Kryon Book III

The Kryon Writings, Inc.

Publisher:
422
1155 Camino Del Mar
Del Mar, California 92014
[www.kryon.com]

Kryon books and tapes can be purchased in
retail stores, or by phone. Credit cards welcome.
(800) 352-6657 or EMAIL <kryonbooks@aol.com>

Written by Lee Carroll
Proofing/editing by Luana Ewing
Copyright © 1995 - Lee Carroll
Printed in the United States of America
First Edition - First Printing - October 1995
Second Printing - February 1996 - Revised
Third Printing - April 1996
Fourth Printing - May 1997 - Revised
Fifth Printing - December 1998
Sixth Printing - July 1999
Seventh Printing - July 2000

ISBN# 0-9636304-8-2 : $14.00

Table of Contents

continued...

Table of Contents... continued

Thanks!

From Jan and Lee:

Every book has a place where the author thanks those who helped. You usually look at the list and recognize none of the names, and this page may be no different for you. Be aware, however, that those helping with the Kryon work are touching thousands of lives worldwide. It is no accident that these people are involved. Take a moment to celebrate these names, and feel the energy associated with them. Each of the 18 has a cosmic contract to be on page 7 of this book!

Garret Annofsky
Gretchen Aurand
Greg Aurand
Susan Baumann
Karen La Chance
Roger La Chance
Norma Delaney
Barbra Dillenger
Jocelyn Eastland
Janie Emerson
Luana Ewing
Joel Heathcote
Geoffrey A. Hoppe
Ka-Sandra Love
Michael Makay
Petra Mantz
Trish McCabe
Carol Linda Vogt

The Journey Home

Kryon Book Five

A channelled novel!

This is the book that has created "The Journey Home Retreats," held in Colorado twice a year. These retreats take 50 attendees and walk them through the journey of Michael Thomas, as presented in this channelled novel. Perhaps the most profound of all the Kryon books, sacred messages hide in metaphor after metaphor...

■ *Also available unabridged on tape, read by Lee Carroll*

"The Journey Home is the latest work from one of this reviewers favorite authors. It is also his best. Lee Carroll has given us a well-written book that flows like a mighty river. And that river takes us to places like truth, hope, destiny, awareness, and home!"

■ **Richard Fuller, Senior Editor**
Metaphysical Reviews

Published by Hay House • ISBN 1-56170-552-7 • $11.95

Books and tapes can be purchased in retail stores, or by phone
~ Credit cards welcome ~

1-800-352-6657 - <kryonbooks@aol.com>

Preface

From the Writer

Kryon Channeling

Alchemy of The Human Spirit
Kryon Book III

From the writer...

Well, here we are in book three already! It seems that it was only a few months ago that I was cautiously standing on the brink of reason, about to launch strange and weird writings from "beyond." The rest is history.

The success of the Kryon books has astounded me. Tens of thousands of books "out there" on the planet. Hundreds of letters a month... seminars all over the world... meeting famous performers that I have admired for years who are now Kryon readers... and offers to join, and to be, and to go. All of this, and Kryon says to me: "Never stray from the admonitions. Remember that Kryon speaks to the hearts and minds of humanity one at a time. You are one, and so are they." What this means to me is obvious. My channeling admonitions are listed later in the book for you to see. They are the postulates or axioms of the Kryon work for me. This means clearly that my "oneness" is identical to all others. "Be still and do the work, and don't look around too much for it will be distracting." My contract is no grander than yours, whoever you are reading this. Each of us has agreed to some kind of action before we got here. The challenge is to clear ourselves to the degree that we can find this hidden quest and implement it. Since we are each part of the whole, so to speak, some of you will recognize Kryon as family, and not an entity to follow, or to worship, or to depend on for power or peace.

I am grateful to all those of you who have read the Kryon books in this series, and listened to the tapes, and also to the many who have traveled to the seminars to sit within the Kryon energy and soak in the love. Now you know what I look like, sound like, and you know more about who I am as a human. I can't hide anymore within the anonymity I enjoyed so few months ago (it seems). My contract for the planet was Kryon. My contract for myself was walking into the fear of ridicule, thereby potentially bringing the loss of friends, colleagues and family. Indeed this work on myself is still ongoing, and there is still discovery around applying the principles I am channeling to my everyday existence. Kryon wants me to "live" the standards that I am giving out to you so that I will be able to feel what it is like. I suppose that's only fair.

At last it is also well known that my wife Jan Tober is the other half of the Kryon work. Most don't get to see this except those in the seminars. The seminars are a venue where I get to explain how she had the patience to wait nine years through my unbelief for me to finally arrive logically at decisions about the intangible... and to accept my contract. She is responsible, therefore, for my seeing the connection to Kryon. Because she saw it coming for years (and knew better than to tell me), she looked for opportunities for it to present itself to me in a way that I would accept. It's Jan who took me to the two readers (both traveling through my town) who three years apart called the name of Kryon in session and told me of my quest – which I did not believe even then! Finally I started opening up slowly to something Jan knew all along. As I explain in seminar, this channel doesn't just bring his wife along; he brings the other half of the work. Jan and I always present Kryon *together*. I have yet to do a seminar or a book signing without her. It's true that I channel and write the books by myself, but her energy propels everything forward. I'm the engine and she represents the wheels – and sometimes the horn too! Our vehicle is a bonded partnership in love and in the work of Spirit. We enjoy telling people what we have learned as a couple, for we believe that the information is valuable in the new energy, and applicable to every kind of love partnership. As you continue this book, realize that all the live channelings you read were done with Jan physically at my side. This is important for the male/female balance.

This book is similar in format to the last one, in that the question and answer configuration is again used a great deal. Also I get to talk a bit more, since Kryon wants you to have my perspective as a human for insight into the words and meanings of Spirit. Since the last book I now have had hundreds of hours of experience with humans in transition. This has given me far greater wisdom as to the interpretations of the Kryon messages, and how they apply to everyday life.

The word *alchemy* is used to paint a picture of what Spirit would have you see around the new energy, as applied to your life. We are in a new spiritual paradigm now. (The word *paradigm* is becoming New Age jargon meaning "pattern" or "model." It also means "the way things work" in the context of this book.) The strength of the magic connotation of *alchemy* is on purpose, and so is the firm idea of transmutation. Kryon speaks of the urgency of our time (more on that later). He also speaks of new human empowerment, and says that we all metaphorically "stood in line" to be here on the planet at this particular time! Can we really become different? Can we actually create our own reality, or heal ourselves? ABSOLUTELY!

Dear reader, I invite you to travel these pages with me within the comfort of your own eyes and your own timing. As you read, realize that the entire purpose of publishing this work is to give you information that will translate into empowerment **for yourself**. Nothing to join, nothing to contribute to, no doctrine to commit to... and no spiritual penalty for putting this book down. The Kryon message is presented in the purest love form I have ever experienced. Those of you who know what I mean will find the same energy here that you found in Kryon Book One and in Kryon Book Two. The reason is simple. It is Spirit speaking to you as an equal, and the love transmitted will have the same energy today as it did when the planet was formed. The energy is pure, familiar and non-threatening. If the feeling reminds you of home, then you really have a grasp on the truth of who you are!

Chapter One

Human Alchemy

Human Alchemy
Chapter One

Greetings! I am Kryon of magnetic service. At this very moment each of you finds yourself in an interesting situation. It is no accident that these words are finding their way into your minds and into your spirit, for all of you are in a mode of discovery. Even since my first communication to you several years ago, your energy has shifted remarkably! You now find yourselves deep in the midst of transition at the highest levels, and some of you are disturbed by something so grand.

I will not begin this new series of publications without telling you again how much you are honored. As you read these words, please understand a few things: (1) My word "you" refers to the entity whose eyes are reading this sentence. (2) I know who you are. (3) It is not accidental that we are having this communication.

When I tell you, dear one, that I know who you are, I mean it in the most peaceful sense imaginable. Just as a dear friend looks carefully at a crowd and recognizes a beloved partner, so I see you now and know your name. You are known to me individually because we have met before. There is no entity on this planet who has not seen me or has not participated in the ceremony of my energy from the Great Central Sun. How can this be? you might ask... for there is a sea of entities on this planet. Billions of them! I say to you that there are far fewer of you than there are stars, and I know of all the stars. Your concept of serial communication and numbers limits your ability to understand how I can give you all my attention at this moment. The "now time frame" that exists for a universal entity such as myself gives me the ability to sit opposite you and take my time as I honor your valuable entity and give you advice in love.

Each of you has been selected for your time here. Yes, even the ones who are dying of the diseases of the forest, and the ones dying from the diseases of war. You didn't just volunteer for this duty; you actively petitioned for it, and then planned the contract that you now carry. It might seem odd that some would be selected to be here just to die. If you wonder at that, then you do not see the overview of the play that you are in, or the importance of your agreed part in it. The play that I speak of is the one that places you on the planet as an all powerful entity selected among countless others to participate in the grand event of becoming human, and then having all that you are hidden from you! In addition you are given the overlay of not even recognizing your mission, or your brothers and sisters. Again I tell you that it is with great honor that I view you in lesson now on the planet. Here you sit reading the words of the Kryon. You hunger for Spiritual information for you know something is different on Earth. You are feeling urgency and unrest and don't know why. You look for some great sign, or long for God to come to your side and give you comfort. All this, and because of the duality of humanism you don't recognize your power, or who you really are.

The truth is that you sit before your **servant** Kryon! My partner bursts to give you the reality of who you are. I circle you with energy and love, for I know exactly what you have been through for your entire life. You do not yet recognize your empowerment or your potential, when I already see the greatness. You do not know who you are, and I see your incredible lineage. If you know how things work, and have read my past communications to you, then you also know that you have had many incarnations in the Universe. This is your service and your group. Therefore your lineage is awesome, and it dwarfs anything that most of us have as our colors.

Many times in this book you will see transcriptions of my words to you in live channelings as my partner fulfilled his contract to communicate the Kryon over your great planet. Some of the messages will seem similar as I repeatedly speak to many different individuals about how I honor them. You will also hear me speak about your colors. Let me explain this again more clearly.

When I first arrived, I requested that my partner try to represent the look of the publication you are reading with some sense of changing color. The color is never the same as you look at the Kryon name on the book. It changes depending on how you look at it; and if you move, the colors change. Each of us has this exact attribute as an entity of the Universe. Our shape and our colors tell those around us our "names" and our service. In addition the colors tell the others where we have been and what we have done. The Kryon has a splendid shape and many colors, and some of you have even seen them.* They tell of my service to the Universe, and of the various places I have been doing the work that I specialize in. My underlying color is what you might call a shimmer, and so is yours. Overlaid on that is a light vibration color that you cannot see as a human. This light vibration color is the actual beginning of my "color story," as opposed to the shimmer which tells of my service. Just as you are able to read these words, so it is that you might see me as a universal entity and read my colors and shape. You would understand immediately that my source is the center, for this color attribute is my strongest, and carries with it the highest vibration of all. It represents the creative center and the Brotherhood of Light. All entities of the Universe know of this. As I have mentioned before, this center is not a command. It is simply a part, and does not have a hierarchy of importance as you understand it. The weight that it carries is that it is honored for its purpose and for its service. The "importance" is therefore one of celebration of purpose, and not rank. This is very difficult to explain to those of you who are still thinking like humans (cosmic joke).

* See Kryon Book One, *The End Times,* Chapter three, for Kryon colors.

Imagine two entities walking down the road. They stop to speak to each other, and suddenly they recognize that one is the brain and one is the heart! The brain is in awe of the heart! For years the heart has never failed to be the pump of life. Both had been partners creating life for the whole, and yet they never occupied the same space until now on this road. The brain wanted to ask so many questions of the heart about how it felt to be so important an organ, and what it was like to massage the liquid of the human system and keep it flowing so well.

But the heart is also in awe of the brain! For years it had been dependent on receiving the needed clock rhythms from the brain in order to operate. The heart wanted to ask the brain so many questions! What was it like to contain such an electrical system and be so complex that it could also communicate with all the organs at once?!

So these two parts, completely different, sat down together and spent a grand time informing each other of what it was like to serve the whole. When they went on their way, each one knew he had met a celebrity that day, and each one walked away feeling that he had been enriched by the experience.

So it is with you and me. We have worked this planet together for years, you in your capacity and the Kryon in its capacity. It is now that we meet each other on the road; and although you may look at me in awe as I represent Spirit, I am the one who looks at you in awe and tells you again and again that I am from the Love source... and you are loved dearly! The main difference, dear ones, is that until now you and I have never occupied the same space. Now we do, and you have earned it.

And so it is also that each time you descend into humanoid form on any planet, you earn a badge of color that intermingles with the ones you already carry. Like stripes on an Earth tree it tells a story to those who look on it. All of you on Earth at this moment have something in common. Your colors are the ones that tell the story of Earth. This is the great story of an eleventh hour upset (as my partner wishes to call it), and a victory of astounding value. Any universal entity looking at you right now will also see the story of your great lineage. You were the ones who planned and executed one of the greatest of all tests and experiments, for your work has changed the future of the entire universe. Too grandiose, you say? Then your duality is working well, and the imprint that you carry that hides the truth is functioning at full capacity. Believe me, the story is all that and more! There will come a day when you will again know that these words are truth, and that you are far more than just biology walking the planet with human names.

Because of your work the direction of the actions of the universe will be altered. Entire worlds will now have a plan that has substance. This is again difficult to explain to you. When you issue paper monetary value, you back it up with gold. The gold is the substance that shows that the paper also has value. So it is with your part in the place of many worlds to come. In universal terms, the outcome of your journeys and tests as humans have provided the substance and precedence for the value of certain actions to come. You therefore are the GOLD. (Do you remember the two New Age colors I spoke to you about in earlier books? Find them and you will have a good laugh at this analogy.) You have shown that in a void the natural tendency of an entity in the dark is to motivate to the love source! Although this may seem like an overly simple statement, this fact was never actually shown to be so until you proved it on this planet. The significance of this will astonish you in its universal importance when you finally take off the mantle of the biology that you now carry.

There will come a time, when you travel the universe, when all who meet you along the road will stop and stare in awe at your colors, and will recognize your celebrity. They will ask you what it was like to participate in the experiment of Earth! Like massive badges and awards, your colors will tell the story of the group of warriors who did so much for so many! The legends of your work will be universally known, and the word *Earth* will mean so much more than just a planet. It will be used synonymously to communicate the energy of "beginning." Is it any wonder that in the middle of your battle I come to you in love and honor? Is it any wonder that I wish to sit at your feet and be of service to you? Is it any wonder that each time I see you I metaphorically desire to wash your feet? You are right in the middle of a tremendous event!

The Great Transition

The pages of the upcoming channelings and the prior communications (Kryon Book One and Book Two) will clearly tell you the story of what has transpired in the last few years regarding the Earth. My entire reason for being here is due to your work. My service is in response to the change of the planet, a change that you have created. As an individual person you might say, "I don't remember doing anything special. What did I do?" As a planet, however, humans gradually lifted the vibration of the Earth to allow for a future that was not foretold... by anyone!

Now there are many changes for you to confront. And my work here is not only to facilitate the magnetics to allow for your growth, but to give you loving information about what is happening. Everything that I do here is focused into one purpose: to give you peace over the change, and to give you information that will make so much sense to you that you will self-enable your entity and take the power which belongs to you. These changes can create great fear in those who regularly feature drama in their lives to keep them stirred up. There will always be humans who do this to feel comfortable. Beware of the doomsayers who spread fear for the purpose of control or fame. The prophet who tells you the sky is falling will receive far more attention than the one who says it is not. This responds to an old energy concept, and is no longer appropriate for you. The new system of energy in this New Age is Love based. Think about it. Isn't it time that your way of life and your innermost thoughts started to correspond to the ways of the many masters who have walked this planet that you have respected so much? Those you think most highly of spiritually have all had a love-based message. And around the love messages were wonderful miracles and a peaceful countenance. You have separated these entities apart from you and labeled them as special. Many of you have set them up as examples, and some of you even worship them in error... hoping that this action will bring you closer to God. Now I am telling you that **the New Age system is Love**. It will agree with your changes when you move in a direction with those attributes, and will cooperate with your life as you co-create with it. It will do the opposite if you do nothing and don't move at all spiritually. There is no punishment implied here at all, just a lack of growth and a shorter life of being uncomfortable and fearful.

The feeling that much of humanity is experiencing now is the uncomfortable one of sitting in a familiar easy chair that is changing. The chair has served you for eons. True, it is dirty and not very comfortable, but it is familiar; and therefore you can count on it always being the same. For some this easy chair of familiarity contains anger, victimization and a complaining nature. Why not? If it worked well and always gave the needed support of sympathy while passing on troubles to others, then why change? Suddenly, however, the mechanics of these actions will not get the same results... and the reaction of humans to this will be fear. What would happen if you awakened one morning and none of your mechanical devices functioned in the same manner? Switch A made action B. You turn on your lights and water appears at the tap. Can you imagine your disorientation until you relearn the switches? Now place this in a venue of the mind. If you have always been a certain way, and people around you have always reacted to you in a certain way, this is a stable thing (even if it is negative).

If that suddenly changed and humans no longer reacted in predictable ways to your old methods, this imaginary situation might challenge your sanity (to say the least).

And yet this is what is happening to you in your various cultures right now. All around you there is a feeling of completion. Many are in the process of celebrating the closing of an era and the opening of a new one. The oldest tribes on the planet are very aware of what is happening, for their calendars predicted it. The change, however, will be different than expected. It will be the age of graduation instead of an ending of life. It is the graduation of the Earth and the entering of it into new areas of the galaxy (formerly hidden). It will be the graduation of the human being into a new consciousness, and new ways of life (formerly hidden).

Although I will continue to give you some of the detailed personal changes to expect, if you want a two thousand-year-old view of how you are expected to be, then read the original list of nine honorings by Jesus (which you have called the Beatitudes) on page 89 in this book. This is the blueprint for the New Age human. Odd, isn't it (you might say), that you had it in your lap so long ago? The master of Love himself brought this new paradigm to you in a form you could read about and study long before you needed it. Now you do.

My messages in this book will give you much to consider of a practical nature regarding your life. And now I would like to specify some of the changes you may be **feeling** as a New Age human. I do this in order to help you identity with the truth of what I am speaking.

Earth Changes

No human welcomes the kind of change that a planetary upheaval can bring. As I have mentioned before, the human and the Earth are not just related, but are interactive and considered as one entity. When universal entities refer to the "Earth," they actually mean the physical dirt and rock of the planet, the humans there, and the other entities in support of the whole. All are seen as one system, and measurements of the vibration of the planet include all on this list together. You cannot raise the vibration of humans without also raising the vibration of the land!

In the past I have spoken of the fact that you must consider the Earth as part of your life. The ancients knew it, and honored the planet greatly at every chance. They also were careful to create balance when they took of the resources, giving back at every opportunity. I will not give that message again at this time (since you already have it), but I will remind you again of why the planet must change physically.

The magnetic grid is the science that affects your duality. It is constructed to allow for how much spiritual power you recognize, and how much of your "real self" you get to see. The new adjustments in the grid are for your duality, but are actual attributes of the planet. Again I invite you to realize the logic behind the mechanics of this. Why should I adjust a physical Earth attribute in order to change you? The answer should be obvious: it is because the Earth is your parent and your partner. The two of you are symbiotic travelers through the galaxy, and need each other's respect on a continual basis.

The grid change will affect the land. I have spoken in the past of the fact that the magnetic grid of your planet is being shifted. I have also spoken of the fact that your sun is the engine of the grid. This fact is not being taken very seriously at the moment, for it is unrealized truth to your Earth science. Only later when you start giving and receiving intergalactic messages will the part of your sun become clear... for all communications will be through it, given to the grid, and passed to the new portals created for that purpose.

As the land changes, so do you. Earthquakes, weather, and volcano activity can actually define your moods and change your personalities. "Certainly," you might say, "because I am afraid of being killed!" The kind of personality change I am speaking of, however, is where an earthquake on the other side of the planet makes you change in the location where you are. You cannot explain why it is, but you are becoming uncomfortable. This feeling is not worry regarding your safety, but rather an anxiousness regarding the planet itself (because you are becoming tuned with it). Some of you are getting a planetary awareness for the first time in your life. Many of you never thought of these things until the last year or so, and now you are more than casually interested in what is taking place within nature. What can you do about these changes? Let me explain again that this is a transitional period that will settle within the next eight years. During this time you can be very peaceful with the changes, even if some of them take you by surprise.

Take responsibility for the event being appropriate for the planet's new path. This doesn't mean claiming responsibility for death and destruction and sorrow. This means claiming the fact that you are a part of the whole, and the whole is experiencing growth. Therefore it is appropriate, expected, and is not the end. Your ancients knew how to do this well. After many great storms that pruned the land and terminated life, and even made food difficult to find, they celebrated the event as being a growth cycle in the overview of how things worked. What wisdom this was! There is so much irony in the fact that you are now so close to finding the truth through science, and it has removed you so completely from your connection with the dirt. Help others around you with this concept so that they do not hate the planet for things that will happen to them during the shift.

Don't feel victimized by anything that happens to you! Can you stand in the midst of fearful events and sorrowful times and realize that the overview is that you helped plan it? Some of the parables of Kryon later in this book deal with this exact thing. You have your choice when the lessons come to you. You can be a victim or a victor. It's your choice. The New Age human understands the difference completely and has peace with it. God (or the planet) does not gang up on humans to make them victims. Then how can you be safe (you might ask)?

The question and the communication with Spirit isn't "How can I be safe?" or "How can my children be safe?" The creative energy you now have should say "*I co-create in the name of Spirit the ability to be in the very center of my contract.*" There is no sweeter spot for you than this. Remember that we want you to stay and do the work, just as much as you do. This means that it is far better for you to remain here and continue your spiritual light work than to be terminated, come back, and take another 20 years to grow up again. Doesn't this make sense to you? Even though you cannot know the future, you can co-create the ability to be in the right place at the right time (even though you don't know where that place might be). This may sound strange... like making travel plans without knowing the destination. It is so, nevertheless. This seeming puzzle has to do with the new energy and living in the "now," rather than the way it used to be where your happiness depended upon a linear view of your life, and the concept that you should always be preparing for what you thought was ahead. In other words, the sweet spot is your safe spot. Following your contract places you in perfect alignment.

Dear ones, the finest thing you can do for the planet is to comfort others during the time of Earth change. The hurt of the heart is the worst hurt of all, and fear is the enemy of the New Age. When you realize the potential for peace during turmoil, and can practice it yourself, then you are encouraged to give it freely to others. When things get tough, there will be many you never thought would be in your home who will arrive there with fear-struck faces. They will want to know the secret of your peace. They will ask for answers to questions that you don't feel you know. Share with them the message of Love for the planet. Share with them what you know about these times, and the honor that Spirit has for them now. Give them the hope of the future that the Kryon gives to you. There is no greater singular thing that you can do than this. Many of you will be in the very center of your contract when you do, and will realize for the first time that your path is to share the love. Simple, but potent.

General Human Change

Let me speak of some of the changes for those who are not light workers, and would never be caught reading this communication. The events that will happen to these dear ones, who are every bit as important to the planet as you are, will be as follows.

Due to the Earth changes, many of these will experience fear and seek out answers. They will find good answers in places that are teaching about Spirit in many forms. Some will find faith through a spiritual quest of many varieties. The quest for God is a valid and true answer to fear in this new energy, for it promotes Love and a closeness to the Earth. Honor this in all its forms. It may startle you to see the humans who come forward at this time of change. Fear does that.

It is important that you realize a basic universal truth regarding others who do not believe as you do. Do not judge them! Do not make them wrong in your mind simply because their path does not correspond with yours. Do you remember when you might have believed something different than you do now? If it served your vibration then, you were in the correct spot. To have advanced it prematurely would have spoiled the wisdom that you now enjoy on your current path. So each human is responsible for his own place and time. Your admonition is to respond to those who come to you. Do not go out and recruit others to believe as you do. Try to view all the others in the context of appropriateness for who they are, even the ones who ridicule and hurt you, for those are the ones who have a karmic contract with you. If you have called for the implant (more on this later), then it is less likely that they will be in your life, for your change will have disabled the need for the karmic interaction.

The humans who reject the spiritual change will become more angry than before. Sad to say, but your problems with crime in your culture may actually become worse before they settle down. This is a direct result of the conflict within these humans feeling that they are being victimized by the planetary changes (which they cannot identify as planetary changes) with no hope for the future. The reaction for these will be more fear and anger. The other sad thing that will take place (but will eventually frighten many of these into changing) is that their life spans will shorten dramatically (due to remaining in the old ways while the grid shifts to the new).

Those who choose not to change in the New Age, and go in an opposite direction to the vibratory rate of the planet, will have the seeds of disease released into them by their own biology. They will no longer be able to remain comfortable or biologically balanced in the new energy. This is what they agreed to, and was set up by them in the same planning sessions that you attended with them before you were born. Make no mistake. This is not a punishment! This is a planned response to a free will human decision, contracted by them in advance. Can you imagine the changes in these when they dramatically see that they are dying early as a group? They will accuse you of sinister covert actions that are affecting their kind. They will become paranoid, and most will never believe that you are not killing them with some kind of new unseen psychic technology. Since the ones affected won't have taken responsibility for their lives, their fears will only grow stronger and they will turn their anger toward you as they slowly perish.

I tell you these things so that you can understand that the Earth is not going to become some kind of instant heaven (as you have perceived heaven to be). There is much work for you here. That is why you stood in line to be here! Some humans will flow with the new energy, and some will not. You also knew that before you got here. This is the planet of free choice, and remains so! The main change for the present, however, is that enough of the population of Earth has evolved in consciousness to a level that has changed the vibration for the entire planet (as measured during your Harmonic Convergence). This change goes much deeper than what is taking place within your own culture, which does not represent even half of the humans on the planet. This consciousness change has earned humans a New Age and the self-empowerment that is now upon you. It is why I communicate to you at all, and the reason for my extended stay here.

As proof of what I am telling you, notice that within your culture you are beginning to see far more interest in the New Age kind of subjects. Your mass media, which is driven only by economics, has chosen to highlight the attributes of this New Age! This means, of course, that there are many of you who are watching these transmissions, driving the economic numbers to allow for them to remain. As regular fare, you now have subjects on Angels and Guides, discussions on visiting galactic entities, and miracles. You would not have found these things in your main-stream entertainment or serious discussion venues had it not been for a mass consciousness change. Think about it. It has only been since I arrived that this has taken place. Does this correlate to any timetable that the Kryon has spoken of?

Changes in You

I speak to the light workers now. It is imperative that you understand some of the mechanics of what is happening to you so that you will not have fear. There is going to be a new way of feeling "normal" for you. There are also going to be new feelings within your biology for you to get used to. The plan is for you to become comfortable with the new ways of being.

Important: What follows is generic to all light workers regardless of any implant action. Those who understood the first Kryon messages about the acceptance of the karma-voiding process (implant), and did it, will quickly proceed beyond some of the following items. Those who did not take the implant gift are light workers who will have a longer learning cycle until their karmic attributes are cleared in the old manner. But all of you should study the following message.

All of you are now aware of the new energy. This awareness happens in that part of your being that you call mental. It is also the part that the teachers call the crown chakra. It is also represented by the development of what you have called the "third eye." Whatever your view of it is, it represents a tremendous increased vibration within your head (that is where you will perceive it). As you communicate with your guides, co-create, and have a much stronger relationship with your higher self (God self), some interesting things will take place.

Meditation: The first thing that happens will be a disconnection with the old methods. Those of you who meditate may suddenly find it difficult! Isn't it odd that meditation would be the first casualty of an increased awareness? Here are the mechanics of what is happening so you will understand why. Meditation is the time spent **listening** to the Universe, or Spirit. You have become used to sitting quietly while you gain great insight into yourselves and to the Earth (which some call nature). It has been the old method of communication between your God self and your human biological self, and has worked well.

Suddenly we are telling you that the veil has been lifted slightly, and that the grid is helping to facilitate that change. As the veil lifts, your communication methods will change; therefore your meditation will also. Here is an example: when your technology became so sufficient that you no longer had to write long letters and have them physically delivered to others to accomplish regular communication, you stopped writing long letters. Instead you used newer technology to immediately and instantly speak verbally to the others over long distances, and they were able to answer instantly as well. This had the effect of speeding things up in your every-day lives. No more waiting for the hand delivery of written communications just to get ordinary answers.

Much the same has happened spiritually. The long letters you used to write are much like the meditation you have become used to. Now you have the ability to have instant communication with your God self... and the answers come quickly. Some of you (out of habit and a feeling of guilt) feel that unless you sit and meditate anyway, you somehow are not honoring the God part of you. Get used to the new method. For many this will mean never meditating in the old way again!

New Age energy meditations will become **action sessions**, where the main purpose is to involve others with you to give direction of love for the planet. We look forward to those of you who understand this to begin the protocol for these sessions. Some of you are already doing this because it feels like the natural thing! If you fit this description, then you are honored indeed for seeing the change and moving with it.

So if you are one of those light workers who feel that your meditations are just "hitting the ceiling" (my partner's words), then please stop to consider why. Nothing is wrong. You have new spiritual technology now that allows you to get what you need in a fraction of the time. You have a new gift, and have accepted it... but the gift remains unopened. If you feel that you are not "feeling" the same response from Spirit that you used to have when you meditated, YOU ARE CORRECT! Get used to the feeling of being in charge. Get used to the new paradigm of normalcy as a light warrior who is enabled at every step! Your wisdom is now instant. This is much like the feeling of channeling for my partner. The love and wisdom of Spirit happens as you need it, and the love is always there pouring into you day and night through the crack in the veil. No more sessions are necessary where you create a tiny stream of love that squeaks through and makes you feel a certain way for an hour or so. Now you have the full mantle of Spirit to put on, and we invite you to do it! This makes the long letters of meditation inefficient and unnecessary for you personally.

Now, am I telling a planet of light workers not to meditate any more? Some will think so. Please understand that all this changing happens gradually. Some of you are still meditating and having the kinds of results you expect. Continue. This message is for those who feel that their meditations are faulty, and I have given the reasons why. If this fits you, then start accepting your power and understand that what used to take periods of time doesn't any more. This corresponds to the universal change as you slowly move into alignment with the "now" that I have explained many times. Change your former solo meditations to group meditations (two or more) and assign an energy purpose for each session (so that you are coordinating your vibrational intent). This is the best thing you can do for yourselves and for the planet. If you are willing to spend that much time before Spirit, make it count for the planet! You don't need it personally in the same way any longer.

Biological Balance: Here is another feeling you may be having. There is currently a lack of vibrational consistency between what you have called your mental vibration and the rest of your biology. The message I and others are bringing to you is a spiritual one. Even though I involve the physical planet, you perceive your growth in a mental and spiritual fashion. You slowly grow into a tolerant, peaceful person with a wise overview of others around you. These are almost exclusively mental processes for you, even though the truth is that they are astral attributes. You "feel" it in your head, however, and your attitude is seen to be a product of your mind set.

What happens next will seem familiar to some of you. Spirit knows that the rest of your biology needs to "catch up" to your new mind set (crown chakra). In order to do this there is much work being generated for you at the biological level. This process actually goes back to the 11:11 period when you were informed of the code that was passed to all humanity (more about that in this book). Your biology was given permission to change with your astral growth at this time, and the mechanics were given to the magnetic portion of your DNA for this purpose.

The results of this non-synchronization is that many of you are feeling "worked on" while you sleep. Some of you will have metaphoric dreams about hands touching you all over, or very small creatures administering to you throughout the night. Again this is a new process that is working in your favor to bring you health in the new energy, but it can again create fear if you are unaware of what is happening. The main fear most of you have is that there are entities attacking you in your sleep. Be aware of the differences between the cooperation of your own biology and an alien attack. The main difference is how you feel about what is being done. If you have any doubts, then simply create the solution by the procedure I have already given you in the past: (1) practice lucid dreaming, where you have total control over what is happening to you while you sleep. (2) If you suspect that what is happening around you is inappropriate in your dream state, then demand any inappropriate entities to leave. You truly don't appreciate your power to do this. It is absolute, and no astral or other dimensional being can continue if you do not give them permission to. After you do this, you will be left with only the appropriate things taking place; and if you still feel the changes going on, then you can relax and smile at the workings of your own biology. (3) Honor and look forward to the process.

What if you can't sleep because of this? you might ask. Here is an axiom of Spirit. Your healthy biology will always take the sleep it needs, and often leave you awake if it doesn't need any more. This may be boring for you, but it's correct. Many times when you are being worked on, the energy transmitted to you during the work will replace the energy you would have received through hours of sleep. Therefore your worry about losing the sleep is not valid. In fact the worry may itself cause a real sleep imbalance! If you feel that you are having sleepless nights because of this work, then out loud request of your body that it do the work over a longer period of time. This will help you relax in the sessions where no work will be done, and will honor your request to feel like you are getting more sleep. Do you start to understand the control you have over these things? So often the answer to health is to take control yourself. This is an understatement.

Slowly your lower biology will catch up with your head, and the other chakras will balance themselves to the same vibrational level as the top one. In this process be aware that what you call the kundalini energy will seem odd indeed. This is just another feeling that will be different from anything you have experienced before. This kundalini energy is the energy that actually touches all the chakras at once. It is also the only energy that moves about in response to the others (whereas the others are static). This will show up in your life as unrest, or anxiousness of mind. It has you walking around feeling that something is going to happen, so you'd better not relax very long. This is a false trigger, and is not a negative thing. It is very much a real chemical reaction. You are dealing with brand new alignments and new feelings. We invite you to get used to this surge of energy and recognize it for what it is. For some of you this surge may continue well into the next century. You must learn to relax with the new feeling. It is simply a new vibration between your biological portals. It is the new normal!

No more dark: There is yet another attribute that some of you are experiencing which is minor but needs explanation. The human experience with biological sight in the old energy is different from what it will become. Your biology is actually being tuned so that you can see some astral attributes in the future. This means you must receive changes within your eyes, the connections from your eyes to your brain, and your brain itself. Here are the symptoms: many of you now shut your eyes in total darkness only to find there is still a redness present, as though there were still a light on in your room. For those who got used to everything going black when your eyes were closed (the old way), there will have to be a period of adjustment and understanding of why this is happening. In addition to the subtle redness, you may also experience geometric patterns! This is pure science, and an absolutely natural response to the work you are allowing to balance your biology. Some of you will understand the geometric attributes as you continue with the messages in this book.

These things, in combination with the others mentioned will also tend to get in the way of your sleep (as described). You must, therefore, take this entire package of biological changes with a peaceful overview. We encourage you to relax with everything that is happening, and honor it. In the process of honoring something you don't understand, you become part of it. This alliance promotes a faster conclusion to the work, and also makes you feel loved in the process. This, of course, is the Kryon recurring theme for the New Age.

You are the reluctant enemy: How many of you have thought of yourselves as someone's enemy? Most of you who have accepted the love-based message of the Kryon would step far to avoid such a label. In fact it is much the opposite for most of you.

You wish to have the tolerance and peace of the Earth's finest masters, and you wish no ill will to anyone.

It will then disappoint you to realize that to align with the new energy will be to draw a battle line with many human religious organizations all over the planet. We have spoken in the past of the sadness surrounding the fact that so many of your love-based religions feature a doctrine which excludes everyone but those who sign up to believe exactly the way the organization asks them to. There will be so much fear around what is happening on Earth that these organizations will make you the culprit, and actually call you the devil. The great irony is that they will point at the channelings of their prophets for proof of this. You, of course, will not be given the privilege of pointing to your channelings.

They have no space for change; therefore they cannot accept an Earth without a bad ending as channeled in their books. They sit complacent and expect the worst, and have no tolerance with any who have the message of Spirit that says you have changed the planet with your thoughts. Even the highest love-based religions of your own culture will not be able to decide what to do with your good news information... so they will turn against you and try to do away with your message. Their message is one of fear, and in order to save your soul essence in these end times, they say you must give your power over to God... and they will define God for you. Then you will be ready for the end. Does this make you feel good?

What can you do about this? First: do not ever address their doctrine with them. This is an issue of their making and belongs to the consciousness of fear. How they can reconcile it with love will be of great interest, for there will be attributes of their behavior which will not match their doctrine. If a human comes to stand in front of you and says, "I don't like your nose," you have several options. One is to take issue with the statement and defend your nose. If you do this, you have been manipulated by that person into discourse and have joined into a battle of his making. There is no human law or rule that states that every time another human speaks, you must answer. The second option, therefore, is not to answer, and go about your business as though nothing was said. If this sounds similar to the admonition to "turn the other cheek," you have just gained a great New Age irony. You indeed will be using the love doctrine of those who confront you, and thus you will win your own individual victories.

Second: honor their right to believe their own way, and be tolerant of their ways. Never make them wrong in your minds, even if their methods irritate you. Remember that they are total equals with you, and that you all helped plan the changes that are causing the dissension. Many of them may join you later on when they weigh what is happening on the planet in light of the reality of their narrow doctrines. Love is the doctrine of the New Age, and it fits well with the great results and healings they have experienced in their meetings. Many will eventually understand that the only thing that separates you from them is the organization they belong to, and information that is old and no longer valid.

Third: Don't put up large organizations around your New Age work. Your best work will be done with many individuals whose faces change often. There will be much moving around for many of you as you discover your contracts and feel compelled to be in different areas. This does not lend itself to setting up organizations where membership and long term organizational responsibility is desired. This is important: **You can do every bit as much work without a building as those do with large organizations with many members.** If you do not have a building with your name on it, you also become a very elusive target for those who would wish to use their economic and political powers to terminate your activities.

There will be abundance for your work! The old methods of economic community collection and contribution is no longer useful. The new methods will be far more spontaneous. This is a difficult concept for those of you who need old energy monetary institutions and old established methods of income to make you comfortable. Our admonition in love is to become willing for the solutions to economic needs to become closer to the actual need. You will be given what you need at the point of the need. The Universe is very abundant, and you are indeed part of this plan. You will slowly watch many of the old monetary methods of the old energy fail completely, with great surprise and shock to those who must support large buildings and organizations.

Those of you who must have buildings for your healing or educational work must keep a low profile. Remember, dear ones, that your awareness and consciousness is not an evangelistic doctrine that invites others to join. Yours is perhaps the most personal belief system that has ever existed on your planet. It is a true miracle of Spirit that so many will receive the same information and come to the same conclusions without any human leadership or guidance to organize such a thing! No stadia filled with people, and no mass media pushes for economic support will push you on. Those who would cast you out as "the devil" will not understand the New Age way of organization, for it will be on a level of communication that they have never seen. There will come a day when you will be able to meet at a place for world meditation without even one invitation being sent. This is part of the "new sight" that you are being given.

There will also be those from your own beliefs that will reject the good news of the new energy. They will be angry that their methods are now being changed, and will not rejoice in the fact that many are now receiving the power that they intuitively had in the old energy (see page 184). This is a real test for them, for the very fact they were given sight in the old energy was to bring them into this time of testing. Their test will be to surrender the old ways to the new ones, and increase their own power tenfold in the process! Love them. Their work represents much of the reason why the planet has changed so much, so fast.

As you read this, remember that this is available to all humans at this time, even the ones who do not believe it! It is your birthright as a sovereign person on this planet. You all have earned a chance to take this new information and weigh it in the light of what is happening around you. Some will cast it aside, and some will not. This is not a proprietary message for a chosen few. It is the wish of Spirit for all humans to know of these things, then for them to go inward and use their intuition for advice on the truth of it all. When they do this, that part of them which is God itself will shout at them that they are very close to why they came here at all. Many will fall down weeping in thanks for the discovery, and will go on to embrace the new energy with eagerness and joy. Many will fight the feelings with the seed fear that I have spoken of in past writings (Books One and Two), and run from all of it.

Those who run are loved by Spirit every bit as much as those who do not. The rules of this planet are free choice and non-intervention. You come by design, but your actions are always in the NOW, as we call it. There is always spontaneity and surprise in what humans will do with the information of Spirit.

Because you are reading these words, again we tell you the following. Dear one, it is no accident that you are scanning this page with your eyes. We know you by name, and have placed before you a loving message from home. We know what you have been through, and what is happening in your life right now. There are entities who love you and have been with you for life that look over your shoulder while you read. These entities are often your best friends, and yet this is hidden from you while you are on the planet. They are rejoicing at this very moment, for you are reading a message which is about them and you. They long for you to acknowledge them, and begin to learn about the duality that keeps you from seeing each other in the dimension you live in. They long for you to recognize who you are, and to finally start the process you came here for!

There is great honor in their eyes, for they serve you completely. There is no judgment either, for they are truly of Spirit consciousness, as you were before you came. Do you ever tell them of your love? Do you ever try to remember who they are? Is it too weird or unusual for you to image such a thing? Even the most skeptical of you is honored for being on Earth during this time. We do not come to pass judgment on you, but to serve your planet with information about what is before you in this New Age of Love and science. In the process of that honor, we have to tell you many times of the love Spirit has for you. It is incomprehensible for you to fathom the depth of this love. You have changed the very fabric of the universe, and the very thing that keeps you from realizing it is the very thing you are honored for. The work you are doing is amazing when viewed from any place in the universe. All know of your path, and we stand in awe.

You are indeed dearly loved.

Kryon

Chapter Two

Questions About Human Alchemy

Questions About
Human Alchemy
Chapter Two

From the writer...

Again we follow the question and answer format, but this time almost all of the questions are from readers or seminar attendees. Where possible I have asked permission to use letters and comments, and give credit. In other areas I have been unable to contact those who have contributed their thoughts, so I only use initials. In some cases the questions have come from a live seminar, and the name and face are long gone in my memory, but the burning questions remain. Sometimes the questions were unanswerable in my own wisdom at the time, and so I gleefully give them to Kryon with a sigh of relief.

Question: How, if at all, are the listeners and readers of the Kryon differentiated from the billions of souls currently inhabiting the planet? Are we healers and teachers by virtue of simply being somewhat elder brothers and sisters of the same family, or by virtue of perhaps being the in-lesson portion of a service team from elsewhere? In either case would you speak more about the differences between the process of healing and rejuvenating ourselves and the process of healing and rejuvenating the world?

Greg Ehmka
Akron, New York

Answer: There are two parts to your question, but the first part shows wonderful wisdom in its context. Those of you reading the words of Kryon right now are indeed a special group, but not a karmic one. Your group consists of those who have passed through the most karma of the centuries to end up at this moment with the best grasp on the reality of who you actually are. It is therefore no accident that many of you have realized your importance to the planet, and to those around you, and have become altruistic. Many of you are healers and facilitators, addressing the concerns of your fellow humans. All of you are aware of Spirit in a way that the others are not. Therefore, in the school of Earth you are in the higher grades, since you have done more homework. These higher grades don't mean you have greater visibility or planetary fame; rather it means that you have greater insight and wisdom. You will be the first to take on the new gifts, since you are in a position to understand what is being offered and to see the many changes that are upon you and the ones around you.

The equality of humans on Earth is real; yet you look around you and obviously see some with less and some with more. You also see those with opportunity and those with none. Harder still is for you to see those who seem *by chance* to be born into war or violence. Yet we tell you that all humans are created equal. The equality relates to your contract opportunities and your time windows of action. In other words the equality is in regard to what you have done with it over time. When you see a person in a war ravaged country, you are looking at an entity with lifetimes of karmic overlays (just like you). You are also seeing a lesson plan that they themselves have created for their own path. Therefore the equality of humans on Earth is a long-term overview and not a "one lifetime attribute." Those of you who are healers and metaphysicians are the ones who have been through much of what the others have, but have moved more quickly through your opportunity windows and have graduated through lesson after lesson successfully.

Your group, therefore, does not have a heritage that is different from the others, nor are you part of an elite group that has been placed for a purpose. This is where the honor from Spirit comes from! You all start with the same overlay of contract potential. You have been the ones to move the fastest, but you come from the same seed as all the rest.

The second part of your question is interesting. You wish to know the differences between healing yourselves and healing the planet. There is no difference. One will create the other. Understand that you have no choice between these two goals. If you decide to skip the work on yourself and concentrate on the planet, you will fail. But when you concentrate on yourself, the healing of the planet will be automatic and will happen simultaneously. Even though you look around you and see so much to be done physically with Earth, we are telling you that your self-discovery and your inner work will bring these planetary changes. Why? Because of what the Kryon has been telling you from the beginning of the messages: The Earth is you. It will respond to your work as part of your body responds to your overall health. As you improve and take the gifts of Spirit in the new energy, you will be given great insight to new physical ways to implement planetary clean up and peaceful coexistence. The proof of this is what has happened in the last 50 years. As you did work on yourselves, the Earth became more peaceful with great political and environmental awareness. You toppled governments with your inner work, and made millions aware of environmental issues that would never have been seen before. This all started in the hearts and minds of humans who consistently walked through their karma and moved closer to their contracts. Can you see how all this relates?

The next time you feel selfish when Spirit is asking you to work on yourself only, think about this and understand the overview of how your work is affecting the whole. Your individual contribution isn't just one of many; each of you is like a pillar in a vast building construction project. The more of you who make personal changes, the stronger you support the building.

Question: (Speaking to Lee) I honor your work for the Kryon, and I want to believe all of it, but I can't help but feel that it is a kind of "Pollyanna" approach to a complex problem. As I look around me in my city of Los Angeles, I don't see this raise in consciousness you speak of. In fact all I see is anger and violence. How can this coexist with what you are speaking of? The Kryon words don't seem to fit the reality of what I observe around me.

> Attendee at Seminar
> Sedona, Arizona

Answer: This question is greatly related to the last, and is why I have asked my partner (Lee) to place it here. When the Earth was measured at the Harmonic Convergence and found to be of high vibration, and ready for a much different future than imagined, it didn't mean that everyone was suddenly going to be happy and healed. The measurement itself was a vibrational gauge of contract fulfillment, and your potential future because of it. You were therefore found fertile for the change of grade, not already graduated.

It truly marked the beginning of a massive shift for humanity, one which would actually intensify the anger of many, as opposed to mellowing it! When we call you "Warriors of The Light," do you now understand that this connotes a battle of some kind? In this case the battle is between new energy enlightenment and old energy stubbornness. It is the struggle of many old energy individuals to enter the new energy paradigm kicking and screaming with fear. The battle therefore is one of individual self-improvement or individual self-denial... and the self-denial will appear to be the more logical human path!

When you look around you, therefore, you see an even greater contrast of dark and light than ever before, instead of an improvement. This is the very attribute that will be responsible for relocating for some of you. Many simply will not be able to exist in an area of low energy vibration with those who actively choose not to be part of the shift. It is important, however, that none of you should feel like you have to band together into communities of enlightened consciousness. This is an old energy concept and won't work! Try it, and you'll find out why. Your task is to carry your piece of God to the area that fits you best, and live normally with others around you who are also ready for the shift. This is one of the reasons for the implant, for it gives you the armor for such a task, where you will be able to coexist with those who need to see how your life works. Like the example of the tar pit (*Kryon Book Two*) you absolutely must stay in the mainstream of human culture for this battle to be won. Others must see what you have so that they will have the recognition of the same energy within them. Therefore the catalyst for them to change... is YOU!

It won't take much to change an entire area. Even the darkest, most violent areas of your cities can be changed by just a handful of enlightened humans. Instead of moving, some of you will be on a path that invites you to stay and change the areas around you. This is similar to the mechanics of those healers who choose to stay during epidemics. Whereas the others wisely leave in order not to suffer, the healers who stay not only aren't infected, but heal many, often stamping out the epidemic completely. Which one are you? (you might ask) ... the one who should move to another area, or stay and heal the area you are in? These are the decisions which you will make calmly and intuitively without much drama around them. We have spoken often of your path being your "sweet spot." It is the place where your passion for your contract is fulfilled. It will be obvious to you!

Perhaps you are looking around for proof that the world is changing before you accept this information? If so, then you will be an observer for a very long time. If, however, you recognize your part in all of it now, your work will actually bring about the very change you are waiting to observe! It is human nature that in a group of resting laborers at least one will have to get up and start the work before the rest follow; otherwise they will all stay at rest. You therefore are the catalyst for the very change you are trying to observe. Nothing will happen around you without you changing first. Feel the information intuitively. Don't wait for others to start first. Spirit is excited about your potentials. Although we expect you to do the work, we are giving you the tools to accomplish it.

Question: People can relate to making choices, and for having good reasons to make those choices. Can living in the new energy be simplified to one's making choices for reasons of love as opposed to reasons of fear? If so, since the evolving individual will learn either way, what are the practical consequences of either path?

Greg Ehmka
Akron, New York

Answer: One of the attributes of the new energy will be the absence of fear-based decision making. Of all the facets of the New Age, this will be one of the most universal. With the kind of self-awareness that recognizes the piece of God in each human, reasons for doing things will become based on a completely new way of thinking. Love is the driving force of living, decision making, working and being in the New Age human's life. Responsibility awareness is the backing behind the logic of it all. There used to be a time when explorers feared falling off the edge of the Earth as they moved forward to unknown areas. This was a logical fear due to what they observed, and due to their ignorance of how things worked in those old times. Now no explorer fears this. No exploration decisions are made based on this possibility. Why? Because the truth of the way things work has been shown; the proof has been validated over and over. This is the same with the New Age path. Once the truth is known and the path is validated, fear will cease to be a player in everyday life for the New Age human. **This is indeed the Alchemy of the human spirit! Going from fear to Love is the Alchemy process.**

It's easy to answer the last part of the question. Fear-based decisions will bring poor results in the new energy... over and over. Love-based decisions will elevate a person into new areas of discovery. Therefore the evolving human (who takes responsibility for all that happens to him) may try both, but it won't be long before the results speak for themselves and the fear-based decisions are discarded. I have spoken many times of the new gifts of Spirit for you. The implant is just one. Knowledge of the way things work and co-creation is another. These two gifts alone can change a human's life drastically and forever. Intent is the key, and appropriateness is the permission. So many of you are ready to live a different kind of life, free from fear and worry. We literally sit at your feet begging you to look up from the negative things which keep you glued to your past, and consider this new information. Weigh it in the light of how you feel. Check it with your inner consciousness. See if it resonates with your soul! Take the challenge that you might be wrong to ignore it. If you are a spiritual person, ask for God to show you the answer. Then choose for yourself.

Kryon

From the writer... again

While doing the Kryon work I have met many wonderful meta-physical professionals in publishing. One of the absolute high points in my path was meeting the publisher of *The New Times* in Seattle, Krysta Gibson. It's Krysta's words that grace the back of the Kryon book, *Don't Think Like a Human*, released in August of 1994.

The New Times is one of those publications that is created from the heart, and is produced by a small group of dedicated employees who are there no matter what the time of day to crank the paper out on time under Krysta's direction. I am always impressed by the fact that each *New Times* publication seeks to make a change in people, not just to publish news about New Age personalities and activities. When you sit with Krysta, there is no doubt in your mind that she is exactly where her contract says she should be, and you can't help but honor her for this quest to run a paper of this quality, changing lives with each issue. The responsibility of this is not lost on her, and plays an important part in her choices in what to do and what not to do in the pages of *The New Times.*

In January of 1995 I came to read her editorial comment. It caught my eye due to the title, "How to Handle the Predicted Earth Changes." Since this book features many letters and questions from readers all over the world, I felt comfortable in including this article in its entirety. Even though it may seem to deal first with the issue of Earth changes and predictions, it actually deals with the Alchemy of the Human Spirit. I found it refreshing to see these concepts presented out of channel, by an industry professional, to thousands of readers. It made me realize that the messages of Kryon are right in line with others in high profile places who are responsible for leading our New Age movement.

JANUARY 1995   Vol. 10   No. 8   *CHANGING AND ENRICHING LIVES SINCE 1985*

How to Handle The Predicted Earth Changes

I magine life without fear. Imagine the feeling of living in total trust and faith, never doubting that only the best will ultimately come to you and those you love. Such a life is possible, although it won't happen without intention and devotion to one's purpose.

Most of us live life rooted in fear. We fear not having what we need: love, safety, money, friends, a job, success, status, knowledge. Most of the decisions people make are based in fear. The problem with using fear as our foundations is that fear has no substance and can't hold us up like we hope it will. A life lived in fear is a barren one.

One of the first things I was told about when I became involved in the metaphysical community were the "coming Earth changes." Of special note was the planetary shift. The Earth was supposed to shift on her axis, turning us topsy-turvy, sometime in the 1980's. At that time there was a small group of people who gave workshops on how to prepare for this event while others moved to geographical regions which were supposed to be safer than the rest of the country. Seattle was due to be buried at the bottom of the ocean. People in east-ern Washington could be cheered at the prospect of suddenly owning beachfront property.

Over the years, various dire predictions have come and gone, but there continues to be a consistent focus on planetary disasters. With much of the information now going prime time through such programs as *Ancient Prophecies*, there are many people who are living their lives in terminal dread. People fear not only for themselves, but for their children. What will happen if disaster does strike, they wonder. Is there somewhere they can go to be safe? Is there something they can do to prevent the predictions coming true?

Fear is an odd thing – it originally existed as a warning device to keep us safe. When it is ever present, however, it closes the heart and clouds the mind. If we are in a constant state of fear, we are unable to think or feel clearly. We can't begin to live to our potential if we're constantly afraid of being hurt, killed, or abandoned.

At various times people have asked me what I think about the changes and what my plans are. I look at the planet and see that she is and has been in a state of disruption for some time now. The Earth changes aren't coming; they are already here. The planet has been going through disruptive changes for eons, and chances are it will continue to do so. Will I be in the path of an earthquake, flood, or volcanic eruption? Will you? I don't know. Perhaps. Maybe not. It doesn't matter.

"What do you mean, it doesn't matter? You mean if you knew you were in the path of a tornado, you wouldn't take some action? Wouldn't you want to know so you could protect yourself and your property and loved ones?"

What matters is that we live from our center. What matters is that we have done our internal work and cleansing and that we have an intimate relationship with the divine, whatever form that may take for us. If we are relatively clear, and if we are in touch with the divine essence of life, what is there to fear? We will be in the right place at the right time, and if that is in the middle of an earthquake, then so be it.

If there is an earthquake and I am in the middle of it, there will be a reason for me to be there and my job will be to do whatever is required of me. If I am to make my transition in such a dramatic manner, I will.

All fear comes from the fear of death. People fear disaster because they're afraid they will die. It is instinctual for us to want to live and we will, but the truth is that all of us will change our bodily form someday. Even those who plan to ascend with their current body will still go through a death of sorts because it will be a major transi-tion from one form of life to another. Living in fear of changes, Earth or otherwise, is allowing ourselves to be distracted from our real purpose for being on the Earth at this time.

How do we handle the changes? If it makes you feel better, take the necessary physical steps to ensure the highest form of safety and comfort you can. Have enough water and food available. Be sure your home is properly stocked to handle emergency conditions. Then let it go and get on with living your life.

Has it crossed your mind that maybe the Earth changes won't touch you? That you will spend years being worried, not living to the fullest, and then it will pass you by? Won't you feel foolish to have lost so many good years that could have been spent in creativity and furthering your evolution as a person?

Another thought to chew on is that maybe the predictions are wrong. Maybe circumstances have changed enough so that many of the predicted changes won't even happen. That is certainly what has been said in the Kryon materials. Kryon says that the consciousness of the planet has changed enough that the major disasters which had been in store for us are not going to happen. Most of the fear being generated is being done so on out-of-date predictions!

Every century has had its predictions of doom and gloom. Some of it happens and some of it doesn't.

Living one's life based on the maybes is a sad waste of human potential.

There is a way to live without fear. That way is found during times of prayer and meditation. When we focus our thoughts and energies on the divinity in life and begin to feel its omnipresence, fear vanishes. When we truly know and feel that everything, including us, is an expression of God/dess in form, what is there to be afraid of?

Some people like to have a lot of drama in their lives. They would be unhappy and bored if they experienced an overwhelming sense of peacefulness. Life lived on the edge with lots of upheaval, chaos, and uncertainty makes them feel alive and real. Even these people, though, can learn to experience the divine within the soap operas of life. They can have their excitement without terror, if they choose.

Instead of spending your time and energy focusing on the maybes of life, start focusing your attention on the here and now. Who are you to become today? What are you to do? How can you contribute to planetary peace within your own life today? Have you set aside time to turn within, become centered and have a personal experience of the divine? Are there people or situations you need to release in order to move forward with your life? Is there some thing or condition you can create today which will alleviate suffering or bring joy to someone else?

Befriend your fears by spending time with them, finding out what they want to tell you or teach you. Most fears only need to be acknowledged in order to loosen their grip. Others require a bit more attention. Some need to stick around until we learn whatever lesson they are here to give. There are no circumstances of which I am aware where fear needs to rule one's life or where it needs to be given the supreme dominion some folks want to bestow upon it.

If you fear disaster, if you fear poverty, if you fear death, the best action you can take is to begin to live your life to the fullest. When life is being lived in faith and love, there is no room for consistent doubts and fears. Should uncomfortable circumstances present themselves, you will be guided in what actions to take, where to go, who to see. Any anxieties will be transient guests rather than permanent roommates.

A great New Year's resolution would be to live in the present with conscious intent to love and honor everyone and everything around us as well as to love and honor ourselves. Such a life would be one of joy and peace no matter what might happen in the outer world. Can you think of a better way to live?

Krysta Gibson - PO Box 51186, Seattle WA 98115-1186

Chapter Three

Three Live Kryon Channels
About The New Age Human

...itings

)el Mar - #422

92014

yon:

The love, the euphoria I feel attempting to express to you my indebtedness; reading one of your books, listening to Kryon in my mind, or just walking across one of my grassy fields on a warm sunny day, answers more questions than I ever knew how to ask.

The elimination of habitual negative thinking, temper tantrums, insecurities, fears and hideous mood swings take time, but there are those moments when exposure to one more portion of the great puzzle says you're heading in the right direction. Something mighty is unraveling here; not enough, or fast enough, to appease my horrendous appetite, but it seems I'm the one to blame for the stagnant periods. It's as if I'm being challenged to find the key to one obstacle after another before I can continue onto the next step. If I could successfully manifest one wish, it would be to become so spiritually enlightened in this lifetime that I could motivate and/or help anyone, and everyone, who wants to master the art of life as much as I do.

With love and appreciation,

Cecelia M. Villarreal

Raymond, Washington

Kryon

"The 12:12 Channel"
Channel of December 12, 1994

Del Mar, California
Special Kryon Light Group

The Kryon Writings, Inc.

PMB 422
1155 Camino Del Mar
Del Mar, California 92014
[www.kryonqtly.com]

"12:12"

Live Channel
Del Mar - December 1994

> *This live channel has been edited with additional words and thoughts to allow for clarification and better understanding of the written word.*

Greetings dear ones, for I am Kryon of magnetic service. We will take a few moments to adjust this room to the energy level that we wish to impart to you this night, and as we do so, we wish to tell you a little bit about who is here. For the entourage which is coming in at this moment, to fill the cracks and the crannies between where you sit and where you lie and where you stand, belongs to you. It is Spirit this night that comes to wash your feet. For that is the love we feel for you. There are many of you here tonight who have come in pure enlightenment, who know their path so well and are ready for the change, and who see who they are in all their splendor and magnificence. For those of you who are in this state, we say "be prepared," for all that you wish is yours! We will fill you up until you can contain no more and will send you away with joy, and with a cup that will run over for years. Such is the power of your own intent.

There are so many of you here this night who in all appropriateness are here to celebrate a grand event, and one which you have come here to know more about. And we say to you also that your intent is everything! All you have to do is give the word, give the thought, to be filled like the others. For your magnificence will astound you and will shock and surprise you when you face it, for you have no idea who you are. And we will fill you as well. And you will feel the loving arms of spirit around you as we come forward with those who are joining us now. You can be changed this night. For the Earth will allow it; you have earned it.

We wish to tell you at this time of the great lineage of the dates which have occurred to create the event which you are celebrating now as you sit before Spirit. We wish to tell you briefly how it started, and even as we speak to you this night, there are some who are so aware that there is more being transmitted than words. For many of you are receiving energies of what we call the third language, transmitted through the facilitators who sit next to you, which remain unseen at this time. Remember, we know who you are. Perhaps you think it's a coincidence that you are all here, an accident that has brought you to this place? We say this is not the case, for all of you had an appointment. Take advantage. Feel what you can.

August 16, 1987 of your year on Earth, was a phenomenal time. For this was the time as we have channeled in the past, that the Earth was measured; and much to the surprise and the joy of those on my side of the veil, we discovered that your planet had a much higher energy level than expected. This was the beginning, dear ones, of what you celebrate now on the 12:12. For without this time and without this measuring, nothing would be happening as it is now. For by design and by plan it was set out that the measuring time would be at that moment. The Earth had changed dramatically in the last fifty years, and as many of you know who sit in the chairs in front of Spirit and are reading these things now, this was a time of great celebration. It was the time when the Kryon was summoned. It was the time when the master guides were summoned, and all entities in the universe, from the great central source outward, knew it. For it changed what would happen in the future of all of us, and I speak universally. You may not be aware of how Earth could change the Universe but it has, dear ones, as channeled in the past. And as we arrived to facilitate the changes that you have made for yourselves, we found that you were indeed ready. Things were moving even faster than we had imagined, and we are here in force to facilitate this now.

Then on January 11, 1992, the most astonishing thing happened in the history of humanity! There is nothing that will ever diminish this date which you call the **11:11**. And it is my wish at this time to tell you more about what happened, so that you will have a greater appreciation of this day as you sit in front of Spirit. My partner wells up at the thought of the joy that Spirit has in the honoring of you this night. For on this date which you call the 11:11 all of humanity received a code. And the code went out to every human being on the planet which said, "We are changing things and opening a door, and enabling you as humans to walk through it." Now, dear ones, this may sound like so much rhetoric or fantasy, but we wish to tell you what happened that day. For the code that was transmitted to you was magnetic; and that, dear ones, is why the magnetic master speaks to you at his time. For it was done through the magnetic grids and given to every human on the planet, including those not yet formed. Now you may say, "I was here then, and I felt nothing." And we say it is thus: imagine yourself facing a very long hallway which is your life. Down in the darkness, years away from where you are, silently a door opens... but what a door it is! You felt nothing and heard nothing, but your biological imprint and your magnetic imprint knew that the door had opened, for it represented a grand enabling of your spirit! An enabling of your humanity to pass through to a place which was barred from you before.

It is the new age, and the door of enablement was given to you to eventually grow into the status which we have called ascension. This was the day, the 11:11. Now you might ask, "How was this done, Kryon?" And so we will tell you now for the first time that **each of you has a magnetic code system that wraps around your biological one**. These magnetic strands, if you will, correspond and give coded messages to your body's biological strands. And we speak now of the human genome, your DNA. And for each one of your biological strands there are two bipolar magnetic ones (this totals 12). This is your imprint. This sets your duality. This will be very hard for any of your scientists to ever see, but we will give you clues in the future that will show that it exists. So this is how it was done, for the shift of the magnetic grid alters your consciousness and your enablement. And this magnetic grid "talks" to those magnetic imprint coded messages, which then in turn talk to your biology and allow for the changes. You may wonder about this, but let me expound further.

Did you know that your bodies were designed to last forever? Did you know that they rejuvenate themselves on a regular basis? Did you know that most of your cells and your organs are designed to be infinite, to last for eons of time... and that they regenerate themselves over and over and over? You have proof of such things. So why is it, dear ones, that you grow old, and that you age and pass on? "What is happening here?" you might ask. It is the magnetic imprint that is talking to the DNA, that is generating chemicals which you have called the death hormone. This old energy code gets in the way of the regeneration process, and cooperates with the slight lack of cosmic energy which allows for your aging. It is appropriate, and it is by design, and it is as you planned it. It facilitates the plan of incarnation and karma, for it keeps you aging. And it keeps you passing and coming back incarnation after incarnation to facilitate the raising of the vibration of the planet. This is what is being slowly voided, and is part of the door that opened on the 12:12.

Now you may say, "How is it that we have not seen this before in our science?" Here is another revelation for some of you: you may have thought in the past that magnetism damages your cells, as radiation does. It does not, for **magnetism gives your cells instruction sets to act differently** and do different things. For proof of this we ask your science in the future to expose cells to small magnetic fields of all kinds. Use different kinds of human cells and watch the result. We'll guarantee that you will see these cells secrete chemicals that you have not seen before in these circumstances. Some will even grow quickly. The cells will not be damaged, but when they are exposed to the magnetics they will act differently. Now you know what the Temple of Rejuvenation was all about in the place you called Atlantis! For this was a magnetic engine, and the target human had his magnetic imprint altered. The magnetic instructions voided the death hormone and allowed the human three more years of youth, until it reverted back to its original design in this lowered cosmic energy. This is why the elite of that place you called Atlantis lived for a very long time, and the reason their slaves did not. For the technology, as channeled before, was not shared. This is the process, dear ones, that created the code that was sent out on the 11:11.

Now, a dear one has brought you this news in the past, and we speak now of the angel **Solara**. We encourage you now to revisit this information, for **none of this information is old**. The most astounding event that has ever taken place was the 11:11, for it truly was the enablement of mankind and humanity. The messages put forth in the channelings of Solara should be looked at each year and remembered, for the message is one of splendor, and will never grow old. For it is wise, as this channel was sent here so that you could see these instructions for all of your life. Revisit them often! We encourage you. Such an event should be celebrated until the end of your age. So it is that all channeled messages that you receive that have to do with this new age should be treated thusly. There is a tendency for humans to put the old things away and look only to the new. And we say to you now that there are many things that have been given to you which should be put on a high shelf and looked at often. These things are high in honor and in celebration, for the news is the truth, and it will not grow old.

April 23 of 1994 began the shift that you now have completed today. For dear ones, you need to understand that as your planet has grown, there have been "place holders" holding the energy and the vibration of the planet so that it could survive in balance with the grid system. The grid system is partly an engine of the sun. When you understand the colors and magnificence of what you call the solar wind, and its reaction to the grid system, you will know more about that engine. And the entities which hold the balance within that engine have been here since the beginning. For you should know that not always have there been so many human beings on your planet. As the human energy sum grew, the other entities gradually reduced. But the ones with the most power always remained, *for they were needed as place holders to create an energy balance on the Earth that the humans could never obtain in the old energy.* But this place holding entourage started to leave on this April date in 1994!

And they left the planet in great celebration, for they knew that it was the beginning of something amazing: an enablement of planet Earth, and the beginning of what we will call your independent planet. We will use the word enablement a great deal, since there is no better one than this. It frees the shackles of an imprint which had been yours for eons, and allows for marvelous gifts for human beings. So it was on that date the beginning of the **passing of the torch**. Many of you felt it and celebrated it, for it was foretold. This was the process that had begun because of the Harmonic Convergence. And because of the 11:11 code passing, it was now possible. First was the measurement, then the coding, and lastly the action; and the three together will change the planet forever.

In your year of 1994 all of these things have happened in a quickening pace. Look at the distance between the first event in 1987 and the second in 1992. Then look at the distance between 1992 and the third event in 1994, and finally the 12:12 now. You can understand the mathematics of what is taking place is not linear, for things are happening in a quickening pace and will continue to in this fashion. For the passing of the torch in April of this year was the beginning of what you now know as the 12:12. Those of you now in this room who wish to know what the 12:12 truly is, we say this: **it is your independence day**. For this is the time when the last of all of the balancing entities which have been here since the Earth grid system was set, will leave. And dear ones, of the most powerful entities that leave now and say good-bye to you, there was 144,000. It is with great honor and celebration that they departed, and also with some sadness, for they have interacted with you and know who you are. But as they departed they chose you to continue. They throw the challenge into your court, for 144,000 of you will take on their energy! Of the entire planet this day, this is the number of humans who will choose the path of ascension. For the ascension posture is the energy necessary to hold the balance at bay and to keep it where it belongs planet-wide. It allows the enablement to continue.

So the 12:12 is the completion of the passing of the torch. Even though the 11:11 was perhaps the most astounding event in humanity, the 12:12 is honored as well, *for it is truly an honoring of the entities that held the* energy for eons of time. The 12:12 consummated the new energy; truly the new age is here... the age of enlightenment and enablement for each and every human who is sitting in this room and reading these words!

You may say, "I have not necessarily seen much of a change in the planet. I have been here a long time, and it doesn't seem like there is much changed." We encourage you, dear ones, to look at the overview as Spirit does and see the differences that may be subtle, but would shout that there have been changes in consciousness already, even within the last ten years.

There are those who have channeled for many years who said that this would be the end. You have six years left to the millennium. By now, in a very important area on your planet the sands were to run red with blood. And if you go to that very spot this day, you will find two countries that are not running red with blood, but sharing their water information, planning to build dams together, opening embassies one with the other. Did you notice? Granted it has been slow, but did you notice?

There are four countries on this planet whose rulers sit in the chair of importance and premiership, who only a few years ago were in the dank dungeons of their very countries, enslaved by their own governments! What happened to bring them back to power? What does this tell you about the consciousness and tolerance of this era? Did you notice?

The new age in the new energy creates tolerance, and those who negotiate do it with tolerance and in deep earnest. Even though they may not be what you would call enlightened, they are still a product of the new energy and they feel it as well. As you look around your planet, are you aware that you have gone from the threat of global annihilation just a few years ago to a situation where every conflagration that is taking place that you see now is tribal warfare. The tribes will be at war for some time, but in the new energy their battles will bring only sorrow and not victory... and they will tire and beat themselves up in the process.

Dear ones, we have a parable for you now. This is the time my partner enjoys, for he gets to see and feel what takes place. But before we do this, let us just take a moment to tell those of you in this room who have come expecting something special that you may have it now if you choose, for you are in the midst of Spirit speaking to you. For Spirit never changes and the truth remains clear. And we give to you in all grace what you have come here to receive. Many of you know what we are talking about, those of you now who have come expecting this. And so those of you who have the gift of sight may look forward and see the auras of those who sit in front of you... and also of my partner; so there is verification of what we say. The words "I AM" will be meaningful to you, for it represents the essence of Spirit which you and I both share. And it is the love that pours forth from Spirit, and from the same place that these words come from, and from the great central sun, that shower you now with honor for having done these things as humans. And for all those who want to, we shall push into you as much of this power as you wish to receive this night.

The story of David the Indian.

There was on an island an Indian named David. And for those of you who wish to know more about why an Indian was named David, you will have to analyze that later (cosmic laughter). The island that David lived on was a good one and was abundant. And David was of the lineage of royalty on the island, for his grandfather was the chief. David lived a fine life on the island; there was an abundance of food and much grew and could be eaten. David's village and his tribe lived well for many many years.

Now the island was surrounded by an odd attribute, for there was a great fog bank that was very thick surrounding it three miles off the shore. It surrounded the island completely, this fog, and since the fog never came onto the shore, the days on the island were generally sunny and clear. The fog remained three miles off shore like an ominous sign, and no one could ever see beyond it.

Now, David grew up with this fog, and those in the village had experienced it generation after generation. They did not understand it, but they feared it, since every so often there would be a villager who would journey into the fog bank and never return. Even as a boy David can remember one of the older tribesmen who was near death who chose to get into his canoe and go into the fog. There were many stories of what would happen if you went into the fog, mostly told at night by the light of the campfire.

The villagers were taught that if anyone was ever to go into the fog, the rest of the villagers were to go into their houses and their villages and not watch, for there was great fear around this fog. But David, being of royalty, got to watch these few events with the elders as a child, and later as a teenage boy. But the only event he really remembered was of the old one going into the fog. He remembered that as the old one went into the fog bank, he saw him pick up his paddle while his canoe slid gently into the fog, and as expected, the old one never came out again. Just as the elders had said, "No one who ventures into the bank ever returns." And the royalty stayed for many hours watching the fog after the old one had disappeared into it, waiting for something that was foretold would happen. For often, after a time they would hear a giant muffled noise, a fearful noise, that would strike fear into their hearts, a muffled roaring sound that they could not understand. David would remember it for the rest of his life. Who knows what that could have been? Perhaps a monster on the other side of the fog bank? Perhaps the sound of a giant whirlpool or waterfall, there to claim the lives of those who would go through it?

Now it seems odd that David in his thirty-fourth year would have made the decision he did, but David felt a pulling to the fog! He felt that there was something more in his life that he was missing. Perhaps it was a truth that had been lying dormant for years, and somehow the fog was the answer? It is true, no one had ever come back, but that didn't mean they were gone, thought David. And so David set out, without telling any of the elders or villagers, with courage to see what was on the other side of the fog bank. He got into his canoe slowly and gave ceremony about what he was about to do. He thanked God for his life and for the revelation of what was to come. He knew that no matter what happened to him, at least he would have knowledge, and that was what drove him on.

And so David paddled silently and gently toward the fog bank. No one was watching, for he did not announce what was taking place. Soon he was on the brink of approaching it, and it was coming ever nearer. Then David noticed a strange thing; no one had ever purposely gotten close to the bank before to observe anything this close, but it was pulling him into it! The element of fear at this surprising event started to grip him. David did not need his paddle any longer, and so he picked up his paddle and put it into the boat. The canoe disappeared into the fog with him in it. It was still and quiet as David was in the fog bank, as the current kept pulling him forward. It became darker and darker, and then David began to reconsider what he had done. "I am a young man; I have failed my elders, for I was in the lineage and I have chosen a foolish, foolish thing!" David was now afraid, and the fear came over him like a blanket of death, and the blackness started creeping into his brain, and he shook with coldness and emotion as the canoe sped silently along.

David was in the fog bank for hours and it seemed like it would never end. He cowered in his canoe, for he knew he had made a mistake. "What if nothing ever changes?" he thought. "What if I am here for all eternity and starve in this canoe?" David suddenly had a vision of fear where all those who went before were now floating endlessly in their canoes as skeletons in the dark fog. Would he see the old one from years ago? Would anything ever change? "Oh, where is the truth that I sought?" said David out loud in the fog.

Then it happened. David came out of the other side of the fog bank! He was astounded at what he saw, for there in front of him was an entire continent: clear, filled with many villagers and villages as far as he could see! He could see smoke coming from their smoke stacks and hear them playing on the beaches. There were lookouts that were stationed along the fog bank who saw him immediately. As he came through, they saw him and sounded their horns in celebration to let the others know on the shore that another one had come through. Then David heard a giant roar come forward from the land. A roar of celebration! A roar of honor! And they surrounded him with canoes and threw flowers. When he got to the beach, they came and took him and put him on their shoulders and celebrated his coming through the fog. David began a new enriched life that day.

Now you might say, "I know what this parable is about. It's about death, isn't it?" And we say, "No, it is not." This parable as given to you this night verbally, and as you read it, is about coming into the new energy, and about ascension. It is about what is before you if you wish to walk the path. For each one of you has before you a fog bank, which is your fear, and each fear is a different challenge and lesson of different degrees for each person.

Listen carefully, for we're getting to the origin of the subject now. What is it that gives you the most fear? For many of you unknowingly it is the fear of succeeding, and the fear of being on your contracted path; the fear of abundance. Perhaps it is the fear of enlightenment itself. We encourage you to walk into this fear standing tall. Whatever it is that gives you the most anxiety, that you know is karma in your life, must be walked into face first with a challenge, knowing that it is simply a facade. It is the fog bank in the parable, and on the other side is celebration. But it is not without fear. What are the other fears you might say present themselves this night to you? Perhaps it is the fear of relationships – being in them, being out of them? Each of you is different.

But there is another fear also which is paramount in some of the minds of those of you this night. Dear ones, we know who you are. We know your innermost thoughts. As you sit in your chair listening or reading, do you think you are in some kind of faceless mass of humanity? Hardly! We know your name, since we carry it in our hearts. Some of you have experienced events in your lives which are unthinkable tragedies.

The fear many of you have is a memory, for there is blackness in there that you do not wish to move back into. Events or tragedies that may have seemed inappropriate, and had broken your heart at the time, are not to be revisited ever, you tell yourself. This is your fear, and it grips your heart to think that you'd have to visit it again. Let me tell you what you're really afraid of. At the cellular level you're afraid of the fact that you will realize that you were responsible, and that you helped plan it! And that it was part of your contract. And that it was scheduled, and that your spirit knew of it long before it happened. This is your true fear. To have such a black thing revealed as something that you helped plan would seem unthinkable. Yet it is the overview of things, and will bring you face to face with a learning experience that will provide peace where you thought it was never available!

And so it is with some of you this night that carry this very karma with you. Why does Kryon bring you such a parable? It is to exemplify responsibility. You come here by design with a plan that you know of, but that hides from you. It is revealed in the 12:12. Now is the time of enablement, of responsibility for the entire energy of the planet, and it is the time for you to recognize your path. It's time to look into the eyes of your adversaries and say, "I know you! I know who you are, and I choose to disengage from your karma." This is where the tests are passed and where the vibrations are raised for the planet! For there is no sweeter spot on this planet than for you to recognize who you are. For all of the things that give you grief now will disappear and vanish. Do you want miracles for your health? This is simple. For your bodies were designed to last forever. Remember this.

And so it is with these thoughts that Spirit welcomes you to the new age. **This is the new Jerusalem, and you sit in its** energy. And we say to each and every one of you, this is the time when you can stand in the sun and raise your arms high and shout to the heavens "I AM," and mean it. You are magnificent. We sit at your feet this night in celebration of this new age, of this enablement. Some of you will leave this place upset, for there will be anxiety in your heart. For you know you heard the truth, and your brain will wish to deny it. Do not fear this. It is simply Spirit speaking to you in love. Some of you this night have been healed and you will know it. It is a certainty, for each time a group sits in front of Spirit, this takes place. Claim it and know it is yours.

Some of you during this time will simply have been loved. And we ask you to claim that as well. For this, dear ones, is the essence of our relationship to you.

And so it is.

Kryon

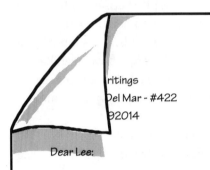

ritings
Del Mar - #422
92014

Dear Lee:

The service you are providing by making the Kryon Writings available to others will do much to raise the vibration of the planet. When I read the books – and it is daily lately – I feel I am having a private conversation with Spirit. The information is so personal, and I feel the presence as I hold the book. I can never explain to you or anyone what those books mean to me. I don't read them; I experience them.

Love and Light,

Pat Rowe Corrington

Awakening Publications
Author of <u>Alive Again... Again... and Again</u>.
Danville, California

Kryon

"Becoming a New Age Human"
Channeled in Kamuela

The big island of Hawaii
Kryon Seminar

The Kryon Writings, Inc.

PMB 422
1155 Camino Del Mar
Del Mar, California 92014
[www.kryonqtly.com]

"Becoming a New Age Human"
Live Channel
Hawaii

> *This live channel has been edited with additional words and thoughts to allow for clarification and better understanding of the written word.*

Greetings, dear ones. I am Kryon of magnetic service. Never fear, my partner, that I would not be here when called. It is the current theme of the Kryon each time we meet with you, to tell you who are assembled in this room that the Kryon never speaks to groups of Humans, for the Kryon speaks to the individual hearts of each one of you. So it is this night that the Kryon comes before you and says, "You are dearly loved." And it is the intent of Spirit this night to sit before you and wash your feet, for you are indeed the exalted ones. Before I say more about this, let me tell you what is taking place in this room right now. For as you get used to my partner's voice, un-

derstand, dear ones, that the translation and the thought groups coming to you now speak with the same voice as came from the voice that instructed Moses. It is the same voice that halted the arm of Abraham with his dagger ready to plunge into the chest of Isaac. It is Spirit that is translated to you this night, for you sit here listening and reading by appointment.

It is no accident that you individually hear or read these words at this time, for we are filling this energy portal with love. We are inviting in at this time the entourage which accompanies me to fill this place with a cone of love, so that during the words spoken tonight, or read at this time, will be transmitted via the third language which speaks to your third eye, regardless if you hear any of the English words. There will be power and healing and love transmitted this night to those who are here. And so it is with all these groups that there are three kinds of people here. Humans each one, we speak to you now, for there is a group of you which comes enlightened and ready for a great soaring of energy in your life. You are the ones who will walk away from this meeting healed! And you will receive this through your own power. But you will hear the truth this night, and energy for healing will be transmitted to you. You are the ones who will walk away and vibrate for three days and have sleepless nights, for there will be instant changes within your spirit. You are greatly honored, for you are the ones who are truly prepared and ready to hear these words. And we honor you greatly.

There is another group of you that is here at the beginning of your actual path, that sweet spot that spirit talks about that will change your lives forever. But you are here to know more about it in anticipation of what is to come, and you are honored, for it is appropriate since you are here by appointment. And when we say you are here by appointment, we mean that you physically desired with intent to sit in the chair that you are in. The third group are the ones who came here because they had to. Perhaps they are here by obligation to a friend, or they're with a partner who they did not wish to leave for the evening. Perhaps they were only curious. And we say to you dear ones: you are loved every bit as much as any Human being on the planet, and there is no judgment for your consciousness this night, or for your reasons of being here or for your intent. If you will be open and receptive this night, you will receive information. It is not necessary to believe any of it, but let the seeds fall within your mind, for someday it will serve you. We guarantee it! Know that none of what happens this night will harm you.

Kryon wishes to tell all of those Humans sitting here this night that we know your name. We know your Earthly name and we know your angelic name. We know why you are here. We know of your path, and that is the reason we honor you so greatly, each single one. We see you and know who you are as you sit in that chair. See us clearly, for those of you who have sight can see the aura of my partner change this night. That alone will prove that spirit speaks to you through love from the great central sun. Changes will abound in this clear energy through translation this night. The information of the Kryon is the information that changes Human hearts and souls. It is not information that will change the doctrine of any organization. It will not change where you go to worship. It will not change the love you may have for any ascended master. It is simply information about the new age and the gifts of the new age. Some of you are already receiving the love and are feeling it as it flows into you. Oh, dear one, we know who you are. But we know of your trials; we know of your thoughts. And this is why we honor you so, for you are the ones who have chosen by plan to be here this night... warriors of the light each! You are the ones who have chosen the hard path: to be born in biology on this planet in order to raise the vibration. Over and over you have chosen to go through this, for even the Kryon cannot say he has done that. I see your colors, each one, and I know where you've been. For the badges of honor show through clearly even as you sit in your chairs.

The past lives! Are you aware of your karmic group, dear ones, this night? It may amaze and surprise you. For here you sit pretending not to know each other. Ah, for in this very place so many years ago (that it is difficult to count), you were part of the great continent called "Lemuria." And each one of you in this enlightened state in this new age of this planet were shamans and holy men and priests and priestesses. And so this is your karma. As a group it brings you back together now – perhaps not for long, for you will go your own ways in this new energy. We thought you might be interested in knowing who you are, for all of you coming together this night have had a lineage which is great on this planet. It is no accident that the group comes together now to hear the admonitions of Spirit.

Walk through the fear of enlightenment! It did not serve some of you well when you were here in Lemuria. For you faced termination shortly after your enlightenment, and the fear of that happening again is in your face, so to speak. It is a real fear indeed, to walk through this night. It is a seed fear for the persecution you received seemingly at the hands of Spirit itself, as this, your civilization, was terminated so many years ago. So we welcome you back, and we honor your very presence. For those of you who are in this place you call Hawaii, we tell you this – not to generate fear in any one Human soul, but in love – that the Earth is under construction here.

When the Kryon works in order to alter your magnetic grids, you can be certain that the Earth will change as well – and we will speak of this later even in this channel. The Earth is part of the whole, and you are part of the whole, and you must **both change** to facilitate your own consciousness. The Earth is not dead; it is not a rocky barren thing. It has essence as well and must change with you. So it is in an area such as this that we tell you that it will not be a very long time before there are rumblings and movings of the Earth here. We say to you, each and every one of you, do not fear this. For as long as you are walking in that sweet spot which is your path, you will be at the right place at the right time. If some of you may lose items around you because of these things, do not mourn that, for your essence is what is most important. You will be alive with your higher selves to the degree that you will have peace over this. You will stand as the lighthouses here for those who are in fear, and you will be able to comfort them with your knowledge and your enlightenment. We give you this information, not to create fear in any one of you, for the little ones here tonight will be safe. But it is with honor that these changes take place on this planet.

Let me tell you now of the new age Human being. I wish to paint a picture for you, as the love is even intensified for you in this room, about the attributes of the new Human. Oh, dear ones, sometimes I allow my partner to see you as I do, and he has asked that I not do this very often, for it overwhelms him. Each one of you is magnificent! ... and about to become even more so. Let me paint the attributes for you of the new age Human being. The new age Human being is the one who has a weakened duality. The duality, as the Kryon and Spirit sees it, is that name which is given to the barrier between you as Human beings and your "higher God self" which is also you. Sometimes you think of God as being someone else. You are part of the whole, just as Kryon is. And when you co-create, you co-create with Spirit and the guides and yourself. So the **weakened duality** is the attribute of the new age Human. The veil has been lifted slightly so that you can connect in a stronger way to your higher selves. And because of this, the next few attributes I will speak of are possible. For the new age Human is one who has seen the opportunity of the new energy and has voided his or her karma. And whether it is heavy or weak, the new age Human being has been able to cast it aside. This, the first stage, allows for all of the other attributes to fall into place.

The next attribute is one of **responsibility**, and it has two parts. The first is the overview. The new age Human being understands that he is totally responsible for all things that are taking place in his or her life. What this means is a knowledge at the intuitive level that what is going on has been *planned by yourselves*. **You are not predestined to do anything**. You may have your own life, and it will exist for you as you choose it.

But the windows of opportunity are planned by you in advance, and one of them is here tonight as you sit in this chair, for it brought you here! Think about that. It finds you here listening to or reading these words – not predestined, but by your own choice. This overview of responsibility means that you, none of you, are victims of anything! No one or no thing does anything to you. For you understand that even though it may feel that way, it is by your own design and choice for you to walk through these lessons. Many things will take place in your lives which will make you stop and think, "Why did this happen to me?" Then you will have the answer through your intuition, for you planned them long ago and they are at the cellular level, waiting for your own discretion and discernment for answers.

The second part of the responsibility is something that perhaps you have not thought of until now, and again remember that Kryon tells you this through Spirit. **You are responsible to the planet.** You may have thought of this planet as simply being the vehicle of your Humanism; that is, something you walk on, or something that you breathe, or something that you simply enjoy. Nothing could be further from the truth. For Kryon is here to alter your planet. The magnetic grids are only one piece and part of what makes your consciousness work. **For all of it is alive and has essence**, and it is important that you greet this planet with great responsibility and say, "I am here with you and you with me for the new energy, and together we will change the vibration... together as a whole." And so it is important as you begin any meditations from this point on in a way to remember these things. Using the pattern of many of your ancients, greet the Sky, greet the Earth, greet the Winds and the Waters. Before you meditate, give honor that you are all together with them. Give verbal honor that you are a part of the whole, for one cannot exist without the other, and the system is complete when one honors it and has responsibility to it. And believe me, dear ones, when you start doing this, it will honor you as well. It will harbor you and keep you safe. And we speak now even of those about to take long journeys... honoring especially the waters under which their journeys will be taken.

The new age Human is one who is **enabled**. Now we have used this word before, and what it means is that an enablement is a Human who is co-creating. This perhaps is one of the highest gifts you have in the new energy. For to co-create means that you and Spirit and those around you create your own reality. This may seem like a paradox to you, for you have been told only to co-create for yourselves. But what happens when you start to co-create for yourself is that those around you are affected in a positive way. We call upon you to revisit the parable of the tar pit which has been published (*Kryon Book II*), so that you will know of what we speak. For this is the way co-creation works. As you co-create for yourself, others are touched and helped; some are even enlightened! ... and all because you co-created for yourself.

There are several elements of co-creation which we must visit for your culture so you will understand these things better. The first is abundance. Spirit uses the word abundance in translation to mean sufficiency, but Spirit means sufficiency on a day-by-day basis. And if you are always in the now, that means that each day will also be in the now. A sufficiency, therefore, means a sufficiency for life as lived in the now. This is abundance. Would your definition of a wealthy human be different than a sufficiency for life?

And yet we say to you that it is one of the hardest new ideas for you to grasp, that you have control over these things. But indeed, it can be done. As you graduate, intending the neutral implant as a new age Human, you will begin to learn how to create your abundance. Now we have used the example of the bird in the past, and you may say it is oversimplified. But we say to you, dear ones, the bird awakens hungry, yet the first thing it does is to sing.

It knows of its abundance and its sustenance, for it will co-create its food on a daily basis. It does not worry where the food is coming from, for it knows that it feeds daily and has gotten used to it, and that it will be provided for. Yet some of you will say, "Yes, but how can you compare a bird to a Human being? After all, Human beings have intellect and intelligence and will tend to worry, and are far different from the bird." And I will say to you, Human, that perhaps knowing that your intellect and your intelligence does this to you will give you insight as to what the intellect and the intelligence do against you! For we will say again that the intellect without intuition is your enemy. You may intellectualize yourselves to death, into disease, and into imbalance, but when you combine it with the spiritual self, the intuition, and the higher self – Ah! together that partnership is strong. And they marry one with the other. **Therefore your intellectual nature and your intelligence, together with your spiritual self, will be the balance of the new age Human.** The triad here isn't subtle for some of you who understand, again, the power of the three.

The next attribute is that of **relationships**. This attribute we don't have to tell you is sometimes the most difficult one. We speak now of relationships of all kinds. We speak of mothers and daughters, and we speak now of fathers and sons, and of partners. The whole area of relationships was given to you for tests. Each time you have difficulty in this area, you are invited to co-create your way out of it. And when you do so, and it's in a partnership level, watch how you change! But more than that, dear one, as you change, watch the reaction of your partner. There are miracles here for you in this area if you will accept them. Some of you are still waiting for the correct partner. We say to you that these things can be co-created with marvelous results, and we ask you for patience, for your windows of opportunity are being prepared even as you wait.

The next attribute of the new age Human comes in the area of **health and healing**. The new age Human has a grasp on self-healing, for she or he has discovered something important. And it is that the marriage of the **intellect** and the **spiritual** and the **intelligence** to the biology is critical (the triad again). You cannot walk around with your Humanism and your biology thinking that your Spirit resides in your head while the rest of you is simply meat! (Audience laughs.) And yet some of you do! And when things go wrong with your body, you say, "This or that has malfunctioned," or "This or that hurts me." Start practicing a marriage to your biology. Ask it to talk to you and be one with you and when something irritates you or has pain, examine why. Start thinking of your body as "we" instead of "it," and this will serve you, for the new age Human sees them as one. This is critical information for those who wish to live a very long time. And speaking of such things, we say to you who have voided your karma, "The engine of karma is indeed death and rebirth; and when it is voided, there is no more reason for death." Therefore, what we are saying is we invite you, the new age Human, to live a very long life, longer than you ever had imagined. Slow the aging process down, and spiritually co-create the death hormone to be eliminated. As we have channeled in the past, this is all within your ability, but practice will be necessary. Not all of you will be able to do this immediately, since it is very new to you, and is against everything you have been shown to this point.

The next attribute of new age Humans is that they are the ones on the planet who can **hold the magic**. As my partner has spoken to you before, what this means, dear ones, is what was explained on the 11:11 and the 12:12. The entities who are gradually leaving this planet are passing the torch to you. This new age Human that you are can hold the magic! **Oh, rejoice in this, for it is the first time we have ever told any Humans this**! Those who wish to move into ascension will hold the magic. Those who wish not to move into ascension, but wish to be light bearers and light workers, will also hold the magic. All of you to some degree may hold this. "Place holders," each one... holders of the enlightenment and guardians of the truth; this is what you are. For the torch is passed to you by the devas, and by those in the rocks from the lands they are leaving at this time. And as they honor you, and smile at you, and leave this planet, they do so in honor, not in sadness, for they never believed such a thing could happen. Honor is the key word here. All of the magic you attributed to these is now yours! You are the sole holders of the energy space of the entire planet, and you no longer have to share any of it with those who held it for you for so long. There is no sadness in their leaving, believe me!

The new age Human is **peaceful**. He is peaceful because he or she sees the overview and understands what is going on. We sometimes have called this "unwarranted peace." This translation may surprise you, but it's the kind of peace you feel even though things around you are in disorder. There may be chaos taking place in your immediate vicinity, and yet as you look at the ones in chaos, you feel peace. **For you feel safe in the plan that you have created, and you feel peaceful regardless of what is going on.** And we say to you, dear ones, that even in the face of the passing of loved ones, you may have peace, knowing full well that they planned it before they came. We have spoken of these things before, and the appropriateness of the grief of missing someone. Perhaps some of you have lost dear ones recently, and we say that they are among the ones in this very room loving you now! Do you see the overview, the comings and the goings? ... and the oneness of the planet for all of you? The one who is the new age Human recognizes that he is his own ancient! The karmic humor of it! ... imagine leaving messages for yourselves over and over, to dig up and find. Of all kinds of cultures and colors are you, even as you sit in this room or read these words. This is the attribute of the new age Human.

The final attribute of the new age Human is that which is difficult for many of you; but you will learn it over time: **Patience and tolerance**. For we tell you that it is the new age Human who is tolerant of his neighbor who is not enlightened, and as simple as that sounds, it may be difficult for you to realize until it comes at you. When others criticize you, it is your tolerance and your peace and patience that will love them back, for you will see them in their own process and you will not judge them. It is the marvelous trait of the new age Human when accused, rather than thinking of himself, instead to think of the accuser and to love him within his process. It is not a difficult thing to do, for it will be your nature as the new age Human. And although your adversaries may seem difficult, you still will not judge them. For you will see them as part of your own process as you planned it. They are in your life by agreement, but with your karma voided, they're up against a brick wall trying to push your buttons. And in their own process they are appropriate being in your lives. Dear ones, it is critical for you to know this. Some of them may never receive the kind of enlightenment that you have, and yet they are on their path just like you. They are no different. They have planned in advance with you to be here, and they have a path and journey of their own. So to criticize or judge them would be to criticize yourselves. To judge them would be to judge yourselves, for each one is part of your collective plan.

We wish to tell you something now that you may have already noticed on your planet, and that has to do with "tribal awareness." We wish you to look around you and see what is happening on the Earth. For in the new energy and with the shifts going on, there will be this element of awareness for you; and not surprising, it has to do with **lineage**. Dear ones, all of the major conflicts and the minor wars of this planet, at this moment as you sit in this chair, are tribal. That is what it has come to at this point. It is no longer nation against nation, or country against country, as in the old energy. For now it is tribe against tribe, and this was expected. To some degree there will be some of this for the rest of the time on the planet, for not all will become enlightened.

This is appropriate, this tribal awareness. It's interesting to see what Spirit wants you to make of it, for it represents the awareness of the "seeds of the beginning of the tribe of Earth." For as you join the other tribes of the galaxy, we wish you to feel your lineage, and right now you are feeling it as individual lineages of the tribes on the planet. We ask you to join these feelings into one feeling of human lineage, because, dear ones, **you will be forced to later**. For in the future you must negotiate with other tribes of the galaxy as one human tribe of the planet Earth. And so we ask you to hold this thought. These things will be clearer to you as time goes on.

Another admonition we have for you is that we call upon the leaders of the tribes to translate the ancient languages and bring them together as one. And what we mean by this are the languages which are at least ten thousand of your years old. We ask that the spiritual leaders of these tribes, no matter what the lineage on this planet, bring these teachings together and compare them. Look at the similarities and honor them as the truth as they show themselves. Do not depend upon the writings which are any younger than ten thousand years. This will become clearer also, as time goes on.

These are the admonishments of Spirit in the new age, and the honor that we have for you as Human beings in order for you to exist now in this new age. For Spirit cannot do this itself! You are still Humans walking the Earth in lesson, and there are so many lessons left for you. Not karmic ones, but Earth ones... and later there will be the galactic ones. But for now, as you walk the path as an enlightened Human, you will be peaceful about each one as it presents itself... without fear even though you face the unknown. This is indeed the new age Human!

(Comment for the reader. This channel was delivered within days after the Japan Earthquake of January 95.) We stop for a moment before a Kryon story in order to tell you again in this communication how Spirit views you. Oh, dear ones, at this very moment there are thousands who used to be Humans on this planet, who have picked up their essence in the cave of creation and are standing in the hall of honor! For the ones who have recently left this planet, about whom you are sorrowful, are in ecstasy and joy at this moment. If you could see this, and if I could show you the awards ceremony where they are receiving their colors, you would be in awe. In the "now" of time each one of them has an unlimited opportunity to stand in the presence of Spirit and be honored by name for his immediate past incarnation and for fulfilling his contract. You would have an entirely different feeling about Human death if you could see this.

And now let me tell you the story about the father and the son. Let the love saturate every pore of your body as the truth of this real story unfolds to you. Now is the time for the healing that you came for, and are reading this book for. Yes , I'm speaking to you. We know who you are!

And so there was on the planet Earth, the father. Now he was not yet a father, but was looking forward to it, for the birth of a child was imminent. And he so hoped it would be a son, for he had great plans for a male child. He was a carpenter and he wished to teach his son carpentry. "Oh, I have so many things to teach him. The tricks of the trade, and I know he will be excited and will carry on the lineage of our trade in this family," he thought to himself. And so when the birth occurred and indeed it was a son, he was overwhelmed with joy. "This is my son!" he cried to everyone. "This is the one who will carry the lineage of the family. This is the one who will have my name. This is the great new carpenter, for I will show him everything I know. We will have a grand time together, my son and I."

And so as the baby grew up and became older, he loved his father. For his father doted over him, lifting him up at every opportunity saying, "Son, just wait until I can share these things with you! You're going to love it. You will share our lineage and our craft and our family, and we will be proud of you long after I am gone." But something unusual happened along the way. For as life progressed, the son slowly felt smothered by the father's attention, and he began feeling that he had his own path, even though the son did not recognize it in those words. And he began rebelling. When the son became the age of the teen years, he was not interested anymore in what his father had to say about carpentry or lineage. And he said to his father, "Father, please honor me; I have my own wishes and desires. There are things I'm interested in that are not carpentry." And his father could not believe what he was hearing, and said, "But son, you don't understand! You see, I'm wiser than you, and I can make decisions for you. Let me show you these things. Trust me. Let me be what I was supposed to be, as your teacher, and we will have a grand time, you and I." And the son said, "I don't see it that way, father. I do not wish to be a carpenter, nor do I wish to hurt your feelings, sir. But I have my own path and wish to go my way." That was the last time the word "Sir" was used, for the honor between father and son gradually disintegrated and diminished until it became a void of blackness and darkness.

For as the son grew even more, he realized that the father continued to badger him to become something he did not wish to be. And so the son left home, not even saying good-bye to the father, but instead left a note that said, "Please leave me alone." The father was mortified. "My son," he thought, "I have spent twenty years waiting for this time. He was supposed to be everything... the carpenter, the grand master of the craft with my name. I am ashamed. He has ruined my life!" And the son in his life thought of his father and thought, "This man has ruined my childhood, and shaped me into something I had not chosen to be.

And I do not choose to have affection for him." And so there was, indeed, anger and hatred between the father and the son, and it remained all of their lives and to the point of death. And when the son had a child of his own, a beautiful daughter, at that moment the son thought, "Perhaps, just perhaps, I should invite my father to see this child of his lineage." But then he reconsidered, thinking, "No, this is the father who ruined my childhood and hates me. I am not going to share anything with him." And so the father never got to see the grandchild.

And so it goes that in his eighty-third year, the father died. And on his deathbed he looked back and he said, "Perhaps now, as my death is imminent, I will call for my son." And so in his moment of wisdom, nearing death, feeling his intuition and knowing what was coming, he sent for his son. But the answer came back that his son would not join him. "I don't care about you, for you ruined my life. Stay away from me." And then the son added, "I will be glad of your passing." Oh, the anger and the hatred that was there!

The son lived a good life. And it was also in his eighties that he passed on, surrounded by a family that loved him dearly, mourning for his essence that would no longer walk the planet Earth. And this, dear ones, is where the story really begins. For the son passed to the cave of creation. He took the three day journey where he picked up his essence and his name and moved on to the hall of honor. And he spent a long time in adoration there, where literally millions of entities, in a stadium which you cannot begin to fathom, applauded and honored him for what he had gone through while on your planet. You see, dear ones, all of you have been there before, but we cannot show you this, for it would spoil your time here, and give you too much remembrance. But you will be there again some day to pick up the next color. For these colors are seen by everyone in the universe when they meet you. Your colors are an identity badge indicating that you were a warrior of the light on the planet Earth. It is hard for you to conceive of, I know, at this moment as I tell you this, but it is true nonetheless. You have no idea of how important these unique Earth badges are. Some day you will remember my words when you meet me in the audience at the hall of honor.

And so the son was there receiving his accolades, and his new colors were placed into his energy to spin into his other colors to show those around him who he was. And when this time was over, the son, in the cloak of the real entity that he is as a universal entity, entered into an area where he immediately saw his best friend Daniel.... the one that he had left to come to the planet Earth. And he saw Daniel from across the void and said, "It is you! I have missed you so!" And they came together, so to speak, and embraced, intermingling their energies. And so it was with great joy they spoke about old universal times that they had enjoyed together before the son went to Earth.

Frolicking around the Universe with his friend Daniel, one day he said to him, "You know Daniel, you made a grand father on Earth." And Daniel said to him, "My best friend, you made a wonderful son. Wasn't it amazing what we went through as humans? How complete the duality was that separated us as best friends while we were on Earth. How could something be like that?" The former son replied "Oh, it was because the veil was so strong that we didn't know who we really were."

"But the planning worked so well, didn't it?" said the former son.
"Yes, it did," replied Daniel, "for we never once had a glimmer of truth as to who we were!"

And so we leave these two entities as they head toward the next Earth planning session. And we overhear one saying, "Oh, let's do it again! Only this time, I will be the mother and you be the daughter!"

This precious story is told especially for some of you reading this now, who have yet to recognize the gift of what is taking place in your life... or have yet to recognize your best friend.

Dear ones, look at the love that it took for these entities to agree to go through this! We gave you an example of anger and hatred, but they were only karmic attributes. They were fears to be broken, and I tell you now that had either the son or the father during this lifetime recognized who they were, they would have walked into the fear of the hatred and the anger, and come out with love. **The other one could not have resisted it, and things would have been different for both of them.** This is the new age Human lesson. Regardless of what you think is in front of you, and the way it appears, it may only be a paper-thin fear ready to be dissolved, ready to move into love.

Love is, dear ones, the greatest power of the universe. This love energy isn't just the thing that gives you peace. This love energy isn't just the thing that gives empowerment. This love energy is also responsible for your silence in the face of accusation, for your universal truths, and at the same time it is also responsible for the most unenlightened things that you can imagine on this planet! For the source of your karmic set-up is also love. Sometimes it may take on a strange face, such as hate and anger, but love is the king of the plan. It has substance. It has thickness. It has logic and reason. It is the essence of the universe, and it is passed to you this night.

For we are here now to meet you by appointment, and all the words that have been spoken this night have only been spoken so that you personally can enjoy an earned change of heart, or a change of energy. And so my partner comes this distance to give you these messages: that he is loved in no greater way than you, that his task is no greater than yours, and that it is to receive the gift of the new energy and become one of these new age Humans.

And in the process, reach out and touch your guides and feel the electricity and the magnetism of the love which Spirit has for you right now. Kryon is only one among tens of thousands who are unseen entities in this, "your" Earth.

We hope that this time together will have given you a broader overview of not only who you are, but indeed who is the one who sits next to you and pretends not to know you, but who may very well be your best friend or former partner. There is irony here this night, that within this gathering may be the only time that you see each other as humans while you are in lesson this time. Such is the cosmic humor of Spirit that the workings of group karma has you coming back over and over to see familiar faces that you do not recognize! Fathers and sons, mothers and daughters, sisters and brothers: we tell you that you all know one another!

Now, as we surround you with love, we remind you of the family that you are, and that the tribe that belongs to you is that of the planet Earth. And so we close this time saying that what you have felt this night that has spoken to your cells can never be discarded. For it will be part of you from this time forward, even if you do not remember the words. Receive this gift, if you choose. Spirit honors each and every one of you who has made the trek to sit in this chair this night, or read these words. And we do not necessarily mean the trek of the past few hours, but rather we mean the path of your life to this point. For you are in the "now" with us here. All those reading this are experiencing the same exact time frame and energy as those listening to these words in chairs on this great island.

Do you really feel that you picked up this book by accident? Our love for you is absolute, and given freely in appreciation of who you are.

And so it is.   *Kryon*

The Indigo Children

Lee Carroll and Jan Tober

The New Kids Have Arrived

*Can we really be seeing a spiritual evolution in the kids
today? Are they smarter than we were? Why do so many of
our children today seem to be "system busters"? Some very
fine minds are brought together to discuss and expose this
exciting premise, first published in Kryon book 6.*

■ **This book is a must
for parents!**

"The Indigo Children is a helpful and informative book.
I highly recommend it"

■ **Harold H. Bloomfield, M.D.**

Published by Hay House • ISBN 1-56170-608-6 • $13.95

*Books and tapes can be purchased in retail stores, or by phone
~ Credit cards welcome ~*

1-800-352-6657 - <kryonbooks@aol.com>

Kryon

"The Beatitudes"
Channeled in Bellevue

Seattle
Kryon Seminar

The Kryon Writings, Inc.

PMB 422
1155 Camino Del Mar
Del Mar, California 92014
[www.kryonqtly.com]

"The Beatitudes"
Live Channel
Bellevue

This live channel has been edited with additional words and thoughts to allow for clarification and better understanding of the written word.

Greetings, dear ones. I am Kryon of magnetic service. You are all loved dearly! It is true that this is the voice that was heard from the bush that burned. It is Spirit that comes before you this night. It is Spirit that sits at your feet as you listen to my partner's voice. For you are indeed the warriors of the light. And we ask you in all love to prepare yourselves and open your hearts to the message of the Kryon this night. In addition, because it is a very special occasion, this being the sweet spot I have put my partner in, where his contract is being fulfilled now, we ask for verification of this channeling this night from the sensitives that are here, and we challenge them to feel Spirit and to know what is taking place. To see the auras change, to feel the power of love as it walks the aisles of this place, and to know that it is real and it is truly happening. For each one of you is a very special entity indeed and Spirit sees you for who you are as you sit in these seats before my partner. Spirit knows much about who you are. Spirit sees a time when there will be a great celebration when you are no longer here. A time when all will know you from the badges of colors that you carry, for they will say, "Ahh, you were the ones in the planet of lesson. You are the ones from the planet of free choice that lifted itself up. We honor you. We can see from your stripes who you are." For this is the mantle that you carry with you even as you are here now, one of tremendous honor!

The message this night may surprise you. It is an internal one for you. There have been those who have said "Kryon, you have not spoken at all about the other masters who walk this planet. You have given very little credence to the one who went into the cave and came out with the Koran, and yet there are millions who follow him. You have not spoken of the ones in India. You have not spoken of the Babas, or of the Avatar. And what about the Buddha? There are so many masters, and yet you have given us no information about these." And the answer is thus: that the other channels in the other cultures will do the work of the exposure of these. For they all had a message of love, and they all tie with Spirit. But it is this day that we wish to examine other messages from the New Age master you called Jesus, which we will refer to as the Jew Jesus. For there was a time when, close to the town which He called Galilee, He gathered a crowd before him and gave the nine declarations of blessedness, which are the new age blessed declarations. These will this night be reinterpreted, and then you will see how this master of your culture was indeed the first master of love for your new age. What follows in these reinterpretations will be the essence of what was meant at the time these channelings were given. Go slowly my partner, for you do not reinterpret the scripture without fear (audience laughs).

These declarations of blessedness are for you, dear ones. Listen carefully, for they are ordered in importance. There are nine of them and they are given with the one which carries the most energy first.

Before we do this, there is an entourage that I bring with me that is in the aisles of this place as you hear (or read) these words, that sit next to you and raise the vibration of the room. This entourage, the Kryon entities, along with others that have been invited, are here to respond to your needs. They are in love with you, and they are here to serve you. We cry out "honor!" and we say to you, get used to this, this love that pours out from Spirit, for it is the way of things. It is the way Spirit works. For each of you is loved exactly as the one next to you, no greater and no less. And the entities that I bring to this arena this night are here to serve you and your guides, which you have also called your Angels. For they are very excited, and know there are no accidents and that you are here by appointment. It would not serve you if you did not know this.

(1) Here is the first declaration of blessedness: Honored are the poor in Spirit for they are family. Now you may ask, "Who are these who are poor in Spirit?" This phrase has been misinterpreted to be those who are humble. Dear ones, in this assemblage this night there are so many of you who have had spiritual past lives and incarnations. With great cosmic humor we see how many of you who are here wore sandals in your past lives! And the sack cloths, and all of the incarnations spent on your knees, bowing your backs and prone on your noses before Spirit. You could not come to a place of enlightenment at this time in your planet's history without having gone through these times. Many of you are familiar with this, and have had these past lives analyzed and know of what I speak.

But dear ones, I am here to say that the one who is humble is not the one about whom we are talking. This humble one is not the one who is poor in Spirit. For humility through the eons and your own past lives has only produced sore backs, sore knees and sore noses. No. We speak now of the one who was exemplified in the parable given about the prodigal son. Now, this parable briefly is about a family that had two sons. One son stayed home and honored his family and his father. This son took responsibility for the things that he knew he was to do, and did them well. The other son did not. He did not see his responsibility within the family, and he took his inheritance and left. He spent it foolishly, and did as he chose. All of the things he wanted to do, he did. And as the story goes, and as you know, there was a time of reckoning when the wayward son recognized his responsibility and returned to the family. Now, this parable (you may think) focuses on that returning son. Indeed it <u>does</u> <u>not</u>. It focuses on the son who remained. For this is the son who was doing the work and had the responsibility. This is the one who was mortified at the celebration of the one coming back! For he did not understand the logic that said that although he had stayed to do the work, the celebration was all about the one who had not! Dear ones, this exemplifies a situation which has the returning son as the one who was unenlightened becoming enlightened. And it shows how you are to view the ones who are not enlightened who are walking among you now. For these indeed are the *poor in spirit*.

These are the ones, each and every one, who have the potential for being wonderful Spirits of enlightenment. Yet the timing simply is not right. So as you sit and as you watch these, see them each as a prodigal son, one who is poor in Spirit. The hierarchy of importance has this example first, and you may say, "Why is this?" It is because Spirit loves these unenlightened as much as you. They simply are not in the family yet; but they will be. And so the declaration of blessedness and the admonition that comes with it is that when the celebration occurs, and these unenlightened become family, rejoice! Do not see this situation as something that slights you. Honored indeed are the poor in spirit! The poor in spirit therefore represent all those around you who do not see themselves in your New Age, and yet Spirit's compassion is first for them. Understand the wisdom of this, and you will indeed understand God.

(2) The next honoring is very important. Honored are those who mourn, for they shall receive peace. Dear ones, nothing touches the soul of the human being more than the mourning for a past human being. And Spirit is well aware of this, for Spirit understands that it is unique to you as humans. Spirit does not mourn like you do, but we understand that there is no greater hurt than the hurt of the heart.

There are those this night who have had recent mournings. There are those this night who are still clutching at their hearts for humans who have passed, whom they called family. Dear ones, this night I wish some of these to fill these aisles, and to let you know that although you mourn their passing humanness, they are still here to shout to you this night;

> "WE ARE ETERNAL! We go on and on and on, and so will you... and we love you dearly. We see your mournings and we wish you to have peace with what has taken place. We honor you as does Spirit for being here, and we also want you to know of your own eternalness. For there is *no such thing as death*. Celebrate the life that is yours through Spirit, and know that WE ARE STILL HERE!"

The ones who crowd the aisles of this place are the ones who have recently passed and are now here to revisit. Ahh, some of you do not believe this, but there are those among you who know it is true. They are here, and as my partner is filled with emotion for what is taking place, he says "Honor those who mourn, but realize that they mourn for some who are living and alive and are standing in the aisles here this night."

This declaration of blessedness is near the top, for it involves how much Spirit loves you for what you go through as human beings. For you are so honored indeed for wearing this mantle, for coming into a planet where you cannot even see who you are, and for mourning those who are past. You are eternal... eternal.

(3) Honored are the meek, for they shall inherit the planet. Who are these meek, you might ask? They are not the weak ones, as some have told you. These meek ones are the warriors of the light. The meek ones are the ones who are slow to anger in the face of situations which would create anger. These meek ones are the ones who are slow to defend themselves in a posture where defense would seem to be called for. These meek ones are the ones

who tolerate the intolerable. These meek ones are the ones who sit before Spirit this night! The warriors of the light. This meek person is YOU. For you are the ones who have seen the love and the peace of enlightenment. As far as inheriting the planet, be aware that you are the ones to be looked up to. You are the ones who are going to lead the others through this New Age. For you know what is happening and they do not. You are the new leaders. Honored indeed are you, the meek ones.

(4) Honored are those who seek the truth, for they shall have it. Dear ones, we have spoken of intent, over and over. Those of you who seek the truth are here this night, for you have given intent to learn about Spirit, and to learn about yourselves. This piece of God that you carry with you wherever you go is ready to be exposed to yourselves individually. You are honored for your quest of this, even as you sit before Spirit this night. For intent is everything. Do not give it unless you mean it. And when you give it, speak it out loud so your humanness can enjoy the proclamation! Honored are those who seek the truth.

(5) Honored are the merciful, for they will receive mercy. These merciful ones are those who are kind and have empathy, and they represent the group of you which has voided your karma. For you see, one who is kind and empathizes cannot be one who has a critical Spirit or a critical nature. For a critical nature in a human is a display of karma which has been unresolved, and unresolved karma creates rage and anger. One who carries rage and anger cannot be a merciful person, and so Spirit honors the merciful, and therefore honors those who have walked through their karmic lessons and have popped the personal bubbles of fear. For the bubbles appear ominous before you, and they generate fear for you; but they pop so easily and they move aside so quickly, for they are phantoms indeed! When they are voided, the merciful person is exposed... the one who is empathetic genuinely, and the one who is kind genuinely.

(6) Honored are the pure in heart. Oh dear ones, this has been so misunderstood. Who is this pure in heart? I would like to address the mothers among you, who would generally be the females... (laughs) ... cosmic Kryon humor. Can you remember the first time you had a child? And as you carried that precious life within you, you looked at other children around you and you often said, "mine will not be like that, for you see I'm going to teach mine better. I'm going to expose mine only to the finest of truths and only to love in the home. I'm going to shield it and teach it well. And it's going to be a glorious child who loves me greatly."

Then to the horror of some of you, the little one came out with a set of attributes you could not believe! There was anger, fear, jealousy, self-centeredness, and yes, even trickery. He did not learn that from you... did he? Is this not proof of the imprint all children born into this planet carry as attributes of karma? No mother had to give them these things. In fact the opposite was true, for those of you mothers who saw what was taking place quickly realized that your job was to help unlearn these things! Yes. The one who is pure in heart is the one who has taken responsibility for his contract, and understands that there is no such thing as a victim. Each one of you has a set of circumstances in your life that you are walking through which you planned yourself. And as odd as it might seem, and as strange to you as it might be, whatever situation you find yourself in now, you planned it! You planned it with help from the others around you, even some of those whom you say you do not know. For they are indeed very knowing of you. You know each other and you don't even know that you do. Such is the strength of your duality. You planned it and you are responsible for the situations that you sit in now. And when you have full knowledge of these facts, you are one whom Spirit calls pure in heart. For your heart understands very well the planning that went into the creation of the situations you find yourself in. You might say, "How can this be, for so many of them are negative?" And Spirit says to you, "On purpose you have asked for these things so that you may walk into the face of them. The tiger can be exposed and the karma can be fulfilled." Those of you who have opted to take the gift of the neutral implant automatically become pure in heart. For your cloud of karma is voided, and the clarity is exposed. Honored are those who are pure in heart.

(7) Honored are the peace makers, for they shall indeed have peace. Dear ones, there lurks in your human consciousness an enemy. For without the integration of a certain part of your brain with another part, you have an enemy within you. We speak now of your intellect. For without the marriage of the intellect to the spiritual, you have a killer living in your body. How many of you as human beings know of the feeling of being awakened early in the morning only to have your active intellect say to you, "What is it now we should worry about that will keep us awake? Let's do the 'what if' schedule. What if this happens? What if this does not happen?" It is typically a human trait where there is part of your brain not participating in the duality that would take you on a journey to the worst of all scenarios, repeatedly. And in that activity you become unbalanced and you get dis-ease in your body. For the worry will create the chemical imbalance, and therefore your intellect has done you no good whatsoever. We wish this night for you to fully understand the mechanics of this attribute, for you are the peacemakers. Not necessarily the ones creating political balance between nations, but we speak now of internal peace. We speak of a peace where peace has no reason to be, existing alongside problems and situations which would normally cause imbalance and fear. Instead, you claim peace and you own it! This is the peace maker. This is the one who has married the intellect with the Spiritual... for you see it is a catalytic power. That enemy of the intellect becomes very powerful when married to the Spiritual. For not only is your greatest science going to come from this, but your greatest peace as well.

For the intellect will then wake you up at three in the morning and say, "Do you know how much you are loved? Do you know who you are? Do you know that your guides are with you right now?" Quite a switch wouldn't you say? This is the peacemaker; the honoring is great. Oh, don't you long for this, those of you who do not have it? It can be yours even as you sit this night by appointment in that seat (or by appointment as you read these words). This is Spirit that speaks to you now, not a human being. We know who you are; we know what you carry with you. We know of your desire for peace and we say, "We honor this and we implement it at your beck and call." You may have it now, and leave this place as a different person.

(8) The eight and the ninth are similar only in intensity. Honored are those who walk with the truth among those who do not. For Spirit understands what it's like to be among those who look at you and laugh... and who roll their eyes and muse and do not see who you are, or do not believe you when you talk of these things which are precious pearls of truth in your belief system. For you have indeed absorbed the way things work, and yet there are so many around you who do not acknowledge this at all. And for some of you these are family, and for some of you these are work mates. Again, we honor you for this journey, and we encourage you to see each of these as the prodigal son, and each of these as a giant light worker. They just don't know it yet. For each of these can be just as previously described: filled with mercy, honored for mourning, pure in heart. Their timing has not caught up with their contract. But you walk among them as a light, and there will come a time when they may ask you about your light. Be prepared to share what you know quietly and reverently as personal truth. Spirit honors you for what you must endure, and asks for your patience.

(9) The ninth declaration of honor and blessedness is for those in this room (or reading this) who are in graduate status and

ascension preparation who are now living the truth. Spirit honors them in the ninth place, and although it is the last of the declarations of blessedness, it is truly important. Honored are those who are living the truth and walking the truth, for they will indeed change the planet. Not only that, dear ones, but for those of you who know who you are in this condition, be ready and prepared. There will come a time when these prodigal sons will show up on your doorstep with terror in their eyes and fear in their hearts, and they will ask you for help, the very ones who have ridiculed you. For when the things are dark for them and the changes press them, and they feel fear in their hearts, they will be awestruck with terror, and will not be able to handle it. They will not know what is taking place and their biology will fail them. Their brains will rush wild, and they will come to you and beg you for information. To them you will be the shamans; yes, the meek ones who are inheriting the planet.

This is the new age message. These are the nine declarations of honor and blessedness as given that day so long ago by the first master of love, the Jew Jesus. These are the reinterpretations in this new age that you may take with you this night, understanding and knowing what they mean for you now in this new energy.

We ask you to examine the Kryon and know that I am just the mechanic. There is so much more to know and to be facilitated with the other channel groups, and the other ones bringing information who walk among you in different dimensions. Now my partner wishes something very special; he wishes the music to return. This is something he has not done before, that I have asked for. (Live harp music begins.)

Be aware of what the vibratory tones do with your soul and how important they are to how you are fed spiritually. Dear ones, this night as we close this channeling, we have an invitation for you. There are those who sit here (and are reading this) who have come by appointment. And when we say appointment, we mean that there are no accidents or coincidences that find you seated before Spirit, with Spirit loving you in these messages. And if you walk away this night with information, that will be good. But if you leave this place healed, it would be even better. There are those of you who do not believe what is being presented even as my partner presents it. And I as Kryon, and Spirit, say to you that you are loved dearly, and that the seeds of truth are being planted this night for you. And that there will come a time when you will remember what these words were and will respond. Let your heart be your guide as to the truth and what is ringing true to your mind.

There are others of you this night who are prepared for what is going to take place. For the entourage which is with me, the Kryon group, offers you this night... intervention. In this planet of free choice you have the choice this night to make a change. This has to do with healing. We are here in love and purity. We see your higher selves clearly. We examine your colors and we know who you are. There are those who need to be healed of fear. Oh, yes. There are those here who need a biological healing, and we ask you right now to know who you are, and to examine if this is the time for this to take place. For dear ones, if it is, it is yours this night! For many of you may walk from this place a different person, a human being who has been touched by Spirit and changed... one who knows of the higher self and feels the intervention from that other part of you that is unseen. You see, Spirit is you. You are asking to be touched by that part of you which is God, to reach down and make the changes that are necessary. There is nothing here that is impossible. There is no biological anomaly that cannot be redirected. There is no thought that cannot be redirected. There is no situation which cannot be turned around into a winning situation. There is no fear represented here tonight that peace cannot replace instead.

And so we ask you to give intent, as you sit here quietly, for this to take place. Feel the entities as they are in the aisles this night, talking to your guides. For the facilitation for many of you is at hand, and that is why you are here. That is why you are hearing these voices right now. Much can be accomplished in the next three days with you. I am speaking to you! You know who I am! The sensitives recognize what is happening at this moment. This room is different than it was a moment ago. There is no evil thing that can touch you. There is no dark force that can interfere with you. You are at this moment pure love, the way you came in and the way you will return. This is the way we see you, dear ones, as we honor you within Spirit. We wish you to own what has happened to you and walk from this place healed.

When we speak of the new Jerusalem, we say you are in it! It represents the new Earth, the New Age, and the new energy run by those who mourn, and are meek, and seek the truth, and are merciful and pure in heart, and enduring of ridicule... and represent the love energy for the entire planet. YOU.

And so it is.... And so it is.

Kryon

Dear Lee:

This is probably not one of the letters you would want to add to your next book, since I had many physical signs that I was going through the implant process.

I had decided that I would host a picnic to discuss the Kryon books in a group. This is what started our monthly Kryon meetings since August of 94. By the time of the picnic, I was in my change. Besides my other problems, my most uncomfortable problem was that no matter what I ate, I got sick. I was not the most loving person to be around. By the time these problems were over the sinus and headaches started. After three months of trying to explain why the healer could not heal herself, I went to my sanctuary and had a very clear talk with Kryon.

I told him, through all my tears, that I can't take anymore. I'm sick of being sick, crying all the time, feeling so alone, having no money. I don't know how to explain what happened but my candles went out and my tape player stopped... and I stopped crying.

Since that time I have not cried, except tears of joy. I've had no more sickness. I was so happy to feel good again, but more important is that I look at life with a brand new meaning. My life, my children, and all my friends and students have benefited from my three months of change. My heart is so full of love and oneness that I can't remember what or who ever bothered me... with love and respect,

Kathie Greene
Tonawanda, New York

Chapter Four

The Implant

The Implant
Chapter Four

More about the new gift of Spirit

From the writer...

The neutral implant has been one of the most wonderful yet misunderstood aspects of the Kryon writings from the very beginning. If you don't know what I am speaking of, then you should seek out Kryon Book One, *The End Times*, to read about this new age gift.

As I have said before, I wish there had been a better translation for the word IMPLANT, but it's the word that was given to me to use. There is no English word that actually means what the implant is. If I could assign a phrase to it instead, I would say "catalyst for clearing."

Yet with the information of this wonderful earned gift of clearing, some have been immediately hung up with the word, and the semantics of the negative potential of its dark side. No matter what was said around it, all that was "heard" was IMPLANT: A CONTROLLING AND NEGATIVE ENSLAVING DEVICE. Something aliens place into your bodies to control you... or something certain governments are expected to do to you. Despite the truth, and the compelling love energy around the Kryon message, there still have been many who have not let anything break their own fear perceptions of what the implant is. I remember that Kryon has said many times in live channelings that when left alone in a dark room, humans will turn to fear scenarios first before all else. He honors this, since it is the strength of the duality that allows for such a thing. The opposite reaction, manifested as love and peace and lack of fear in the face of uncertainty, **is a learned attribute through self realization of the truth of who we are.**

If you have attended a Kryon seminar, then you will excuse me for now repeating an example I always give regarding a visualization of how the implant works. When I was in high school chemistry class, our instructor gave a wonderful demonstration. One day he unveiled a glass container filled almost to the brim with a vile dark green liquid. It looked like a cross between green slime and motor oil, but with the consistency of water. The glass container was large enough and placed high enough so that the whole class could see it. It was also obvious that the concoction was so discolored and seemingly polluted that none of us could see though it. It was opaque.

For high school students it was an immediate YUCK! We had fun making faces and ugly sounds to show our distaste at the horrible stuff that the teacher had exposed. Without much being said, the teacher then poured himself a small glass of yellowish fluid from another beaker next to him, and held the newly prepared glass above the icky green stuff. What happened next shocked us all, and is the analogy I wish to impress you with regarding the implant.

The teacher slowly poured the yellowish glass of fluid into the disgusting green stuff and then proceeded to pull a wooden dowel out of his lab coat and stir the whole mess. The room got quiet, and we were wide-eyed with amazement as slowly the repulsive green batch began to clear. Slowly stirring, the teacher grinned widely as the substance in the glass container, formerly so vile, became crystal clear... as clear as a mountain stream. Then to our utter horror the teacher took a paper cup from the dispenser by the door, dipped it in the now clear liquid and drank it!

The chemistry lesson was all about catalysts, and the wonderful, often dramatic result of a small catalyst on a larger volume of fluid matter. Being the kind of student I was, I have completely forgotten what the chemicals were, but remembered the example all my life (kind of like remembering a nice face for a very long time, but forgetting the name that went with it).

Our karma is accumulated from past experiences, and placed into our container of lesson. It is heavy with color and purpose, and is carefully mixed and colored by ourselves before we arrive at each incarnation. We carry the container like a dark weight, and the test is to see if we can slowly recognize what to do with it and pass through the tests to clear it. As we find enlightened solutions to each test, the color becomes lighter until it is finally crystal clear. When it clears completely, we put the container on the ground and walk away from it. We are then without karma, but still alive and well on the planet. Being without Karma doesn't mean death (as some have feared). "What do we do after we have cleared the lessons we came for?" some have asked. The answer from Kryon is, "Now that you don't have to spend time unraveling the past, get on with your contract!"

The new energy on Earth, as described by Kryon and many others, is what is allowing the great new gifts of Spirit to be passed through the veil to us. Kryon tells us how we earned it, and has explained many times (including messages in this book) about the details of how it happened. One of the greatest new gifts is our ability to void all karma without having to take the time to work through it... simply by intent. This was the initial message of Kryon. He called this new voiding gift "the neutral implant." Like the example, it was the spiritual catalyst implanted (or poured) into our dark green karma jar that when stirred for about 90 days, cleared it completely. Through nothing more than our intent, we were told that we could void a whole lifetime of upcoming karmic ties, relationships, lessons and happenings.

Many questions arise about the process. How do you know when you have it? When you did everything Kryon said and nothing happened, what did it mean? Could you have actually had it happen to you before you ever heard of it? What is the difference in experience between those who have a very dark jar of karma, and those whose jars are almost clear now? I encourage everyone to read the short parable of the tar pit on page 123 of Kryon Book Two, *Don't Think Like a Human.* This one paragraph example tells you what happens to those around you when **you** become clear. It's good news, and yet many still write and ask in fear what will become of them and their families if they give intent for the implant. Some do not understand it is a gift, and have assumed that it is something they "should" do... like taking medicine.

The truth is that the implant is universal for the new energy on the planet. It is a gift freely given in Love by Spirit to allow for the enlightenment and peace for any human wishing to embrace it. It isn't a "have to." It isn't a "should." It even happens automatically in many cases by intent of the higher self! In what follows examine this trait carefully, for it happens over and over. In my opinion this is proof that the implant (or whatever you wish to call it) is something that happens when the time is right, and when **we** are right. It truly doesn't have anything to do with the Kryon work other than the fact that Kryon was the first channeled entity to expose what was going on in the new energy, and to honor us so completely for it!

Following is the portion of this book that will transcribe letters from people all over the nation who have gone through this process, in order to give you insight on how this gift has worked in their lives. The stories are varied, and after each one, Kryon will have a response for either the letter writer or for us. This entire chapter is offered to allow good understanding of how the neutral implant process works, now that time has gone by since its original exposure in Kryon Book One.

Finally a footnote before the implant letters begin. The implant information that Kryon brings to us is not the focus of his work. It is simply a qualification of one of the new gifts of Spirit, and it also occupied a large portion of the first Kryon book. It has helped many to understand what has already been happening in their lives, and for many others it has been a revelation on what might happen if they were ready. It has taken a front seat to much of the other attributes of the Kryon work, since this gift can have such a profound result on the human who is ready for it. We all want to improve our lives, so it has become one of the most important gifts to many who have written. Kryon does not ask anyone to request this gift, since he knows that it is a very personal decision and that timing is critical for each human path. Since the Kryon work is not evangelistic, he is simply reporting on what the new gifts are all about, leaving the final decision to us. Finally, he reminds me constantly that these gifts do not come from Kryon. Hardly! They belong to us. We sanctioned them long before we ever got here, and now they are ours. Right on schedule.

Lee Carroll

The Implant Letters

from
Kryon Readers

Dear Kryon...

ritings

Del Mar - #422

92014

yon:

I have experienced all "adjustments" that Kryon spoke about. If you had known me seven months ago, you would have seen the exact adjustment phases that Kryon spoke of. I am a businesswoman with a degree in Business Administration from the University of Hawaii. I thought, and my friends would agree, that I would be the last person talking about enlightenment and metaphysics.

I have reached this enlightened point in my life without the help of others. I read your book only after experiencing exactly what Kryon spoke of. Therefore, I see much truth in his words, and now understand that what I went through was systematic and logical – for not only me, but for everyone.

I also have true experience of the 90-day depression. Because this was before I read your book, I did not have any reason why I felt so depressed. I just wanted to relay to you that there was definite advantage in not being "tainted" with literature and interpretations. Because my experience was untainted, I am living proof of what Kryon speaks of being true.

God Bless you,

Jennifer Nakahara

Ewa Beach, Hawaii

October 6, 1994

Dear Kryon,

I was in a deep depressed state during July, August and September. Some days I didn't feel like getting out of bed and that there was no point in life. No, I was not suicidal; rather, at soul level I felt empty. My soul seemed to be crying out for nourishment, yet nothing seemed to assuage this terrible soul-aching experience. I feel as if I have undergone an initiation of some magnitude. Up until this time I felt attuned to God and my Higher Self.

During this time I started reading <u>KRYON I</u> and realized that in my prayers and meditations I had asked for the equivalent of "Graduate" status without knowing of Kryon's revelations. This has always been a soul desire. I am working on raising my vibrations so that I will be ready for ascension when the time comes.

I am coming out of the depression. I feel one of my guides, but still can't really connect. I feel as if my battery is dead! Old fears have resurfaced and I am dealing with them again, for the final time, I hope. This is a sense of completion and new beginning for me.

Putting these thoughts on paper has brought me a sense of release. I expect this sense of release to bring me an awareness of my new guides and transplant.

With love, light and blessing, I am

Martha King
Montgomery, Alabama

And then later from Martha again... next page

March 9, 1995

Dear Lee:

I feel I must tell you, briefly, some of the things I have experienced since I wrote. I worked through the depression and many things came up that needed to be out, blessed and released. Apparently they were deep-seated, and asking for the implant helped the release to take place – that and my faith in Spirit. I have always known, since a small child, that I was more than Martha Brown King and have been shown this throughout periods of my life.

I have experienced some wonderful happenings in recent months and my faith has become a deep, soul knowingness of Oneness with Spirit and all life. I have continuing proof of what using spiritual energy can accomplish. It is there for us if we will but partake of it. It amazes me, and yet we are told, "All things are possible to those who believe."

Let me close by saying again, thank you. I can truly say I have a love affair with Spirit, and it is the most wonderful feeling to be alive.

With love and blessings,

Martha King
Montgomery, Alabama

Kryon Comment (for the reader): Do you see how this dear one received the gift of the implant before ever knowing of the Kryon information? This is important; the implant is not a gift of Kryon. It is not part of a Kryon "belief system." I am here to give you information about a gift you have freely earned by yourself. I am the messenger of information that will speed up your process, and give you knowledge regarding attributes that are happening to you totally without my intervention. I am here to support your work by adjusting the grid in a fashion that will allow you to continue into the next millennium. The gift is part of your own plan, and is appropriate in timing in this new age.

Many have misunderstood the implant in regard to Kryon. Some have asked, "How can I have this without asking?" The answer is that you did indeed ask. Some of you, as in the case of this dear one, have reached the point where karma is at a clearing point by itself! You have walked through it naturally, and are poised at a point where you are ready for the next step. Your entire contract is about this very thing! When this is the case, then your higher self gives permission to your incarnate self to proceed to the next level. Therefore, some of you are experiencing the implant process without any foreknowledge of the Kryon work. Then you pick up the information and say, "So that's what happened?"

You might ask, "If this dear one was so ready for the implant, why does she have depression? After all, there was no more karma to clear, and so it would seem as though the process would be almost invisible to her." This is an important question. Although she was totally clear of karma work, the "residue" of the contract with the karma still had to be cleared. This is not always the case, so each individual is different in his process. You are each marvelous unique entities, just like the Kryon! We all have our individual traits and talents. I have spoken of this before; never let anyone tell you that the spiritual entities of the universe are faceless automatons, all with the same thoughts. This idea by humans is so humorous!! Did you ever wonder why only the higher lesson entities have a sense of humor? What about the fact that only humans truly have choice of consciousness among the living souls of Earth? This alone should tell you that the closer you resemble the entity you really are, the more special you will become, and the more humor you will have about the overview of all things. Later I will speak about how important this is. Each individual on the planet will have his own implant potential, with his own experience to tell surrounding it, and each will be different.

November 15, 1994

Dear Lee,

I am a Reiki master teacher. As such, I give training and attunements to those wishing to channel this loving, Universal Life Force Energy to help heal themselves, others and the planet. A few months ago a man who had attended one of our AGORA gatherings made an appointment with me to receive his training and attunements for Reiki I. We spent hours talking about the Earth changes and our philosophies, and I couldn't stop asking him "Are you sure you haven't read Kryon?" Although he hadn't read the book, most of what he was saying was in perfect balance (if not almost word for word) with Kryon's teachings.

Needless to say, my Reiki initiate got the book and read it in a day. He called me up and we talked for hours about Kryon's teachings. When he came to receive his training and attunements for Reiki II, he told me that although he didn't officially vocalize his request for the Implant, he felt that the process had already begun. (We have found that many of our group did not ask for the Implant, but by vocalizing their intent to honor their contract and follow their path, they are now in the process of receiving the Implant).

When my initiate came for his Reiki II, he said he felt that he might have his masters in another two weeks. However, as I was giving him the attunements, a most wonderful event took place. My initiate was sitting in a chair, hands in prayer position and eyes closed. As I stood in front of him, I suddenly was consumed and overwhelmed with Love. I felt my masters standing behind me, and "saw" my initiate's three new masters standing behind him. Tears began streaming down my cheeks as I silently greeted them and thanked them for making their first appearance during this special time for him. When I walked behind him to begin the attunement process, they backed away only slightly, while my masters remained in front of him (facing me). Their energy was so beautiful and strong, I cannot describe in words how loved and blessed I felt.

During the attunement process I always ask the initiate's guides or masters that if there is any guidance, gifts or information they would like to give, to symbolically put it in the palm of my hand. I reached to my left and felt wonderful vibrations as the master on the left honored my request. I raised my hand above and behind my head for the master in the center to place his gifts into my palm, and then to my right for that master to symbolically place his gifts into my palm. I then slowly turned my palm over and placed it on my initiate's crown chakra, and felt all of the Love, information, guidance and gifts pour into him.

When the attunement process was complete, I left the room so that he could assimilate all that had transpired. He remained in meditation for a very long time. When I finally heard a "WOW!" I joined him, and we spent the next hour laughing, crying, hugging and sharing this most wonderful experience.

There have been many wonderful "happenings" lately, but I especially wanted to share this one with you. Reiki is a form of energy work. The practitioner channels the Life Force Energy in through the crown chakra, down to the heart chakra, and then out through the palms of the hands. My initiate and I are both being guided to combine the Reiki energy with polarity work in offering healing to our clients, with wonderful results.

Thanks Kryon! Namaste,

Rev. Whitney S. Murdock
MS, MsD, Reiki Master Teacher
Vacaville, California

Kryon Comment (for the reader): Here is another example of an enlightened soul intuitively knowing all the work of the Kryon before reading the books. It is again proof that the process of karma clearing, master guide replacement, and the new age process itself is an event which is an Earth energy event, and not a Kryon event. This precious one was already in the process of all of the changes, and found the Kryon information helpful to clarify what was happening.

The real message of this communication, however, is the role of the new age facilitator within the scope of the new age changes. Look how this dear one was enhanced and was sped through the wonderful process of a guide change. It was no accident that the facilitator in this case was familiar with the Kryon information, for it accelerated the process for the human in her care, and took him through it with joy, peace, and a great deal of love.

The role of the facilitators in the new age cannot be under-estimated. The teachers remain the teachers, and the facilitators are as needed now as much as in any period of human history. If you are a facilitator of any kind, start plugging in all the new energy information into your work. Many of you will have wonderful information come to you in visions and dreams. This is your gift to enhance your work. Don't discount any of it. Use the new intuitive methods you receive, and watch the results in your work. Don't be surprised if some of those you service each week never return due to permanent healing! The word will spread fast that you have new gifts, so do not be concerned about your abundance issues. Your new gifts will greatly enhance your life and those you facilitate in love. Believe it!

October 11, 1994

Hello,

I have inhaled book II and I am whirling with the power of it. Thank you for being the skeptic. How very wise Spirit is. I sent you a letter when I completed book I and it turned out to be a letter of woe and fear and tears.

This letter feels completely different. I am so grateful to you for your courage, and to Kryon – for he speaks to me directly. I did indeed ask for the implant, and within a week all began to change for me. I was relieved to discover that I did not enter into a period of depression and a feeling of abandonment. In fact, I now realize that many of the steps had been happening even though I didn't have the words to title them – and I always seem to insist on words. So much of what was said was intensely familiar, and so much was new – not new as in my not knowing before, but new in that I could finally hear without that ever present "yeah but."

It had been so long since I felt the tingling sensation that alerted me to the closeness of Spirit, and I missed it so deeply that I grieved for it. Now I sit and tingle a lot; and though I never thought they were gone, I was frantic at not being able to feel them. So many "coincidences" have begun to happen – people I suddenly meet who are deeply involved in Spirit, but who I wouldn't have met (I guess) had I not suddenly decided to go to a store or class I'd never been to before; clients for my massage practice that seemed to be failing, and so on. I have no idea where it's all going and it doesn't matter. Knowing and feeling the movement and the love of the universe is bolstering me.

Sincerely,

Karen Kleyla
Grehsam, Oregon

And Karen writes again...

March 16, 1995

Dear Lee,

Although I cannot yet say that my massage business is making my living, I do feel that it is growing and I have no doubts as to where the help I receive comes from. I have clearly explained my needs and they seem to be heeded, but it occurred to me one day to do something more (why did it take me so long to realize it?)

and there was a definite increase in my clients. I simply asked my guides what I could do for them and assured them that I would help them in any way they requested. It embarrasses me that I could be so willing to take, and yet forget for so long to give back.

I realize that it's easy to be serene when not faced with crisis, but there does seem to be a certain calmness within me these days. I used to think of happy as elation; I was miserable if I wasn't jubilant. But now I realize that for me happy is peaceful and very, very quiet. It is my sense of being connected with all that is. Only when I retreat and feign distance do I feel lonely and depressed. Otherwise I feel expansive, as if there were no end of me.

Sincerely,

Karen Kleyla
Gresham, Oregon

Kryon Comment: Karen, your willingness to be in the "sweet spot" of your contract has affected the circumstances around you. Do you see it? In former writings I spoke to you of this principle, and how you are indeed a catalyst for the changes that can take place around you. The seeming coincidences in your life are not. New human associations will bring you new windows of opportunity. You are creating your own reality, and are peaceful with whatever happens, living totally in faith that Spirit will show you what to do. We honor you greatly for this.

Notice what is happening with your facilitation business. The moment you let go of it, it became stronger. Although this activity may not be what you are to do for life, for now it is a wonderul example of the control you have of your own abundance. What exactly was the key to creating more? It was turning inward and loving your guides! What a lesson for all to see! There is a great deal of hidden wisdom in your words for all to examine who read this.

As you become closer to your higher self, your entire overview will continue to change. What makes you happy? What makes you peaceful? How can you be of service to the Earth? Your expansive feeling is the truth of who you really are when you are not incarnate here. It is this intuitive feeling of having "no end of you" that is exactly the proof of the piece of God you really are. All should be so free and balanced to know of this feeling. It is part of the new gifts humans have earned.

February 6, 1995

Dear Lee:

I do call on the Kryon energy daily for increased clarity, closer attunement, and any insights which will further the Light.

One important "by-product" of the Neutral Implant was an overcoming of claustrophobia. I flew in a small plane to and from Nassau and felt none of the tummy-tightenings and heart palpitations of prior experiences. A stranger came up to me in the Miami airport; apologized for being "weird," and told me she saw a beautiful translucent, mother-of-pearl light all around me! I thanked her for having the courage to share her experience! To affirm that Life is Wondrous and I have a peaceful heart is a grand understatement!

Again, love, blessings, and many thanks for all you and The Kryon are doing. I am very grateful and appreciative.

Rebekah C. Alezander
Boise, Idaho

Kryon Comment: Rebekah, just this simple example of what you are feeling will show those reading that the implant process does indeed have validity in the smaller things of your human existence. Also, your new colors will indeed attract those who know of such things. Such attributes will be common in new energy humans.

Some of you reading this have lifelong karmic residue that may have nothing whatsoever to do with anything you are about in this life... but still affect you nonetheless. These are the kinds of things that I have spoken of that will be completely disengaged with the success of receiving the neutral implant. Many unexplained fears will be cleared for you that have only been in place due to the engine of karma, and the residue left over from eons of incarnation. Do you begin to see the inner workings of all this?

September 26, 1994

Dear Lee,

Knowing you will receive an avalanche of stories from grateful readers, the gratitude I feel for the "Rosetta Stone" of metaphysical experience offered through your channeling of the Kryon has nonetheless compelled me to share its value for this Warrior of the Light.

I was introduced to Kryon I by an employee of an esoteric shop seemingly "out of the blue." It happened almost in tandem with incidents which had the signature of being karmic conclusions, yet would have perhaps been misinterpreted as such had this material not been immediately available during the same week that had marked the event testing my relationship/response quotient.

I had just located and read Chopra's Ageless Body, Timeless Mind, and had adopted the basic affirmation given in that fine work. The additional clarification you presented from the Kryon was the most miraculous theosophical/philosophical epiphany imaginable. It brought all the total confusion accumulated during a life of continual tragedy and environmental and relationship disasters into the light of revelation. I am still basking in the serenity and happiness every day holds now. It is not possible to describe the feeling of awe that enfolds me. Everything is suddenly in focus. Negatives are conquered and fear banished from my spirit. The wonder of feeling boundless love for everyone is so glorious that it is as though I will begin to float instead of walk – since the effect of being with other people is so lovely it requires control of the energy it produces lest I get locked away for being so optimistic and happy.

My entire life has been made comprehensible. All of my theosophical conclusions have been verified. It is such an overwhelming relief to finally be assured I've not hallucinated the strange forces swirling through the quantum soup we use to manufacture our version of the world. I have often been amazed at the wonderful camouflage we designed to facilitate our testing.

While very young I became aware of other entities around me, and I am sure due to my intense emotional response to life, they began to affect my karma almost from infancy. The events were so rapid and so peculiar that I knew it was not a typical incarnation. It was definitely structured to try my strength and core values. It caused me to feel overwhelmed and beaten; it made me feel negative and hopeless. It seemed no matter how much grueling effort I put into making a reasonable life for myself, nothing succeeded financially or emotionally. The misery was so severe, not to mention the feeling of insanity, I tried any number of times to suicide out; but no matter how sincere the attempt, it was always doomed to fail... Finally I stopped trying for the most part.

Then I was given Kryon I. It was a miracle to me. My life is as odd as it was prior to the implant in some ways, but I read the first book on September 3 and the second one just three days ago, or September 27. I am transformed. I trust the universe and my guides to offer the abundance I need and want in good time, in whatever fashion is appropriate. In the meantime fear is a thing of the past; and though many of the individuals with whom karmic involvement is still in lesson, and perhaps caught in some sort of residue from the contract in process, I have the serenity to deal with the situations.

There is no doubt at all in my mind that the various elements I've struggled to integrate into a comprehensible view of the world's physics are explained at last by the Kryon data. There is simply no way I can possibly convey my gratitude for your work. I am in your debt, and honor you and the Kryon always, as you must know.

Shy Streahl
Whitefish, Montana

Kryon Comment (for the readers): So here is a dear one who obviously has received a karma clearing, and yet there is never a mention of what we call the "implant." This letter is included here to exemplify the fact that the implant is not something that even has to be called "the implant!" It is a naturally occurring karma clearing process that this dear one went through at the perfect time, only to have the Kryon information validate some of the specifics of what was happening.

I have repeatedly spoken of the peace that accompanies this process, and the overview of wisdom that also results. You can tell by this communication that both are in place.

November 30, 1994

Dear Lee Carroll,
Greetings. Today and yesterday have been a few of the days spoken of in the Kryon writings that can be difficult when one calls for the implant. I am not one of the instantaneous acceptance people! As disturbing as the changes can be, however, this is very different than any ordinary depression, in that there is the hope of trust. The difficulty is viewed as temporary, so the fear is much less; and at the base of it all one feels the strong pull of the Universal Love. Past karma has been coming up strongly. Just now

in meditation, in tears I walked into the black bubble and it popped. I called to Kryon over and over. The tears flowed; I felt the Love around me. I have begun the work.

What I wish to express in this letter is my own validation of a concept from Book II that really spoke to me. It is the concept that one calls for the implant long before they realize it. The following is my personal experience beginning six or eight months before reading Kryon I.

I live in a city and use mass transit every morning to travel to my job (at this time I am laid off from work). I would start out for work at full strength (for me), but when I arrived some twenty or thirty minutes later, I would be very weak and tired. There was extreme sensitivity to the scents of others, especially their breath – and especially ones who drank liquor the night before. The other toxins didn't help either. So I began doing breathing exercises while in transit, and visualizations of not allowing the toxins to penetrate. This helped.

Slowly, over many weeks, I began to pray for blockage of the toxins while walking down the hill to the bus stop (a short walk). I knew of the concept of White Light (protection from the highest source), and would repeat a request for protection. After a while the daily request began to take shape of a poem, or prayer.

This poem came together with the Kryon writings during the reading of the concept of calling for the implant before one realizes it. I thought, "That's my poem Kryon is speaking of!" The "coincidence" of the verbiage will not be lost on you, I am sure.

Two days ago I wrote it for the first time on paper while considering this letter to you. The copy you see is the third time that it has ever been written.

Laura Grimshaw
San Francisco, California

(see Laura's poem on next page)

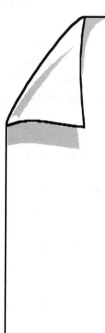

White Light
White Light
White Light

Please fill me
with White Light

So that the Positive
may permeate,
the negative
Deflect

and I
Will do my Part
and I
Will do my Best

because I love you, God
I love you, Guides

So to you,
I leave the rest

Poem by Laura Grimshaw
(see last page)

Kryon Comment (for the readers): Again look at some of the residual karmic effects that disappear when the individual clears and balances. If this process can do this, what do you think it can do with human disease? Think about the control you have over your biology with this new gift! The action element used by this dear one is extremely important to the implant process. It is now time I spoke of the two parts of the implant experience. Notice that all through this communication there was a concentrated effort to combine intent with action. Action is trust, expectation, alertness to opportunity and faith. With the implant process, first there is the INTENT, then there is ACTION.

Some of you have actively given intent for the implant experience, and then sat and waited for something to happen with no results. I will tell you, dear ones, that without action after karma clearing, the only thing that you will experience is boredom, although it will be peaceful (cosmic humor). The key to the success of this entire experience is in the two-part concept for humans. All of those who have communicated to my partner have realized this concept. At the point of the intent there is the understanding of taking responsibility for the karma that they are clearing, and the recognition of contract, and therefore the recognition that there is more to do AFTER THE CLEARING.

Would you purchase a chair to just look at it? Most of you would sit in it almost as soon as it was ready. In addition, how many of you would sit across from it and stare at it, wondering if it would support your weight? Most would not question the fact, and sit in it with your full weight immediately.

The implant process is identical to this. Once you GIVE INTENT for this spiritual process, you then take responsibility for all the karma that is being cleared. Think about this. TAKE RESPONSIBILITY for all the drama around you that is going to be tempered with this process. Realize that you planned it, and are now releasing it. TAKE RESPONSIBILITY for the anger that will be gone, and for the situations that have seemingly victimized you. They all belong to you, and so you must now OWN them as they are cleared. You have therefore purchased the chair (given intent) as a tool to go forward. When the time is right, take action and sit in it!

TAKE ACTION on the fact that you **expect** your life to change! When you feel you are out of the karmic clearing change period, however slight or severe, look around for your mission, and make plans that coordinate with your expected changes. What do you think will happen if you simply sit there and wait for happiness to "drop" on you? You are now in a co-creative mode, and you will be able to create your own reality. Do it. What is your passion, or your mission? Move forward in faith, knowing fully that you will be honored with results.

A few humans have communicated with my partner, telling him that nothing at all has happened after taking the implant. They are still unhappy and poor. Then they go on to say .... "and I thought it probably would be this way, since nothing else has worked in my life either!" Dear ones, you are so greatly loved, but you must understand that to expect nothing is to create it. To expect to be a victim is to be victimized. You indeed will OWN your own consciousness as you lie within its creation. The implant is literal, and will honor your innermost thoughts.

You are the new creative force on the planet, and nothing is going to happen without your stepping forward and making it so. The new gift is an unbelievably powerful tool in the tool box of the new energy, but you have to use it, not just look at it! Therefore the two parts to the process both belong to you. The first one is intent, and the second is action. You create it, then use it. Both require work on your part. This is why you are called "workers." Those of you who expect the honor without the effort will indeed be stuck between the old and the new energy, and will not be rewarded with the attributes of the life you have earned in this new age.

November 22, 1994

Dear Lee,

Here we are close to Thanksgiving, so I write to tell you and Kryon of the deep appreciation of your work. I wrote you before expressing my belief, after reading <u>The End Times</u>, that I had been through much of what Kryon indicated would happen; and after much thought and consideration I did ask for graduate status. Of course the usual loss of guides, loneliness, etc. However, I had an absolutely tremendous experience which I am sure is due to the changes. It has certainly changed my life!!

I was sitting reading <u>Avalanche</u> by Brugh Joy one afternoon several months ago, and in the periphery of my vision I saw something moving. I looked up from my book, and there on the wall directly across from me was a movie going on – about me! I saw myself from the back of my head and shoulders. In some way, my mind projected into my head in that movie, and I saw a large snakelike dark energy which twisted through each lobe of my brain, but also covered the top! At that time I heard myself say, "Okay, if you won't do it my way, I'll leave." Well, all hell has broken loose as almost daily I receive additional information on how what I then termed a casual thought pattern had affected my entire attitude and life. I now believe what I saw was my karmic imprint. I can now see what my major lessons were, and this understanding is allowing me to release and move on. We certainly can no longer blame anyone else for our actions; the responsibility is ours. I feel the love Kryon speaks of, so necessary for our spiritual growth, is beginning to fill me now.

There is absolutely no way I can express my thanks adequately, but I do tell Kryon and my guides daily how much I care. Incidentally, my new guides have finally come in.

Gratefully,

Ɖ. Ꞩ.
Tucson, Arizona

Kryon Comment (for the readers): Again the release of blame is found to be the key to moving ahead. This responsibility issue is probably the most fundamental key to results in the new energy, and this dear one found it in a most visual way... one that could have caused fear, but instead created wisdom. There is one more issue regarding your new energy that the Kryon has not mentioned to you.

The Inner Child, as my partner calls it, is a grand inner source of human happiness and peace, and is necessary as a catalyst for a true new energy transition regarding the implant process. Indeed, you are a complex biological entity; many of you have studied all your days to understand the workings of the human brain. Even those who know nothing of new energy ideas recognize and realize the importance of that part of you which remains intact from your childhood.

You might think that when you grew up from being a child, all the childlike things somehow were erased from your being and replaced with adult thinking. Actually, the part of you that was the infant still exists, and is a vital part of your potential as a complete human. From a new age standpoint, as well as for general human health, this is very potent! Let me explain.

The human child may look to you as though there isn't much going on in the infant mind. Actually there is an extremely strong residual remembrance of where the entity just was on the other side of the veil! It takes months and months to completely "forget" the transition into biology. Naturally the infant can't speak, so you seldom get to hear the dialogue that is going on within. "Why am I here? What happened to the others? What are these new feelings?" In addition, the infant responds purely from a love base. Although needy due to biological helplessness, the infant carries great seeds of wisdom and love in these first few months. How many mothers have gazed into the eyes of their own children in these early days and asked "Who are you, really?" The eyes of the "old soul" shine brightly through the child during this time, and many can easily look into them and see the wisdom of the ages and many incarnations.

Alas, as appropriate, the child slowly "unlearns" who he really is, and prepares for the lessons of being a human with karma. Some of the karma starts right away when he is born into difficult situations, such as family strife and war. However, most infants respond first to love, for it is the state they came from and know the best.

When you were a small child, you had no worries. The intellect that is your human balancing agent for these things was not yet in operation. Everything you needed was taken care of by your mother, and the things that were important to you were likely to be the ones that involved play time. Not only that, but your mother enhanced this by playing with you, sometimes reading to you, and often just holding you close to her so you felt better. Some of you say, "Oh what a time that was! Just think of it... what a wonderful thing it would be to have that kind of peace again." As expected, I tell you that this is exactly the kind of peace Spirit offers you now.

When you are separated from your higher self while you are in lesson, there is the cellular longing for home, and the longing for the love and caring of the mother, which is Spirit itself. This is a feeling of separation and alienation from something much bigger that you remember somehow, and desire so much. "Where can this attribute be rekindled while you are here?" you might ask. The answer is within the inner child of your being. Deep within each of you the child is still intact and ready to surface. Most humans are not ready for this, nor do they necessarily want it. To let the child out is seemingly to go backwards to some, and negate the adult person that is mature. To many the child is buried too deeply and can't come out without help. It is frightened by the internal dialogue of the adult who constantly speaks out loud of negative things and fearful possibilities. The inner child hears all these things and reacts exactly like a real child would if you told him that he is an unworthy individual, and unloved.

So why should you let the child out? The answer is BALANCE! We speak over and over about human balance, and now we tell you that here is a feature of it that you can immediately work on for the betterment of your life. This is no idle attribute, and is absolutely necessary for your work to go forward. In the process, not only will chemical changes take place within your brain and body that are natural and healthy, but there takes place a cellular remembrance of the place you came from... and the security of that place. Most of all it fosters the cellular remembrance of who you are, and your place in the cosmos. Too grand, you think, for a kid? You have no idea how important this is! Hidden in each of you is a full blueprint of who you are and why you are here. The inner child is the gateway to its revelation.

How do you do it? Some of you will find it easy, and some will need to be facilitated. Those of you who regularly love to laugh and play will find it easy to bring the child forward and make it available. Learn to play with the things that make you happy without continually thinking of adult responsibilities all the time. Set time aside to do joyful things, and do not chastise yourselves for doing it instead of working! Find others who will do the same things with you (kids like to play with kids). Learn to relax with the pressures around you that have kept you in the adult attitude of worry and depression. **The inner child is the answer to the healing of a depressed adult.** Watch children play! Remember intuitively the feeling of such freedom from the pressures of life. Is it because the children are naive? No, it is because they feel secure with the love of their mothers, and know that there is no problem that cannot be "fixed" in a moment of time... mom does it all the time.

The traumatized child, on the other hand, is a depressed child. This is an unnatural state, but you can see it in the case of a child who has been through human tragedy. This is a child who has retreated into itself and isn't "present." This is exactly what can happen to the inner child of humans who regularly tell themselves that they are victims and that things can't ever get better. The natural conclusion to that conversation is death, and the inner child knows it and is traumatized by this potential. How, then, can some of you bring out the needed child if it is damaged and traumatized? The answer is through facilitation.

Again we turn to the humans in the new age who understand and work with inner child facilitation. Trust them to help you, and know that the natural state of the child is to play. It won't take long to bring it out, but there must be attitude adjustments, verbalizations, and changes in the way a human goes about life itself. The facilitator knows how, and will guide you through it. Spirit has given these healers intuitive knowledge to help even the most depressed humans at this time. Seek out those with this knowledge and don't fear what they might do. They are here to assist you with life itself, and have contracts with the planet for this very thing. Note how in so many cases of implant transition the facilitator is present and ready to help. Many who communicated the implant experience in these pages related this to you so you can see the testimony of those who have gone through the process, and understand its value.

Spirit has given you the gift of the implant process, a naturally occurring spiritual attribute that clears your karma within this lifetime. Your job is to give intent for the gift, and take responsibility for appropriate action. Part of action is to become consciously balanced. The information to accomplish this task is all around you, including within the pages of this communication. Giving intent for the implant will indeed cause change and clearing; then you will sit in a neutral place with the choice of what to do next. If you just sit there, you are an open slate ready to create more karmic interaction. You must consciously now give intent for action, and the inner child work is part of that action.

The Kryon comes to you in incredible love and appreciation for your work. Many "feel" the love of spirit though this work, and instantly recognize it as the feeling of "home." When I come through my partner in a gathering of other humans, the energy we bring is many times as potent as can be felt by any singular human alone. This is why we have asked my partner to continue to bring this energy to parts of your continent, and to bring the word as directed. Even long after the Kryon timetable of Earth changes is finished, I have asked my partner to continue bringing this energy forward, for I will be there even though my work is done. It is due to the changes you are making each day that allows for the continuation of this channeled work, and the ability of my partner to bring in the new age energy that we have for you.

Within the great love energy of a live channeled event we speak to individual hearts of those present, and healing is accomplished. We give stories and "journeys" for explanation because we know that humans will understand and react to them. In the process much is learned, and a relaxation of the soul is accomplished. Often much astral work is done, with some humans never remembering the words of my partner during the entire event! It is our incredible honor for you that guarantees that we will be there each time my partner schedules such an event, and we have asked him to do it often.

We wish to bring out the cellular feelings of your inner child and play with it during any time you are with the Kryon (alone or in a gathering). These feelings foster peace, and a lack of fear. They support your humanism and give you a brief pause in the lesson of being on this planet. They suspend time and aging, and bring you face to face with your higher self... if you let them. We love you all so dearly...

The Spiritual History of The Implant
1997 Update

I guess I was as surprised as any to find out that the implant/ release was a spiritual gift that has actually been predicted by the ancients of many religions! This not only gives credibility to its workings, but helps us to put into perspective this seemingly strange new gift. To accept the fact that it was foretold, brings you to a greater understanding that the implant is indeed in the spiritual scheme of things that represent the New Age. Kryon didn't suddenly come along and report something wild and weird, as some older energy metaphysicians might report. The implant/ release was to be part of the scenario of new age gifts all along, should we get to the point where the consciousness of the planet could indeed use it. The good news is that we did! And Kryon is here to report that the gift is ready, as predicted, on schedule.

Greg DeLaCastro is a spiritual historian. I didn't even know such people existed! Before I continue with a spiritual article that Greg wrote for the *Kryon Quarterly Magazine* in 1996, I wish to introduce him to you. His article follows on the next page.

Gregory DeLaCastro

Gregory DeLaCastro, President of Scriptorium Ltd. Consulting and Research, graduated with a B.A. in History, Anthropology and Languages (Phi Beta Kappa) from the University of Denver in 1975. He also holds a M.A. in Intellectual and Cultural History of the World and the History of Science, University of Denver 1977. He has also edited *Cosmology, History and Theology* for D.U. and Plenum Press. His intense interest in Sacred Astrology and Feng Shui, and his ability to directly translate ancient texts have led to the rediscovery of over 14 archaeological sites – detailed in his book *The Forbidden Past*. His articles and translations have appeared in *New Pacific, Rocky Mountain Independent, the RMP Journal, The Rocky Mountain Journal of Ancient Religions, and the Transactions of the Ancient Records Preservation Society.* Also the author of The *USL Manual,* and *Astrology Materia Medica,* he is currently collaborating on a translation and study of *Moon Phase Nakshatras.* DeLaCastro is a certified member of the NCGR, and holds many advanced esoteric degrees. He offers Sacred Astrology and Feng Shui consultations.

The Neutral Implant Delineated

Through Lee Carroll, Kryon introduced the Neutral Implant early in Book I: The End Times. Since then, it has been one of the most controversial subjects of the Kryon work. The reactions to the Neutral Implant have run the spectrum, from joy and enlightenment to fear and confusion. Most of us knew little or nothing about the implant prior to the Kryon books. Indeed, Lee Carroll never heard of the implant until it first came out in channeling. Some have even suggested changing the name from "neutral implant" to simply "the release." Whatever you call it, the fact is that it's been around since ancient times, with a translation that means in part, *"The Gift of the City of God."*

One of the time-honored characteristics of all channeled material is that it has its information retrieved in three different forms. These forms are:

1.) Face Value, 2.) historical, and 3.) continuous encoding.

The fact that a single message must track in each of these three dimensions often explains the structural peculiarities or seeming inconsistencies in the face value text. The concept of the Neutral Implant provides us with a case in point.

From a strictly linguistic point of view the term Neutral Implant indicates *latent unused potential that permanently resides in the consciousness.* It cannot be something foreign or extraneous that is introduced into the consciousness by an outside force, because then it would not be neutral. In other words, the Neutral Implant *is something that is and has been a latent element of human consciousness since the creation of man.*

Kryon has repeatedly stressed the fact that the Neutral Implant is a uniquely human trait that has existed long before his current mission. He then goes on to describe the characteristics of the Neutral Implant so that we may recall its use by memory from the historical realm of our dimension.

Kryon says that the Neutral Implant gives us a direct path to the singular love power source, that is only possible through graduation status. This new power will be necessary for you to do the transmutation work for the earth (Kryon 1:43).

What the Neutral Implant actually does is to effect a total karmic clearing (Kryon 2:43) which is voided as surely as if you had walked through it personally (Kryon 1:134).

The Neutral Implant is connected with the biggest set of implants (which) are really "imprints" that... include karma, astrological presets, life lessons (related to karma), magnetics field patterns (auric life colors), star karma, and many more... (Kryon 1:37).

Although this imprint cannot be changed (ever), it can be affected or neutralized by an equally powerful spiritual instrument... (the Neutral Implant) ... variable controls on your imprint (Kryon 1:155).

Astrological magnetic imprints are with you for life, just like your face. You may continue to consult the science for timing issues, and still follow the advice of magnetics. However, the implant gives you the ability to void the attributes that in the past have slowed you down (Kryon 3:265).

We may reasonably conclude from this description that the Neutral Implant has something to do with both Karma and Astrology.

Karmic Astrology is thus the Systems Science of discovering the karma of the individual, as well as its solutions, from the position of the planets and stars. As such, it forms the major component of the Sacred or Tantric Astrology. Interestingly, it is in the techniques of Sacred Astrology, whether among the Hindu, Buddhist, Chinese, Judeo/Christian/Islamic Tradition, or even the Navajo, that we encounter the uniform historical presence of the Neutral Implant.

Kryon uses the term Neutral Implant to describe the astrological derivation of the Dharma Mastery Chart (or Crown of Enlightenment) from the Athla Chart (or Chart of Deeds). In so doing, Kryon actually makes an instructional plan.

In this process the Second and Twelfth House line segment is removed and placed into the first house, thereby forming a bridge. The term Neutral, in the sense of balance, also has meaning.

During the Middle Ages, it became known as the Bridge of Swords, since it cut off over 75% of your karma. To the Navajo, it was the Rainbow Bridge provided by the Sun to his Children so that they could realize their Divine Nature. In Casper, Wyoming, Kryon likened it to walking into a room and then going out the other side, without being captivated by the things inside the room.

In essence, the Neutral Implant is simply a specific special event sequence that allows the Self to forgive itself. The trick is to walk a specific event sequence (roughly 1/12 of your total karma) from beginning to end. It can thus clear 60% to 92% of your karma upon completion. This amount increases to unity shortly afterwards, when it jells, so to speak.

This brings us to the third aspect of the Neutral Implant. In the language of astrology, it reads: *The Life Force of the God of Heaven guides the form and mode of the Work through Grace, the Gift of the City of God. To escape or evade calamity in the twinkle of the eye, exalt the form of the Staff of Fortune in the Lake of the Life Force. Amplify the Opening, work your pole.* Here we have the imagery of pre-Augustian theology combined with astrological terminology that dates back to Ancient Egypt.

The City of God, or the New Jerusalem, is standard term for the Sacred Square Horoscope in the Bible. In the New Testament Koine Greek this is also the proper translation of the word *ecclesia*, which is erroneously rendered as Church.

Because the Houses of the Square Horoscope are triangular, they lend themselves to being described in terms of feminine sexual metaphors; just as a line segment lends itself to masculine sexual metaphors. Thus the instructions to, "*exalt the form of the Staff of Fortune in the Lake of the Life Force*" also refer to elevating the Second and Twelfth House line segment (the Staff of Fortune) to the First House (the Lake of the Life Force) as the individual Life Force or Divine Spark in the Athla Chart.

Should this occasion to take the Neutral Implant be missed, the truth of the matter is that these events can be recalled again through the open Declaration of Intent, or Grace. This is what Kryon talks about when he says we can voice our intent for the Neutral Implant.

Yet, by double entendre, we also now have an image of a Tantric exercise that confirms that one has successfully exercised this option.

In any case, the important thing is that we now have an example of how authentic channeled material honors the three-dimensionality of our continuum by being consciously designed to have its information retrieved in three different forms.

Most of the confusion that surrounds the Neutral Implant has been based on interpretations that do not take linguistic three-dimensionality or Sacred/Tantric Astrology into account. For example, Kryon says that, "*cyclical biological forces no longer apply to those who have taken the Neutral Implant.*" (Kryon 1:60). What this means is that the Athla Age Polarity Cycle between the psychological outlook of men and women will no longer apply. For instance, men and women of the same age have their psychological outlook ruled by opposing signs, as indicated by the table above. In practical terms, this has always favored relationships in which there was a three to nine year age difference. (These make natural conjunctions that are unifying and binding.)

Other relationships with age variance are possible. For example, a two year difference between individuals is a natural sextile, or favorable creative aspect.

However, the point of this is: Wouldn't it be nice not to have to go through the alternate periods of static and tone in a relationship? The Neutral Implant invites you to hear the continuos melody. As Kryon says, "Why wouldn't you want it?" (Kryon 1:45)

Perhaps now we have a broader view of the profound Grace that Spirit and Kryon have extended to us!

Greg DeLa Castro
10101 Highway 73
Conifer, CO 80433-4008

Chapter Five

New Age Healing

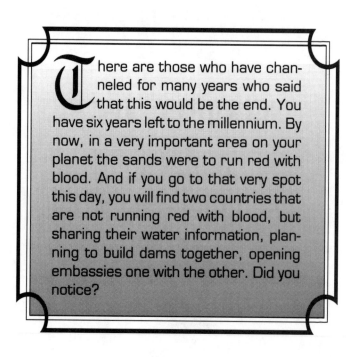

There are those who have channeled for many years who said that this would be the end. You have six years left to the millennium. By now, in a very important area on your planet the sands were to run red with blood. And if you go to that very spot this day, you will find two countries that are not running red with blood, but sharing their water information, planning to build dams together, opening embassies one with the other. Did you notice?

...from page 60

Kryon

"Healing in the New Energy"
Channeled in Laguna Hills

Southern California
Kryon Seminar

The Kryon Writings, Inc.

PMB 422
1155 Camino Del Mar
Del Mar, California 92014
[www.kryonqtly.com]

"Healing in the New Energy"
Live Channel
Laguna Hills

This live channel has been edited with additional words and thoughts to allow for clarification and better understanding of the written word.

From the writer...

"Stop the presses! Hold everything!" I imagined myself shouting to someone. But I'm the guy who writes all the words here, lays out the pages, does the graphics, and takes it all to the printer. So I guess I was shouting to myself (kind of boring now that I think of it).

Anyway, I had put this book to bed, so to speak, and was finalizing the proofreading and getting last minute printing instructions when Kryon did a seminar in Laguna Hills, California. Maybe it's because the seminar was close to home, or that we were so comfortable with the Awakenings Book Store that put on the event (a great store) – but I really didn't expect any surprises from this channel. I was wrong.

Days before our good friend and world-class healer, Joe Gonzales had passed away silently in his sleep. Some of Joe's friends and family were at the seminar, and when we got to the evening channeling portion, it was exceptionally powerful. I think Joe and Kryon had teamed up to bring us a wonderful message on healing! Joe will be greatly missed. I dedicate this chapter to him, as Kryon would wish me to. It represents him so completely, and the love he gave to so many... so often.

Greetings; I am Kryon of magnetic service. As in many previous channels we now invite those who can see, those who are sensitive, and those who know what auras look like and can see other beings, to see the validity of my partner's work. I will surround him with my color, and there will be no doubt that this night Spirit visited you. Oh, feel it, for it is yours for the taking. A lifetime worth of healing can be yours in this moment, for that is why you're here. We respond this night to the consciousness of this room, and of those dear ones who are present who have come into this lifetime with a purpose. And the purpose is that every human being they see, they want to heal! It's a very real purpose, and it requires a tremendous passion. The karmic residue which is involved is not an accident, for we know the ones hearing this voice are the forerunners of the healers of this planet.

So it is we come this night to talk to you regarding healing, and in the process we are going to answer seven questions from this group. The questions are these:

(1) How do I know I'm supposed to be a healer?

(2) What are the actual mechanics of healing from one human being to another? What's really going on?

(3) What can my patient do to co-operate with my healing efforts in order to be healed?

(4) What determines a successful healer? And this answer may surprise you.

(5) Do I really have to be single to be a healer? (Laughter)

(6) Kryon, how can I know I'm on my path?

(7) What is the key to becoming a powerful healer?

Now we will return and answer these seven questions in the order that they were asked in a moment. Do not worry, my partner; I will keep track of them. (*Writer's note: Kryon knows that I don't like 'laundry lists' of items, since I tend to try to keep track of them during the channeling instead of letting Spirit do it. The joke here is that he gave the seven questions right away just for my process! He wanted me to relax and see that I didn't have to concern myself about making certain they were repeated correctly. It's funny in retrospect.*)

Before we can answer these questions, we must tell you about the new energy and healing. We have discussed what is taking place on your planet – of the consciousness change, of the new gifts, of what you have called the implant, the gift of karma clearing. But there are gifts for you facilitators and you healers that will astound you. Before we enumerate them, let us tell you that the basis of what is taking place in the new energy around healing is the **melding of the sciences**. For in the old energy the healers were usually separated into many groups, and they were specific and specialized. So the one human usually trained for one kind of science and practiced one kind of healing. This is now beginning to change, and some of you know of what I speak.

Let me give you an example, and for this example we will use the acupuncturist. We highlight this science because it has great lineage and is very old. It has had wonderful master teaching in the past, so it bridges the gap from the old energy to the new. Miss or Mister Acupuncturist, let me speak to you: pretend that you are poised over your patient spinning your needles. (By the way, were you aware that you are doing magnetic therapy? For the spinning of the needles creates electricity, and that's what acupuncture is all about.) Let me ask you this, and I will understand if you roll your eyes: has it ever occurred to you to use different colored needles? Has it ever occurred to you to color them the color of the chakras?

Are you aware of the color healing potential? Do you know the increase in energy around your process if you were to color them? Let me make this admonishment, however. The needles that are colored should be colored throughout and be solid, not simply colored on the surface. The colors **will make a difference**! So as you approach the 24 meridians, think of the colors that would be best, and if you do not know, then it's time to consult the ones who know about colors! This is a meld. Can you bring yourself to ask them?

Tell me, Mister or Miss Acupuncturist, what is it that your patient is smelling as you do your work? Is he smelling the ancient incenses you have been told to burn that are all generic? Perhaps it's time to change that. Have you talked to the healers that know about aroma? What is the patient feeling who is in front of you? Has he come because he has a back pain? Perhaps there is an organ malfunctioning? Did you know there is a color associated with that? Did you know there is an aroma associated with the state of mind you wish him to be in while you work on his back?

Let me ask you this. What is he hearing as you work on him? Is he hearing pure tones that might coordinate with the colors, that might coordinate with the aromas? When he opens his eyes, what does he see around him? Does he see the lighting that you wish and the colors you wish? We ask you to take all this into consideration, and here's why: you would not have studied with the masters and be doing what you're doing unless you want a full and complete healing of the individual before you. If you will take some of these new energy suggestions to heart and consider them serious, you can increase your healing power threefold. Is it worth it? See for yourself. Don't take the Kryon's word for it. Try it! So it is the meld of the sciences that is new, and we ask each one of you to understand that there may be more to enhance what you're doing than just what you've studied about.

There are five new attributes of healing. Don't worry, my partner, I'll keep track of them. (*Here we go again. Kryon is really having fun with me now. He is doing a list of five items within the list of seven that he has not begun yet!*)

New Knowledge

The first one is new knowledge. For the acupuncturist you might say, "How do I know what colors to use?" We will say that it's intuitive, for you are a healer. If you are uncertain, you can ask the others, for it was intuitive for them. But we also know that when speaking to the acupuncturist, some of you, despite the training that you have had, have discovered new meridians and are trying new things, and have found that there is power in other areas to twirl the needles. You do not tell the teachers of these things, for you are afraid of being mocked, and yet this is the new knowledge. For whatever science you are in and whatever healing you are doing, intuitively, through the gift of Spirit, you may receive new knowledge.

My partner wants to interject something he thinks is humorous, and I will allow it. He says, "As the acupuncturist sits, spinning his multicolored needles into the patient, with the smells and the lighting and the colors, as the old master of acupuncture arrives, he will certainly know he's in Southern California!" (Laughter)

I speak now to those of you who have considered yourselves massage therapists. Have you noticed that you are now in energy work also? For a strange thing is taking place for some of you. Your patients aren't simply being comforted; they're being healed! They're walking away with genuine permanent healing. What is taking place? It's new knowledge, for you are used to touching the human body and you know where and how, and you are sending energy in. Some of you are actually concerned that your practice might be losing abundance, for the ones whom you used to massage are going away healed and not returning. Going away healed, not just comforted! And we say to you that when the word gets around of what you're doing, you will have no trouble sustaining your business. Look for the new knowledge – the different places to touch, the different places in your science to create and pass energy. Think of touching in a bipolar way – becoming balanced, accepting the new meld as part of your work. No one has a proprietary hold on any part of healing. We tell you this, dear ones: It's time to put them together! For when you do, the results will be astounding and you will draw the attention of those who don't believe it could be so. They will have to study it... because it works. They will not be able to ignore the results.

New Tools

The second attribute is new tools in the new energy. Now dear ones, these new tools aren't necessarily physical, but some of them are. We speak of tools that are also cosmic. We speak of mechanisms which you have now which are lying there ready to be used – for you to pick up and know they exist. Let me give you an example – and again for those hearing this in the now, there may be some surprise. I speak now to the energy workers, both classically trained and not. You have learned to move energy. You know how to move it and transport it from one place to another. That is how you balance a human being. You also know how to pass it through yourself to the human, and so your energy work is receiving a great deal of validation, for those who sit or lie in front of you as you work the energy are being healed and helped. Pain is leaving. Things are changing. Health is increasing. So you know how the energy works. You also intuitively know that it passes from one place to another. Let me ask you this. What would happen if you were to place a vial full of an herb in your hand and pass your energy through the vial into the human? Do you think that the human being would receive anything different? And the answer is, **absolutely**. For you have a new gift now, where the transmission of the properties of the herb which you hold in your hand may be passed to the human, in addition to the energy which you are already transmitting. Therefore the herb does not have to be ingested, and thus the herb is not diminished as it's being used! *The herb sealed in the vial is always fresh. This is because it is your energy work that is supplying the "engine." Therefore, no energy needs to drain from the herb. Only the attributes and properties of the herb "ride along" with your energy engine into the patient.* Some will say this is magic. Others will say it's a new gift. So what herb would you use, dear energy worker? Perhaps it's time to consult the herbalist? It's the meld. It's the new tool. Amazing? Absolutely! It's a gift of Spirit in the new age. It's yours. Oh, dear ones, don't take my word for it. Do it. Measure the results. Try it. But in the process become knowledgeable in the other sciences.

Polarity Switch

The third attribute is the polarity switch. Dear ones, your biology is polarized, for your body has magnetic properties. Otherwise you would not be affected at all by the magnetic grid. We have spoken of this in channeling before, and this is not the time to go over it, except to say that you are influenced by magnetics on the planet. The human body is exceptionally resilient to magnetic change. It would have to be this way in order for you to travel from one place to another. Do you know what happens when you take a human being and hurl him at hundreds of miles an hour to another location on the planet? He passes through multiple ley lines of the grid, and his personal magnetics passes through the Earth's magnetics. Those of you who understand electricity know what happens when you pass magnetic fields through electric fields. You get current! That is what you have called "jet lag." It is not harmful, but it is a temporary imbalance, and so we say to allow three full days to recover before you are again totally balanced. So if there is something you must do which is critical for your mental and biological processes to operate perfectly, give three days. Your body will acclimate and become accustomed to the new magnetic posture.

But oh, dear ones, there are some who have a biology which is unbalanced to the degree that a switch like that described can be permanent until facilitated. It is especially so for those human beings who travel between the hemispheres of the north and the south, for this is the greatest potential for polarity shift within a human. So a human going to the south and returning back to the north may have a situation where his polarity has not switched back, and needs to be facilitated. This attribute shows itself, and allows you to measure it and to switch it back. So we say to all of you, it is important that you learn how this is to be measured. It is not for the Kryon to give you this information, for it is already known. Seek it out, for this is one of the first things that you would want to know about a patient who was sitting in front of you. Are they polarized correctly? *It is a measure of a human's polarity for the place in which he sits. It is totally relative to the area, and not an absolute. Many times a polarity switch can change a very ill person into a healthy one in only three days! Incorporate this into your own healing techniques!*

Magnetics

The fourth attribute is magnetics. You are going to see an amazing increase in magnetic healing. Like other healing sciences, however, there are wise admonishments. We encourage each one of you who may wish to be healed with magnets to seek out facilitation and not do it yourself. Magnetic healing is just as critical as acupuncture. It is just as critical as herbology, or any chemicals and substances you would ingest. So it can also be just as dangerous if misused. Take it seriously and get help. If no facilitation is available, then read carefully from appropriate sources before you apply any magnetics to yourself.

Also understand that there is a large difference between what we would call the active and inactive magnets, for the static magnets that you can hold in your hand, which are not connected to current, have a completely different function than those which are active and connected. Here is still another admonition: magnetic healing is a science to be used sparingly. That is to say, like all other healings, it is not something that is supposed to be used 24 hours a day. Use it in a healing mode to rebalance yourself, then take it away. It is not something you should have around you for healing all the time, any more than you would walk around with the needles of the acupuncturist stuck in your body. You must consider the magnetics in the same way, for it is powerful! It also can have an addictive quality, but we will have more on that at another time. (Writer note: don't confuse Kryon's admonition about not having magnets on you all the time with magnetic shielding devices. These devices are not magnets, and can safely be worn all the time. Some are very effective.)

Live Essence Medicines

The fifth attribute of the new age healing is live essence medicines. We speak not of things that used to be alive, but are alive now – some of them taken right out of the human body, enhanced, and given back to you. Some of them are ancient, given back to you. Again we say to you that the admonition with these live essence medicines is that you greet them, and you talk to them, and you give them permission to enter your body. Now why, you might say, would you have live essence medicines at this time, being the new energy? Here is what is special about that. Dear ones, the energy of the cosmos is different now than when I laid the grids of this planet. It is lower now, for there is a careful and consistent balance with the energy of the cosmos. Every time there is a newly created area of the universe, the cosmic overall energy is lessened slightly, for that is where the creative energy goes. Those of you in energy management will understand this.

The energy of the cosmos is constant and consistent, and when it is used in another area it diminishes in the area it was used from. So on the planet right now, although you have a biology which is meant to rejuvenate itself completely, it cannot do it one hundred percent over a long period of time. The reason is because the lowered cosmic energy will not allow for it. Your bodies were originally designed to rejuvenate themselves completely. It is not an error or mistake of Spirit that this lowered energy exists, for, dear ones, it allows for life termination and change. Lifetime after lifetime you have had karmic work-throughs and vibrational changes due to this condition. It is the engine of life to you. But now we're telling you that these things are changing, and as we have channeled before, it is Spirit and the Kryon that says we now wish you to stay. We wish you to remain. We wish you to be clear of your karmic lessons and move on to what you came for – what you stood in line for. There is no healing which is too hard for Spirit! The live essence medicines are the ones to **add the energy back into your body to accomplish the balance to one hundred percent**. They have to be alive, for their life is energy. The live essence medicines that we speak of are the ones that will go right to the thymus. They're the ones that will make that organ function just as beautifully as it did when you were born. This indeed is the rejuvenation of the human biology. One hundred percent... can you imagine such a thing? Watch for these, the live essence medicines.

Now we wish to go back and answer the seven questions in the order that they were presented. And the first one is this: "**How can I know if I'm supposed to be a healer?**"

It may be surprising to know, dear ones, that the people and humans asking these questions are from two groups this night. The first group is of the ones who are just being awakened to their purpose in life. Oh, how we honor you! For you to make this shift during this lifetime is exactly why you came. Do you know what your guides go through when you make such a shift? For they are ecstatic with love and with honor! Even the ones who depart and meet the new ones can hardly wait to speak to you. It's time to say we love you dearly for this, for you have made a lifetime shift. So you may ask, "Perhaps I'm to be a healer?" The other ones asking the question, believe it or not, are some who have been healers all along. But you see, it's changing for them. They are feeling uncomfortable. The humans on their healing table may not be receiving the same results, and the ones who sit in front of them may not walk away feeling as good. So they are questioning themselves and saying, "Should I be a healer at all?"

We say this to both groups: what is your passion? For the passion that you have and the karmic residue that you carry into this life to heal others is real. You have this for a purpose. Yes, you're supposed to be a healer if you share the passion for it. If you do not have the passion and you're just idly wondering, then no, you are not. So again we say to **follow your passion, for that is your contract**; it is your intuition. For those of you questioning whether you should do it, and you've been doing it, we say "nothing has changed in your contract." Learn the new procedures. Understand the new knowledge. Become comfortable with the new energy, and make the appropriate changes. In other words, the old things are no longer working. So stop for a moment; then restart your healing engine with a combination of old intuition and new knowledge!

The second question was this: "**What are the mechanics of healing? What is actually taking place when someone sits before me and I work energy with him, or the human lies on the table and I touch him or do energy work? What is happening?**" You might say, "I know what I've been told. I know physiologically what is supposed to be happening, but spiritually what is really going on?"

For some of the humans here this night the following may be a revelation, but others will say "Yes, I knew that." Although you are called a healer, it takes two to heal. For all you as a healer are truly doing is creating a neutral balance as a "healing catalyst."

Imagine a road with boulders blocking it. A human stands on it saying, "I have to go forward. If I can't go forward, I'll not find food. If I can't find food, I'll surely die. Please help me to go forward by removing the boulders from my path." So by using your healing methods the boulders are removed and cleared away. You leave the scene only to come back a week later with the same human standing there saying, "There are boulders again. Please help." Everything inside you wants to announce firmly to your patient, "When the boulders were cleared the first time, why didn't you get up and move forward?" Did you take responsibility for a "non healing"? ... or did you correctly assign the responsibility to your patient?

Oh, dear ones, the mechanics of healing from your standpoint are truly only half the issue. None of you, even those who prescribe herbs and know the mechanics of what they do within the body, will achieve measurable healing unless the one wishing to be healed gives permission for it to be so. The mechanics, interesting as they may be, are that all healers are "neutralizers."

So the next logical question would be the third question, and that is this: "**What, then, can the human do who wishes to be healed, to cooperate with what I'm doing as the healer?**" The answer should be obvious. He must cooperate to allow the healing to take place! Now this is complex dear ones, for it has to do with contract, and with karma, which is not the healer's issue. It has to do with what he wishes to do in this lifetime, and his readiness for it. Perhaps you sit in front of him, clearing the boulders, but he has no concept of what he is supposed to do. Perhaps it's time you ask him to cooperate?

There are many things that he can do to prepare, but the main one is this: before he ever gets to your space, he might verbalize to Spirit out loud to give himself permission in this new energy for a <u>change</u> – not for a healing, but for a change. Giving intent for change is asking to move forward in the new energy. This is a powerful catalyst to self healing! He cannot look at you and say, "Do it all." He must realize that he has to change, and give his body permission for the influx of energy. He has to give permission for the herbs to work, for the colors to work, for the sounds and the aromas to work. That is the task of the human who is on the other side of the table or the room or the partition. It takes two.

The fourth question is asked, "**How can I measure if I'm successful**"? Now, some of you think the answer would be obvious. How many healings have you done? How many people go away healed? But this is not the answer.

In alignment with the last two questions, dear ones, the answer is: **the successful healer is the peaceful healer!** For she or he totally understands the process that is going on spiritually. When the one who was supposed to be healed gets up off the table, and there has been no healing, the healer can still be peaceful. For the healer has done one hundred percent of his part, and he does not take responsibility for the one who has just left the office. So the answer is **peace**, the peace that comes from wisdom and knowledge, the peace that comes from the understanding of the way things work in perfect love.

We speak to those of you this night who may be asking the question, "Should I really be a facilitator, for around me I see so much pain?" We say the pain is not your responsibility. Your responsibility is in your passion and your science. We say to use it to one hundred percent. Find out what the meld is about and use it to one hundred percent. Let the humans who come to you do the rest, and then be peaceful with your own process. Love them fully, but do not take responsibility for their process. This peace will result in increased power for you. No healer can be at one hundred percent and be in unrest.

Oh Kryon, some ask, "**Do I have to be single to be a healer?**" A humorous question you might say, and yet as you look around you, look at how many of you are indeed single! (Laughter)

Why is that? you might ask. This attribute is a holdover from the old energy, dear ones. What I'm about to tell you now is filled with love. It is filled with honor. We tell you that the same energy that fills your minds and your hands as a facilitator, and as an energy mover in the new age, is the same energy that the shamans have on the planet! It is a priesthood that you celebrate! And we tell you that in the old energy the shamans and the priests were always single. So it is a holdover, or a residue from the past. It is a posturing of consciousness which may now change. For at the cellular level there is part of your body saying, "I cannot have this power and be with a partner." Now we're telling you that this is not so.

Give yourself permission for the partner. Verbally announce to yourselves that the old energy rule is no longer the case. Say, "I co-create in the name of Spirit the appropriate partner for my life." Then let it alone. Important: don't tell Spirit who it should be! (Laughter)

The sixth question is, **"Kryon, how can I know what my path is?** There are so many options in front of me, I am confused. I know I'm a healer but I don't know where I'm to go, or who to be with. What is it I should do?"

Dear ones, we do not ask you suddenly to become wizards in this New Age, for these are indeed the kinds of questions you would ask a wizard. What we tell you is simply to ask for it to be shown to you. Do you have any idea as to the power of your verbalizations and your requests? Say, "*Spirit, I ask and co-create a clear vision of what my path should be. Present the road signs so there will be no mistake.*" Then leave it at that. Don't tell Spirit where you want to go. Simple? Yes. Too simple? No. For already some of you are realizing and understanding the power of this communication. Totally – completely – powerful.

Be responsible to the sensitivity of change, and be alert for new things to present themselves to you. If you co-create this and blindly plod through life, not being aware of subtle new opportunities then you will still be in the dark, just as the human was who didn't know when to get up and move after the boulders were cleared. When you co-create something like this, be extra alert for the signs! Commonly the signs are: (1) Sudden new opportunities that you formerly thought were not for you. (2) New humans contacting you who you never knew before. (3) A seemingly negative happening in your life that actually forces you to change something big. These are all ANSWERS. Get used to viewing them as such, and move with them.

The seventh question is, **"Kryon, what is the key to becoming a powerful healer?"** And we say to you that it is amazingly simple. The answer to this question will be in the form of a story. Kryon has given you this parable before, but tonight it is again time for it.

John the Healer

John the healer was a spiritual man. He had a wonderful practice, and he understood his science well. Many came to John and were healed; however, there were always a few who were not. But John was starting to feel uncomfortable; for you see, the new energy was upon him, and he knew the New Age was here. John was uncomfortable for a number of reasons. The chief one was the fact that his healing practice was not as successful in his eyes as it had been. In other words, he was not at peace. He was having fewer and fewer healings on his table. It made John question whether he should be a healer at all!

We see John sit down to meditate, for John was a powerful meditator. It guided his life, for he understood communication with Spirit, and listened intently to what Spirit said. This had always worked before, and he knew it would work again. Now, we're going to let you in on the conversation between John, his guides, and his higher self. This will be enlightening for you.

As soon as John sat down, his guides said, "Oh, John, hello! How are you?" (They were very familiar and friendly guides... and all are.) John ignored them and began his breathing ceremony (not hearing them). Moments later John was ready, so he was prepared. His feet were in the right position. He was facing north. His hands were upright. His head was in the right position. "Oh, Spirit," John began, and his guides interrupted, "Hello John, how are you?"

John said, "I need help. Nothing is working," and he named the humans who had come to his healing table by name. He said, "What about this one? I have been working on his back for so long, but nothing is happening!" He said, "I pray for help here. Heal this person. Make this happen... give me this... do these things." He hardly knew what to ask for, there were so many requests. And Spirit said, "Oh, John, WE LOVE YOU! All of the power that you need is here, and we stand ready for you." Then they gave him such an incredible wash of love, he knew he was in the presence of Spirit.

John felt he had answers, and he felt that things were going to change. But the next time he saw the human with the back trouble, he realized that it had gotten worse. John did everything that he knew how to do, yet there was no healing. Back he went into his meditation with the same results. He would sit for a long time until he felt he was in the right position, and Spirit would be there and he would feel the love of his guides, and of his higher self. They would say, "Oh, John, indeed we love you. You are so powerful." And he'd beg Spirit, "Oh please, show me what to do in my healing room." And so life went on for John like this.

Now, John had a sister. It was almost adding insult to injury that his sister was also troubled with health, and that he seemingly could do nothing about it. So he sat with her and he prayed, and he sent her energy. He used his science, the things he knew worked, but his sister did not get better. She seemed so troubled all of the time.

Finally after a great amount of time, John had had it. In anger, he stormed into his meditation area, sat down on the couch, and said, "I've had it! Where are you?" And his guides said, "Hi John, how are you?" John was so shocked that he almost fell off out of his chair. "How can you be here so quickly? I'm not ready." "We've always been here John," his guides replied. "We're with you even in the healing room, John."

"You told me I was powerful," John said. "You gave me incredible answers. I felt them in the love that you sent. Yet nothing is happening! I'm at my wit's end. What can I do?" John's guides faced him and said, "Oh John, we're so glad you came. Listen, John: it doesn't matter how good the stove is; the food will never be cooked until the burners are hot."

Now, John was not a fool, and he said to them, "The burners – they're me?" And they said, "Yes." "What can I do?" John asked, and his Spirit and guides said, "What is it that you choose to do?" John answered, "**I want to be in my contract!**" Oh, the fluttering that went on when he said that! For that's all they had to hear. This time John didn't specify whose back was to be healed. He didn't specify what he wanted specifically, or where the power should come from, or which day he should feel better. John said finally, "I want healing for myself. I want to be in my contract. I want my passion to be fulfilled. I want to do what I came here for."

Spirit said to him, "John, it took so long for you to ask that. You shall have it! It is yours, even as you ask."

When John arose that night from his meditation, he realized that things had changed, for he had a new peace. Even before he went back to the healing room, he knew things would be different. Spirit had told him all he had to do was to take care of himself, and everything else would be added. When John walked into the healing room, amazing things started to happen, for he was given new knowledge. "I'm going to lay my hands here today," he would say to himself. "It's different. No one told me to, but I know it's going to be the right thing to do." Results were immediate. John knew that Spirit was standing over his shoulder, winking at him saying "Oh yes, that's right. Now try this." John was beginning to have results like he had never seen before. He told the ones who came to him to get ready to be healed. He had ceremony with them prior to ever touching them. They thought he was crazy – until they were healed. Then even more started coming to him... John the powerful healer.

And so it was that John went to see his sister. John literally danced into her room, all aglow, knowing that healing was imminent. He saw her light up! No more scowls, and yet he hadn't even touched her. She said to John, "John, what has happened? I've been so worried about you!" Everything stopped. Then John realized that his own torment had spilled over into the very ones he was trying to treat. "Spirit told me you're going to be healed," John lovingly announced. He had ceremony with his sister, and she was indeed healed, because John had taken care of himself first – and his power and wisdom had increased greatly.

The answer to the seventh question, "What is the key to becoming a powerful healer?" is to balance yourself first! Call for your contract to be fulfilled. This balance creates new knowledge, new tools, and the ability to see whether polarity is switched. All of these new healing gifts are yours, but they will not be until you take care of yourself first. It may seem strange to you that we say, "When you meditate alone, it is not necessary to give energy to those whom you are going to heal; and yet it is the truth, for your science is your healing. What you do in meditation should be for YOU." Your contract as a healer is what creates the power. The more it is fulfilled, the stronger you will be as the healer. Co-create the total marriage to your contract, and watch what happens!

Oh, dear ones, we have sat in front of you this night, and whether you have known it or not, we have been in awe of you. The feeling that overwhelms my partner each time this takes place is this "awe." That you would have volunteered to come down for such a scenario! ... to be in a weakened biology and not even know who you really were... to have the very fact that you are pieces of God hidden from you while you walk here! To agree to age, grow old, die and come back! Oh, what a task you have agreed to do with your love.

We told you that we know who you are. We have been there at the ceremony that awards you your colors. There is not one of you this night who does not know the Kryon, for I have been there with my colors glowing, standing in the line when you received yours, and we have loved one another before. So we invite you in this brief moment that we have been together to feel the presence of home, to know there is purpose for life, that you are not alone. That the new energy is not here to terminate you on this planet, and that we want you to remain in good health because we love you so.

It's true that the work to be done is completely yours, and that is why we do not give you advance information of your lessons. For the work would not be the work if we gave away all things in advance. But the gifts are amazing, and in all love we tell you that you have earned them!

It is with a welling up within my partner that he translates that we will leave now. There is another fact. This night fathers and sons and mothers and daughters will pass each other in the passageways outside, and never even know they once were related! Oh, such love it takes for you to do this! Is it any wonder that the Universe loves you as it does? Oh, this is a special place, this Earth. This is a special place.

Some of you will walk from this place and vibrate with the energy for days. We invite this. There is nothing wrong with you. You have simply felt the love of Spirit this night.

And so it is.

Kryon

Writings
Del Mar - #422
92014

Dear Lee

The Bible warns us in Revelation of false prophets who will do amazing things and seduce us toward the end times. Is it significant that your Book I is called <u>The End Times</u> ... and how do we know that you are not one of the false prophets?

Will you shed some light on that warning? What was meant, and who are the false prophets? How will we recognize them? (If you are one, you will answer this with a lie, so we will be fooled anyway).

Thanks,

Diane Steen

Seattle, Washington

Chapter Six

False Prophets

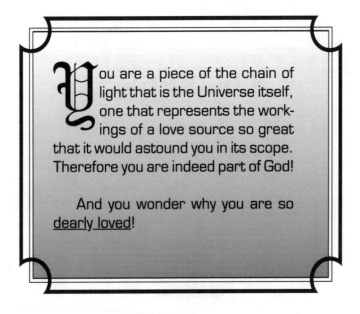

ou are a piece of the chain of light that is the Universe itself, one that represents the workings of a love source so great that it would astound you in its scope. Therefore you are indeed part of God!

And you wonder why you are so <u>dearly loved</u>!

...from page 189

Kryon

"Messages For an Island"
Channeled in Lihue

The island of Kauai in Hawaii
Kryon Seminar

The Kryon Writings, Inc.

PMB 422
1155 Camino Del Mar
Del Mar, California 92014
[www.kryonqtly.com]

"Messages For an Island"
Live Channel
Hawaii - January 1995

> *This live channel has been edited with additional words and thoughts to allow for clarification and better understanding for the written word.*

From the writer...

Here is a live channeling from one of the most beautiful spots on Earth! From the island of Kauai comes an evening filled with love and honor, where Kryon speaks specifically about the feelings of those on this small island paradise.

I have included it in this book so you can share in what Kryon says regarding the island of Kauai and the people on it, and I have included this Hawaii channeling in the "False Prophet" chapter because that subject is discussed midway during the event, addressing the letter on page 162. Typically Kryon also covers topics that have already been discussed in this book... but sometimes we can't hear them too often!

For new readers, I also share that the human teachers Barbara and Michael were there with us. In Kryon Book One, it was these two who provided the venue for the first live Kryon channel in Del Mar within their "temple group," a group of 14 metaphysicians who would hear Kryon's message live for the first time. Barbara and Michael were on Kauai doing work of their own, with clients and groups of appointments, but they broke from their own work schedule to honor Jan and me with their presence that night.

Greetings, dear ones, for I am Kryon of magnetic service. Oh, it is a sweet spot is it not, my partner, to be sitting in your path when it is correct? For you are here by design, as are these who sit before you, and those reading these words. And it is this night that I promise you, my partner, that I will not give any faster than you can receive, for there is much to tell. But first, we say to those of you who are gathered in this place that each and every single one is known by Spirit. There is not one of you whom we do not know by name, and that the reason you are here is simple. Believe it or don't believe it, but you are here so that Spirit can wash your feet! For we love each and every one, and for those of you who have put Spirit on the pedestal, it is time to take him off. For you are the ones whom we are self-enabling at this moment. And so it is with honor and joy that we pack this room with the guides and the energies and the entities that have come to fill it for the short time we are together.

Many things have happened to this planet in these last years, and we have channeled information in the past months all about the specifics of what they are. But in summary we say that the Harmonic Convergence which occurred not too long ago was the measurement by which Earth was judged ready for the new age. And yes, it could have gone another way, but it did not... and that surprised many. But the surprise was then followed up by joy and honor, words we use a great deal in reference to humans. There are so many words and shapes in the astral language that mean honor, but only one word of yours. So we will say it many times until you get the point!

Honored are you for the fact that you raised the vibration of this planet to a point we did not expect. And the flurry of activity around these last years has been in preparation for the new energy and the new age, and for the self-empowerment of human beings all over the planet who wish to take this gift and "see" who they are. A personal message it is from Kryon and Spirit! Kryon does not sit before groups of people, for I am speaking to you, dear one. I know who you are. And I say that you are in a spot tonight occupying a chair surrounded by your guides, with the masters in the back row saying, "Listen to what is being said. Do you know who you are? For you alone can raise the vibration of this planet if you choose. You have shown us you can, and now you stand in a place of self-empowerment to a degree that has never been available before." And this is why you are here, so that you will know more about this.

As channeled before, in 1994 there was a staggering event which could only have happened due to the one in 1992. In 1992 the code was sent out to the magnetic strands which surround the biological strands of your DNA. This was the code that said, "Permission is granted for upcoming change," and without that code being sent out, none of this would have happened. And so you were prepared for 1994, for in your year 1994, starting in the month of April, the passing of the torch began. This has great significance to the planet, but dear ones, it has amazing significance to the island that you are on now.

The passing of the torch was the beginning of the place holder entities of this Earth leaving and passing the responsibility to you. It is thus: since the very beginning there has been an energy balance of the planet which had to be consistent, and whose sum had to remain the same. Humans could not hold it by themselves, and so there were place holder entities on the planet. The magic ones, the little people, the devas, the ones who occupied the rocks, and the ones in the sky. Yes, they were all real, even though many were not in your dimension. And as more humans came on to the planet, they left one by one so that the energy would remain the same. Now, do not mistake the energy balance with the vibration level, for the energy must remain constant. It is the vibration which may change with your work, and it is the vibration which is measured by Spirit.

And so it is that the passing of the torch began in that month of April, until its completion was begun, resulting in the 12:12 experience. And this is what the 12:12 was actually about. It was the time when the last ones would begin to leave, and as they depart this planet, they turn back and look and say, "It is a marvelous thing that the humans have been able to raise the vibration to a degree where they could contain all of the energy themselves."

And so it is that this exodus of these magic ones has begun, and will be completed shortly. And so it is also we turn to you and say, "We need 144,000 of you to become ascended masters immediately throughout the planet, for it is necessary to hold the energy consistent." It is not for everyone, for obviously the number is relatively small. You will know who you are, for it requires great sacrifice. It is an amazing event, is it not, that these would leave after eons of time? Leaving you holding the ball, so to speak, which is the planet Earth (cosmic humor)!

Now, there are three attributes which affect the place where you live, and I speak now of those who reside on this, the portal of energy here on this island... a truly beautiful place on the planet, this island you call Kauai. And because of these three things, you have felt a change here. And because of these three things, there are contracts which are finished here, allowing you to move forward, and stay or go as you choose, whereas before it would have been difficult.

The first attribute you felt immensely, and are feeling even now, for this is indeed a magic place. For in the cracks and crannies of your beautiful valleys there were the magic ones aplenty. For this is an energy center, a portal and a place which sends out a signal to others in the universe saying, "We are ready for you." It is a place which is protected. It is a place that Spirit holds above other places, and it must be cleaned regularly.

And so, dear ones, the magic has gone from the ones who were here, and now resides with you... and you are feeling it! For there is a void where there used to be the devas, and for a certain time there will be an imbalance. Others will come in seeming to fill the void with a consciousness that you would not want, but this will settle out in the coming months. And so this is the first and foremost reason you are feeling a change in this place. Although the rest of the Earth is feeling it also, you are feeling it more, for the magic was indeed great here. But the magic, dear ones, is not gone. It simply resides in a different place. And it is for you in your training to learn how to use it for yourself. This is now your gift and has happened with permission resulting from the giving of the code.

The second thing that is taking place here is my work. For indeed the magnetic grid lines of the planet are changing, and the ley lines that used to be here, that crossed at a certain vibration level allowing for a certain conscious level to exist, are moving. And the ones specifically that you are used to are moving slightly, a number of miles to the northeast. They are centering themselves above what we call the great amplifier. Some of you here will know of what I speak, and for others this will remain a mystery. But it is so, nevertheless.

So not only are the devas gone, and the responsibility is lying on your shoulders, but now I tell you that the grid line has also moved. And if you will recall, I have told you in the past that your very consciousness and enlightenment is altered by the energy of the grid. It is no wonder you feel as you do; it is no wonder. Some of you have felt that the new feelings must reside with you and you alone. But we wish to tell you that this is not the case. For you will feel the changes as a group, all of you. And if you get together and compare how you feel, there will be a similarity, showing that it is not a personal problem that you are dealing with.

The third attribute, and the one that is the most visible, is the one that happened two years ago; and we speak now of the great winds that came. Now, there were many reasons for this. First there was the cleansing of the island and the pruning of the energy. All of these things were appropriate, for **Spirit tends to polish up its finest silver**! But the other reason that Kryon brings you this night is one that you may not have thought of, for it was indeed a test of fear for you. You have spoken of this between yourselves, and Kryon has mentioned the phantom of fear to you before. Oh, what a phantom it was that presented itself in that fashion as many of you huddled in your homes, praying to God that you would be spared! Praying that your homes would be spared as well. It is the blackness part of that time, and the fear that you felt there, that Kryon speaks of when he speaks of the test. Many of you know of what I speak, for fear is what it was about. And the test was passed, for so many of you in those moments prayed in a manner of total surrender. Surrender to your higher selves, and not to just a higher power. And indeed you co-created your way out of it! This is what that test was about when the winds blew that day.

So again we say to those of you who have residence here on this beautiful place, that if you are feeling uncomfortable, you are not alone. We tell you that there is great reason for this. And in all honor, we thank you for going through it this time. For you will be comfortable again if you choose to remain. And we honor you for your trouble.

And so there are many of you reading this right now (cosmic humor again regarding the relativity of the "now") that will also experience this test in the areas and portals that will also change where you live. You may be angry at Spirit in the future for placing you in the middle of something that creates so much fear. You may say, "I thought I was supposed to be in the perfect place! ... my sweet spot!" And Spirit will say to your higher self:

"You are indeed in the perfect place! Feel the potential for human fear and transcend it completely. **Know that you are safe, and feel the responsibility for being where you are**. Look around you and see how you can instantly affect the others who are paralyzed with the phantom around them. You know better, and may walk into the middle of the fear of uncertainty and Earth change. Share your peace and let them see your light shine during the blackest moments! Encompass them with the love of Spirit and watch them settle into the arms of the higher God in themselves. It is at a time like this that your work for the planet is the greatest. How can you doubt that you are in a perfect place when this happens? Do you think that your 'perfect place' contains no lessons or offers no opportunities to show who you are? If that is the case, then you haven't truly understood the message of the new age."

Death of a great warrior – a past life experience

And now we wish to do something we have not done for some time. We are going to take you on a brief journey to one of the past lives of someone who is sitting in this room. Actually, this is a past death. In all appropriateness we give you this in love and in honor so you will understand who you are. And since it is only one of you, the others may listen in appreciation for you and what you have gone through; but it may also inform them of the way Spirit works. We take you to a time not far from here 900 years ago, approximately. You are a male in this experience, and you are not now. A great warrior are you, a sub-chieftain under the service of the dynasty of the King, whose dynasty will have a total of five. It is called the Ten Year War that you are now finding yourself in.

It is the middle of a dark night, as you creep gradually and silently in the warm waters of the oceans to the south, toward this very island. For you have come from another place, and are now gently gliding in boats toward shore with a band of other warriors. Your goal is to land on the south beaches, and to take a position held by other warriors on the island. For this is a holdout. All have joined the Kingdom but for this one island, and it has represented years of trials and battles.

Tonight is an important battle, you feel. As you approach the islands, you are in a group of boats with men totaling 80. Your boats are shaped like two canoes, with a centerboard between them attached to each canoe. On the centerboard between them rests your weapons, your supplies and your sail. But it is time now to take your sail down, for you have learned that even in a dark night there are lookouts on the beach which might spot the profile of a high sail coming. And so you whisper to the other boats in a chain, each whispering to the other to take the sails down. And gradually the sails are lowered.

Then you begin to feel the fear that you have had before each battle in the past, knowing that you will soon land on the shores and face the enemy. The south has been selected because the surf there is light. Now you get out your paddles and start paddling slowly toward the island. Silently you go, and in about an hour you start to hear the surf, and you know you are close to your goal of surprise.

Now it seems there were those already in the water in other boats who knew you were coming, and who attacked you from the left flank out of the darkness. You knew about it first when you heard the cries of those behind you, but almost instantaneously you felt the spear pierce your chest, and involuntarily you fell into the water. Knowing that the wound was mortal, the things that flashed before you were many. But it was all that you could do before you sank in the calm sea, to yell out the name of your King as the warm waters passed over you. It was over in an instant, but this dramatic event is still carried with you to this day.

This, dear one, was an important lifetime for you. And you may say, "Perhaps it is that I should now be afraid of drowning, or perhaps I should be afraid of being attacked from the left." No. For you have had many lifetimes subsequent to that to enable you to clear such karmic attributes. The residual karma you carry from this event now is not a fear, but an apprehension. It is a feeling deep within you, dear one, of unfinished business, for this is the way spirit works with you. And I say to you this night that you are not alone! For there were others here in this very place, and on this island, who were with you and were part of the 80 warriors that did not make it to the shore for their King.

And so there is a feeling of unfinished business that keeps you coming back. And when you leave this island, you are often apprehensive... a feeling that says, "I must go back... I must go back." This residual feeling can now be released, and it is this very night that when you arise from your chair tonight, through intent, it will be dissipated, for you now have the power to void these things in your life. And if you choose to leave this place, it will not call to you in the same way it did before. It is now released within you... for the first time in centuries. Such is the gift of the new age.

This is the power that each of you has as co-creators in the new energy. Spirit honors you for this process of coming and going and coming and going, and of the karmas and the fears that you face. For there is not one of us in service to you that must go through this kind of trial. So we continue to sit before you in honor. There is that word again!

And speaking of this, we wish to honor two who are here this night. For there is the teacher Barbara and the teacher Michael here in this place tonight. We speak to them now, and we speak to all of you now, to say that they are greatly honored. For it is because of them that the Kryon was able to come through my partner who speaks to you now. They may not be aware of the window of opportunity which arose in the year they were given the first Kryon writings. For they had been in the work for many years, and it would have been easy for them to have said to my partner when he brought them the writings: "These notes are nice, but go back and try again. After all, we have been doing this for many years and you have not." But that is not what they said, for they recognized the love of Spirit, and they put their egos to one side. And they saw the truth and said to my partner, "This is truthful, so proceed." For if they had not said that, there would be no meeting this night, and no book for you to read... and the Kryon would have moved to another who also had the contract set up. Do you see how you are in control of your own future? Do you see how no one can sit in front of you and tell you what is going to happen? You create it day by day! And so we (my partner and I) are here because of these dear ones, and Spirit honors them for that.

And so we say to both of you this night (Michael and Barbara), that your lineage is great. Sometimes you are not aware, for you are in the work, of who you truly are (and were). So when we say "brothers of Levi," this will give you a hint of how you have worked together in the past, and your true lineage together on this planet. And dear one, Barbara, when we call you "Daughter of Orion," you will know of your seed. And we say to you also that you are one of the few on the planet who recognizes that the alignment of Kryon is a realignment to something that used to exist, and not something which is totally new. So your gift this night, and from this time forward, will be greater clarity in your work, starting immediately. Look for it. You are gratefully honored. There are tens of thousands who will receive the Kryon information in this new energy because you followed your contract when it was presented!

False Prophets

And now we come to a part of the channel where my partner is asked to be very clear, because it has the potential to be confusing when translated. We have waited until this time within this energy, in the clearness of this island, to allow the integrity to flow to answer a question which may not have been answerable in other energy spots. The question is one which is filled with potent energy, that has ramifications which are great and planetary. A simple question however, it is, and we ask for your patience while it is explained. For the words that are spoken here will be transcribed and published, and the question is too important for this not to be so.

Here is the question: "Kryon, we have been told that in the end times there will be false prophets. Here are the end times, as witnessed by your end times information. Are you therefore a false prophet? In addition, we have been told by the other prophets earlier that if the false prophet is asked if he is false, he will lie. How do we know you are not lying when you say you are real?" Can you see the ramifications, dear ones, of this question?... and what it means to the believers of many different faiths and many different ways?

The beginning of the answer to this question will require that we call upon an old Earth puzzle, one which is already known to those who feature logic exercises, for logic indeed plays a major part in the answer to your question (as it should). We indulge your patience as we take you through this mind puzzle, for it has bearing on the entire answer. Imagine that you are walking alone on a path. Standing in front of you there are two holy wise men. In order to proceed on your path, as the puzzle goes, it is necessary for you to know the attributes of these wise men. For you see, one of them tells the truth, and must always tell the truth. One of them is deceitful, and will always deceive you, no matter what you ask.

Now, as the puzzle goes, you must ask one of them, either one, a "yes" or "no" question. And by doing so, the answer will expose the attributes of each one.

Now, metaphorically many of you actually stand at this juncture in your lives. In all love and innocence of spirit, you are facing many holy men and asking them if they have the truth. So the puzzle isn't quite so remote for you.

This is a difficult logic puzzle for many, for if you simply ask the *truthful one*, "Are you the one that tells the truth?" he would say "Yes." If you ask the *deceitful one*, "Are you the one that tells the truth?" he, of course, will lie and will also say "Yes." You gained nothing by that question. And so the questions must be structured in a way that in advance you will look for a "yes" or "no" answer which will expose the attributes of the one you are addressing.

I will now give you the simple question to ask. As you approach either holy man, say the following to him: *"Dear sir, if I ask the other holy man standing next to you if you are the deceitful one, will he say Yes?"* And by the answer given from either man you will know by the "yes" or the "no" exactly who stands in front of you. Because of the attributes of each, it demands that one must say "Yes" to that question and one must say "No." Ponder this to see how it works. Place yourself in the position of each man to understand what a "yes" means and what a "no" means as to the attributes of who they are.

If you are facing the *truthful one*, he will answer "Yes," for he must tell you the truth of what would happen. If you are facing the *deceitful one*, he will say "No," for he is forced to lie about what the truthful holy man would say.

So what does this puzzle tell you that would have a bearing upon the falseness or non-falseness of the Kryon? It is a paradigm for you to look at that will help you in asking the question at all. Let us examine briefly what the puzzle consists of, for first you must be alone walking down your path in search of the truth. This means that if you already have a holy man in your pocket, you are biased. And if you are believing a truth and have a bias, no matter what you ask of anyone, you will always be wondering if it is correct. So the first attribute for you is to be in a position of clarity and of seeking, where you do not believe that you already occupy a place where you know the whole truth. A true searcher will be neutral, and not a believer in another holy man. This will eliminate immediately many of those who would be capable of asking at all.

Next, the way the question was put. Do you realize the significance of both of these being holy men? For even though one is deceitful, Spirit calls him a holy man. This is something that you must consider. What have you learned by the puzzle? The puzzle says that not only must you examine the attributes of each holy man, but you must ask the one about the other! And so now you sit in front of Kryon. You do not sit in front of the others. So Kryon cannot answer for the others, but he can answer for Kryon. So let me work you through some of the attributes of the Kryon energy, and some of the ways that the question would be answered if Kryon was standing as one of the holy men. Look carefully at the attributes of the Kryon work, for therein lies the answer to your entire question. For this night we bring information for your heart. We do not ask you to join any organization. This is not to say that the joining of organizations is judged as wrong. We are only saying that Kryon brings you only information, and not a system that you must join.

Kryon does not build churches. Kryon does not ask you to attend meetings if you are not willing to. Through intent the meetings are set at odd places and unusual times, so that you may come if you choose, or not. So therefore there is no schedule. There is also no doctrine put out by Kryon, where you are asked to believe a certain way. He only imparts the information of the new age, and invites you to feel the love energy, and invites you to discover who you are.

Kryon does not ask you to tithe of your abundance. Now, this is not to say that those who ask you to tithe are judged as wrong. It is only an attribute of the one who sits before you whom you are questioning. The Kryon does not ask you to tithe of your abundance to him, and for the first time we tell you this: that **Spirit asks you to give of your abundance for yourself**. And for the first time we tell you that it would be appropriate in the new energy for you to set aside portions of your abundance to treat yourself on a monthly basis! Treat that inner child within you, that you remember growing up with, that likes to play. Remember the feeling of being treated as a child, and look forward to it by treating yourself. For it is entirely appropriate in order that you would serve the *God within*. And so we tell you at this time that if you start doing this, you will feel better than if you did not. This also has to do with many of you **learning to receive**. It is appropriate for you to give to yourself. It is so!

Here is a question asked of the Kryon within the framework of the question that is asked about the false prophets. "Kryon, tell me – I am one who enjoys my belief system. I enjoy loving a master who I honor and respect. My entire family does also. We have enjoyed this relationship with our master for years, and are comfortable with it. Can I believe the things you tell me in the new energy and also keep this other belief system?

What a question! For the answer, in all love dear ones, is yes, for the Kryon gives you only information! He does not call you to support a doctrine, and he says that **you are self empowered to believe as you choose**. The admonition here for you is that if you choose to accept the new age information, and work within the framework of another system that serves you, you might choose to be quiet about it. And for this admonition I use the example of the fruit. For there are some leaders who would sit at a table enjoying the fruit that they loved the most, that being the papaya. And in the new energy, if you came to their table with the fruit that you enjoyed most, being the mango, they might say to you, "You know, the papaya is awfully good as well. But I understand that you like the mango. So please come and feast with me. Sit at my table, and even though I do not like your mango, and you do not like my papaya, we will still share what we have in common in love."

In the old energy there would be leaders who would sit at their tables enjoying their papaya; but when you came to the table with your mango, they would say, "What is that you bring here? This substandard fruit!" And they would say, "Give me that," and in front of you they would shred your mango and say, "Sit." And they would cut their papaya, even though you do not like it, and they would give it to you... also saying, "We understand you don't like it, but you will with time." And so we have those who would tell you how to think, dear ones, and we give you the admonition to stay away from this.

As proof, as you look around your culture on your planet, I ask you this, "Who are the ones with the most peace? Who are the those, dear ones, who have not had wars in their lands for many years? Who are the ones who are raising families without fear, who are the most abundant, who do not worry about where their food is coming from, and have shelter guaranteed?" And the answer is almost exclusively the ones who are free to think for themselves, and the ones who are free to have choice over what they do. Think about this.

Finally, there is a great irony involved in the very question about false prophets. For dear ones, as I sit in front of you this night, you are hearing the translations of the voice from the great central sun. It is the voice that spoke to Moses from the burning bush. It is the voice that spoke to Abraham with his dagger poised above his son Isaac that said, "Stop! You are honored." Therefore, this is the very voice that also spoke and said, "*In the end times there will be false prophets; beware of them.*" So it is the author of this very message that you question now.

As you approach the holy man called the Kryon, and you ask the question, "Kryon, if I ask the other holy man if you are the deceitful one, will he say, 'Yes'?" Kryon's answer will be "Yes."

Dear one, tonight you find yourself sitting in the new energy. You also find yourself sitting next to your guides, and they hold your hand during these times. They love you during these times. And it's a real stretch for some of you to ever believe it, yet it is true, and we honor you for the duality that you endure. Before you leave this place, know that this night you have sat in the presence of Spirit. You have sat in the love energy from the great central sun. And regardless of your path, all of these words were meant for you. For again we tell you that you are here by intent and on purpose. We know your name! We hope that you take the responsibility this night for that higher part of you which wants to come in to create a life that you have never seen before, a life which empowers you to co-create your own reality.

And for the ones who have been attached to this place through your King's lineage, we now give permission to leave this place without feeling the attachment. We honor you for your life nine hundred years ago, and for the part it played in this very meeting this night! Who would have thought such a thing would happen?

And so it is.

Kryon

From the writer... again.

We don't speak much in this book about the Kryon seminars that many of the channelings came out of that you are reading. The seminars are always filled with wonderful love energy, music, and occasionally a healing or two. Jan and I always give them together and try to bring the highest integrity to the process that we can.

February 1995

Dear Jan and Lee,

I was blessed! I thank you from the bottom of my heart. All – literally ALL – the things that I had been wondering were answered! The seminar was wonderful! Thank you!

I want to tell you that we were blessed to see the KRYON energy in the room when we entered, and saw the energy around you and through you as you spoke. But Lee, what I want to tell you most is that before I ever boarded the plane to get to Seattle, I had a dream of being healed and saw and felt KRYON talking to me and explaining that I had the power to take this thing into my own hands. Now that I had applied Jan's message to myself, and did the work of the inner child, it didn't take much to surface the truth! He, KRYON, was so loving, and the energy that I felt was like white fire in my joints. He told me that I still needed to find the right kinds of exercise to build bones, and the cartilage would be beginning to grow back, but I had the responsibility of taking the lead in seeking and using the right kind of process to make the changes. He started the flow even before I left home! The night of the channeling in Seattle, as soon as he begin to speak, the white fire of energy began in my joints, and I was hardly able to keep up a clear concentration on what was being said. I was being healed like mad!!! I am so grateful to you for being such a clear and Light channel!

That same night after I went to bed, I had visions and dreams in a period of about an hour, and then I woke up. I needed to lie on my back. I haven't been able to lie on my back since knee surgery over two years ago, because my legs cramp so badly. I did it anyway, and went to sleep immediately. I awoke an hour and a half later, still on my back and no leg cramps. The muscles and tendons were being stretched. I lay there awake for about three more hours and talked to my guides, to Christ, to Kryon, and I felt so wonderful! I did get about 2 more hours of sleep before getting up and going to the plane for home!

This has been a great lesson to me. I had been very depressed about not being able to walk, and this showed me that I cannot waste time being depressed; I must get to work on myself. If the energy that flows through me heals others, then I can facilitate (through God and Kryon) for myself. I know now that I can, and that I am!

Jan, your toning was beautiful. I bought your tape also – great! When we all toned together, I had to marvel at the Light and energy. I am a Vibrational and Sound healer, and the harmonics that I do just had to blend. You two are just so beautifully guided!

Bless you both for the beautiful work. I've never had such an experience of Light through me, except when Christ comes through me to answer letters and questions from others! The truth shines so brightly!

Love you all!

Brenda Montgomery
Tollhouse, California

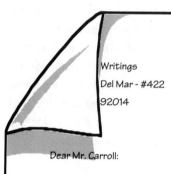

Writings
Del Mar - #422
92014

Dear Mr. Carroll:

Are you aware that in the metaphysical community, nationwide, your books are fast becoming known as an all out counterattack by the dark forces against the <u>real</u> information of love and light and power that is being dispensed from above?

Couched in well-done beautifully written format, using the correct spiritual terminology and concepts, is their way of "hooking" people into the idea of actually doing the exercise. If the BLACK cloud wasn't enough of a clue, then the disappearance of one's guides – feelings of suicidal depression for 90 days – should have been. How much <u>damage</u> do you think this is going to do among the innocent public and well meaning but naive seekers? We are to be removing karmic implants at this time, not asking for ANOTHER one.

I urge you to consider the mass damage you are going to do with these extremely dangerous writings and urge you to stop. This is not hate mail. I am a teacher of these subjects, and the Space Brothers are warning people about you, especially through their human channels in Salt Lake City and San Pedro, California. This is the ultimate in deception by the DARK FORCES.

A former reader.

About the previous page...

How does one respond to such a letter? If the address had come with it, I would have invited the several thousand of you who have had beautiful life changes and physical healings to write to this unnamed individual. Perhaps you were supposed to give them back? A subsequent attack on the entire Kryon work in 1996 identified this individual, and her devout followers. The dark "cloud" is a common metaphysical term for the veil. The loss of guides is also a common challenge before any vibrational shift, recorded in many religions. It even happened to Jesus on the cross. It's documented, common spiritual history. Therefore this trumped up attempt to create something dark and evil around a messenger of light looks silly. Most metaphysical New Age publications across America and Canada thought so too. Kryon reports the gift of the implant as a karmic <u>release</u>, not something <u>added</u> karmically... so the writer of the letter is correct in that we should indeed be *removing* karma at this time. That's what Kryon's message is all about. Kryon begs us to discover the <u>light</u> in each of us.

I present to you the rules that Spirit has personally given me to live by as a channel for Kryon. In every workshop I recite these rules. Weigh for yourselves if these appear to be the attributes of a dark force against the truth.

Rules for Lee Carroll regarding the Kryon work:

- Do not build any churches
- Do not elicit followers for Kryon
- Do not make the Kryon work evangelistic
- Do not surround yourself with a large organization
- Do not channel on mass media! *
- Let the love of Spirit guide your path

What this means is that I cannot go "on the air" and do a live channeling. If audio and video media are offered, they must be in recorded form so that individuals can show intent to play or view them personally. A Kryon channeling should never reach the broadcast airwaves. Humans must always show a personal intent to "want to know" before it is appropriate to experience the energy of Kryon.

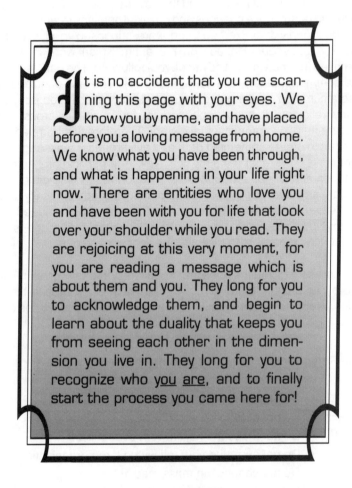

It is no accident that you are scanning this page with your eyes. We know you by name, and have placed before you a loving message from home. We know what you have been through, and what is happening in your life right now. There are entities who love you and have been with you for life that look over your shoulder while you read. They are rejoicing at this very moment, for you are reading a message which is about them and you. They long for you to acknowledge them, and begin to learn about the duality that keeps you from seeing each other in the dimension you live in. They long for you to recognize who you are, and to finally start the process you came here for!

...from page 37

Light

Kryon, on the subject of "light"

Dear ones, you use the words "the light" to mean so many things, and yet they are all so related to the absolute truth. Let us look at the subject from the outside inward:

I come from the great central sun, the creative love force that represents the light. All that is within the Universe is represented by the light that emanates from this source. It is the actual seed in each of you that represents your feeling of "home." It is the source of your joy, and the resource of your relief from fear during trying times. It has substance and can be measured. It is the part of you that is always connected to the great central love source of the entire plan of creation.

The light streams to you from your own sun. You may not consider that it has much of a spiritual significance until I remind you that your own sun is the engine of the magnetic grid system on your planet, and that I am here to adjust that grid system in response to your spiritual nature! Therefore, even the light that comes from your own sun stands in line to be honored spiritually when you define the light in general.

Light... continued

The light is the source of all life and creation in the Universe. It is physics and spirituality all at the same time, for it represents the basic attribute of love. There is no accident that the light allows you to see, for the principles are science, and the attributes are Spirit.

The light is your enlightenment and your acknowledgment of being a spiritual being walking the planet in biology, firmly connected to the light of the great central source. It is metaphorically a release from the dark, which is fear itself. An enlightened human is therefore a worker in the light, and represents a consciousness of planetary vibration intensification... the goal of all enlightened humans.

The light is present in your biology at the smallest level, and is the engine of your rejuvenation itself. If you were a traveler within the smallest darkest areas of your inner cellular workings, you would actually see the light emanating from some of the yet undiscovered parts! The light, therefore, is not only responsible for creating your life, but for sustaining it as well.

Light... continued

Finally the light comes full circle, for it represents the spark within you that is part of the whole. The entirety of creation is made from light, from the largest to the smallest. The part you carry as a love entity from the great creative source is a light so powerful that you can outshine a galaxy of suns, yet so delicate that an individual cell can use it to rejuvenate.

You are a piece of the chain of light that is the Universe itself, one that represents the workings of a love source so great that it would astound you in its scope. Therefore you are indeed part of God!

And you wonder why you are so <u>dearly loved</u>!

Kryon

on Writings

Dear Jan & Lee:

I created a very difficult body this life. In my early 20's I developed lupus, and for 20 years suffered with a struggling and painful body. Finally, two years ago my lupus had progressed to the point that my kidneys were no longer functioning. I was hospitalized and placed on dialysis. During that stay I was given too much of an antibiotic and woke the next day to total deafness. The loss of hearing was an incredible challenge. I cannot begin to express the despair and hopelessness that I felt. Why was there so much suffering? Why was there such duality? Why were we so lost if the basis of God's energy is love?

Then I read book two of the Kryon writings. It was like a moment of epiphany for me. I understood why all of this was necessary. I wept. I felt so free. It was like now it made sense. Now I could get on with it and really be useful. I could go on and on about how differently I feel about everything. It is hard not to go around with a silly smile on my face all the time. I can sense the big picture now, and I stand in awe of my life and world.

With love,

Janice Justice, DC
Tigard, Oregon

Chapter Seven

Karma

From the writer...

There is so much to say about karma! Kryon calls it the "engine of lesson," and tells us that it actually drives the whole process of our actions here on Earth! One question that is often asked that is not covered by the live channeling on the next pages is this: "Can we create new karma while on the planet?" Also, "Can we create new karma even after the implant?" The answer to both questions is yes. Heavy karma is created by willingly moving out of your contract. Normal karma can actually be created by filling your contract! If your contract is to become a wonderful healer, then you build the karmic attributes of a great healer! These are realized at the cellular level, and you carry them back in with you at the next incarnation at the cellular level.

Although karma is thought of generally as lessons, it also represents residual experiences (as Kryon will speak of next). Therefore even with a totally clean slate, you continue to write new karmic attributes. The kind of karma that is cleared by the implant is the strong multiple lifetime kind. It would be very difficult to create that kind of karma again after the implant (unless, of course, you play the accordion).*

Only kidding about the accordion

Another question is "When I take the implant, will it clear out my good karma too?" A full understanding of karma will help you realize that this question is moot. There is no such thing as good or bad karma (as Kryon sees it). The implant cleans the slate of lessons. It does not take away any learned knowledge or any helpful thing that you might have brought with you from the past. Common sense should tell us that what Spirit is offering us in this new age is LOVING HELP. There are still those who are trying to analyze what is going on as though Spirit were some set of static mechanical rules instead of a loving, conscious energy. We should all begin to realize that everything going on around us is based in love... even the things that seem negative. Listen to what Kryon has to say about karma.

Kryon

"Karma"
Channeled in Sandpoint

Idaho
Kryon Seminar

The Kryon Writings, Inc.

PMB 422
1155 Camino Del Mar
Del Mar, California 92014
[www.kryonqtly.com]

"Karma"
Live Channel
Sandpoint

> *This live channel has been edited with additional words and thoughts to allow for clarification and better understanding of the written word.*

Greetings, dear ones; I am Kryon of magnetic service. Oh, there have been some of you who have been longing for this time: to sit in the energy of Spirit. Well, dear ones, you will not be disappointed tonight. For you must understand, as this room is currently being filled with the Kryon group, and as the energy is currently being increased, it is with love for you we come this night. For each one of you who sits in the chair that you occupy has an appointment to be here. It is not chance that has found you here listening to my partner's voice as he interprets the thought groups of Spirit in love for your planet. We ask you to open your hearts and your minds this time. Those of you reading these words in the "now" and those of you hearing this in the "now" will do the same. Know that there are no accidents that find you here reading these words or listening to this voice.

Some of you this night will be taken in consciousness shortly and will not hear much of what goes on regarding the instructions that are given. For you are being worked on by Spirit as a gift because of our love for you. It is the reason you are here. All that has gone before culminates now in this time for you. Those of you know who you

are who have come here with a longing for more, with a mission that is unfulfilled, with questions about what next for you. We wish to give you these answers, but we wish to give them in a way that you will discover the individual answers for yourselves later. So we give them to you in an astral form, but we must take you away for this, just for a while with your cooperation. So at the end of this channel if you awaken and you say, "I did not consciously hear anything," you will know why.

Oh, feel the love that Spirit has for you, dear ones! For Kryon comes to you this night as the mechanic. And as we sit before you, it is the recurring theme of Kryon to say that you are the ones doing the work. It is true that the voice that speaks to you now, and the interpretations, are the same as the ones that spoke to you in the past from the burning bush! For we represent the creative force, the great central sun. We come to you as Spirit, but the instructions and the love and the energy are from the same place. We ask you to feel this as the evening progresses. Even those of you who are reading this in the "now" may experience these things. For our love for you, dear reader, is just as great as for those sitting before the Kryon this night.

And so it is up to you, dear ones, if you wish to take the gifts which are distributed during this short time. The energy is what this is all about. You sit in this place in a sweet spot on this planet. And for those of you who are in this area by choice, we honor you greatly. We tell you that there is work for you here. For there would be forces that would want to shut off this energy, but they are all human forces. Therefore, you have the complete and total power to keep it clean, for it is important on a planetary scale. All will be revealed in time.

We are going to take just another moment before the room settles to the level we wish before we start instructions. As we do, we say to you again, we are here to wash your feet and move among you in these aisles in pure love. You see, we know who you are! We know what you're going through. We know of your deepest inner desires. We know of your contracts. And we are here this night in love to cooperate with all of these.

We wish to take this time for instruction and tell you by example about something that is common to humanity but is often misunderstood. We speak this night more specifically than we ever have before regarding karma. Now, some of you believe that karma can be positive and negative. That is to say, if a human being is having a difficult time on the planet, he must be experiencing negative karma. Or perhaps a human is having something wonderful happen to him; he must be experiencing positive karma. And so it goes that some of you have said that perhaps what is being observed is a reward or a punishment for something which has happened in a past incarnation of the human. This is not the case, and we wish to show you the overview of how Spirit sees karma, and your place within it. Then we wish to give you some examples of some human lifetimes that will show this clearly.

Karma is indeed the **engine of planetary fulfillment for Earth**. What this means is that as you walk through your karmic lessons, you become enlightened, and the planet changes. For each lesson is learned, and with that process comes enlightenment. As your consciousness is raised as a group on the planet, the Earth, the very dirt of the Earth, must respond. For the physical Earth will respond to your changes in consciousness! This is how you raise the vibration of your planet. So as you walk through your karma, you are actually changing Earth. And the individual karma is the most important thing you have; it does the greatest job for all of humanity.

Now, it may seem strange to you that the Earth would respond to your human consciousness; yet this is the way of things. This is why the Kryon is here at this moment, readjusting the grid system for the planet. It is because of what you personally have done in your own lives. It would not be this way had you not changed as a group. So you should understand that the planet physically alters itself in response to what you do spiritually. This is the importance, therefore, and the reason for karma. It is also the reason your future is not set, and will change even as you change.

Let me give you an example. Imagine yourself in a planning session before you were born. And as "pieces of God" and entities of the Universe, you have been selected and indeed have volunteered to be part of Earth's plan. So by choice you go into a planning session where you and those beloved entities around you plan together what all of your lessons will be. And the lessons are decided based upon what you think you can learn from what you have learned in the past. Understand the planning is always on a level where one thing leads to another. Therefore, lessons you have learned in the past will not be repeated. So past lifetime experiences that have been fulfilled karmically will not necessarily be presented again, for those lessons were already learned.

It is a complex planning session, for you are not only involving those around you who are not on the planet, but we tell you again that this planning session also involves the higher portion of those of you who are already on the Earth. What this means, dear ones, is that there are planning sessions going on right now to fulfill your windows of opportunity. They are still ongoing, even though you are incarnate here. So the planning session actually never stops. This makes things seem complex, but it may answer questions from you on how you can co-create! For the windows of opportunity are moved for you as you change your consciousness. This also means that your "contract" will also change as you raise your vibration. Again we tell you that you and your planetary future are interactive. As you change, your contract and windows of opportunity change, and the planet changes. When we ask you to "know your contract," we mean for you to know about the "now." For clarity, we are always speaking about the "now" when we communicate at any time.

Imagine still that you are back in this planning session before coming to Earth. You have arranged for the various lessons you wish to learn, and now you are ready. So when the timing is absolutely proper, correct and appropriate, you make your journey to the planet. And the first place you visit is the cave of creation. We have spoken of this before. This is a real place on this Earth, where there is an energy gem which holds your higher self. There is a name inscribed on the gem which is your astral name, and the balance of your energy then moves into incarnate form at biological birth. This cave of creation is also where all records are kept of all of the entities who have ever been here, and their lessons that have been learned. So this is where the accounting is also accomplished. This is the actual purpose for the cave of creation.

In your biological form you are then given the opportunity, although hidden from you, of fulfilling your lessons. There are no negative lessons, and there are no positive lessons. They are all simply lessons, each of equal importance. And even though some of them may seem negative or positive to you, they are not, for the mind of God is far different from the mind of humans. And when you were not here, you had the wisdom of the whole and fully understood the implications of what you planned... especially when you gave yourself a seemingly difficult challenge.

Oh, this is all about the joy of walking through it! But you must be left alone to do it, and this is the seeming "veil" regarding everything you experience. There is no predestination. The choice of each human is what he does with his own lesson, and it is the choice that changes the balance. **For without natural enlightenment and without full knowledge of who you**

really are, if you are still able to see and make choices that motivate toward the real truth, the planet's vibration is raised. And then when you are finished, dear ones, you pass back to the cave of creation to pick up your essence and your name. What you accomplished is recorded for you, and then you move to the hall of celebration, a non-Earthly place where you greet all those who helped plan your incarnation. This is also where you will see others like myself, dear ones. Remember... I know your name. Those in service like myself are always at the hall of honor; we never leave it. I am there even now, as I am also with you.

And so at the end of all of this, one cycle has been fulfilled and you are back in the planning session again if you choose to be. Since it is a fact that there are more and more humans on the Earth at the same time as your Earth time goes by, it also should be obvious to you that not all of you have been here before. This means there are always new humans coming in. But we will tell you that there is a relationship between the ones in this room to the amount of lifetimes that have been spent on the planet. For the ones in this room all have multiple lifetimes. There is not one here who is what we would call a "first timer." For the ones with multiple lives, and multiple karmas that have been fulfilled, are the ones who are currently on this planet who are the most interested right now in receiving enlightenment. They are the ones who are responding first to the new energy. And so it is up to you in this room to bear this torch to the ones who are coming in fresh. But they will recognize you and be attracted to you. This is all part of your karma and your mission as "past life rich" entities. As we have mentioned before, this is very much like an Earth play. And when the play is over, no matter what has happened within the play, even the one with the knife in his chest gets up. The heroines shake hands with the villains. They hug one another, and then they all go and have a party. So you see the overview may be a bit different than you had imagined. But it is this way, nevertheless.

Those of you who have wondered about group karma are wondering about a very complex issue, for not everyone is in a group. There is appropriateness in group karma, for it greatly helps to facilitate individual karma. If you continue to reincarnate as a group, you have interactive lessons which can continue to be played out because you are with the same individuals over and over. Therefore, groups facilitate individual lessons better than individuals alone. Now I tell you that as you stand and walk from this place this night, you will be walking past mothers and fathers and sons and daughters who are your own... and you will not recognize them! Faces you see that you do not know will be of your own children. Such is the interaction of the group karma in this area. Some of you have belonged to very ancient tribes in this area for eons. And I give my partner the name "Nespars," the great horse ranchers of the ancient time on the very dirt that you occupy at this moment. For your lineage is great in this area.

As we study group karma, we have to tell you there is another attribute that has to do with "energy accounting" that we have never discussed before. It is for your interest only that you should know this, but it may be a revelation to others reading it. For there is one group on this planet that must always remain in the same group; they may never change. It is like a staple of group karma, an anchor or starting base for the system of groups to work. We call these, therefore, the "astrally pure-bred" of the planet. In other words, the group always incarnates into the same group over and over. (Those who step into the group remain within the group until they wish to leave it, never to enter again.) The group is large enough so that this can take place all over the planet, and the newcomers that come into this group will always remain in this group as long as they wish, and they know this in advance. Now, some of you already have guessed what this group is. For it is so often that Kryon takes you back to the lineage of the Jews. This group has an attribute on the Earth which is like no other. My partner continues to be filled with awe at their lineage, and now he knows that this is the reason. For they are the ones who are astrally pure-bred. They are also the ones who have played such an important part in all human history. Being astrally pure-bred carries with it the attributes of a double-edged-sword. Being in the same group over and over strengthens knowledge of how things work. As you work through your lessons, you come in again with cellular knowledge of your past accomplishments. This creates cohesiveness, wisdom, and seemingly an unfair edge over those who change groups often. To compensate for this, the astrally pure-bred have agreed to take on the heaviest karma of the planet.

Now, Spirit does not create a hierarchy of favorites. The astrally pure-bred are loved just as much as any other, and they are not set aside as being God's chosen, except that they are different from other humans in that their karma is pure. We invite you to notice an interesting biological attribute: The Jews are not recognized biologically by your human science as a separate race, yet they act like it, since karmically they are. This indeed is their great lineage, for they helped to found the planet, and were here from the very beginning. There is much to be said around this. Your history has shown the reaction of the other groups to this pure karmic group, and the events that helped create many heavy lessons, all planned by those who decided they wanted to be the astrally pure-bred on planet Earth. We shall leave this for now, for it is only a point of interest within our purpose tonight.

We wish to take you on a number of small journeys into the lives of individuals, so that you can see the inner workings of karma. This is given to each of you this night so that you may understand more about why you are here, and what you might do with certain feelings that you have.

Before we do this, we wish to pause still another moment and ask you to feel the energy, for it has shifted even since we started. And, dear ones, do you know why the shift is taking place? It is because you asked it to. You have ultimate control over what happens in this room tonight.

Mary the Barren

We will talk now about Mary, the Barren. Now, when Mary was a very small child, she knew intuitively that she was born to be a mother. When other little girls her age played with dolls, they played with one doll, but Mary played with six. You see, Mary knew all about children. She knew what made them happy and how to bring them up. She was wise in this area, you see, since Mary had been a mother before. Lifetime after lifetime after lifetime Mary had raised children. Sometimes as many as eleven were hers. Mary was born to be a mother.

As she proceeded along her life, Mary found a partner, a male human who said, "I want a big family." Mary said, "This is the one for me." Together they made plans and they obtained a very large house in preparation for many children. But unfortunately, as life unfolded itself, Mary had no children, for to her shock she was discovered to be barren. And all of the knowledge that she had regarding children seemed to be for nothing. She was distressed and distraught. She was angry at God, and thought such a trick was played on her: to come in to this planet with such a knowledge of children, and then to be denied! Her mate?... he did not last a year. For you see, he wanted his own biological children as Mary did. He wanted to look at their hands and their fingers and know that they were just like his, and that his biology was their biology. Mary was left alone.

Mary got over her anger at God, for she was spiritually aware and she knew it. A window of opportunity had come for her to learn more about the feelings she had inside. It did not make sense to her that God would trick her so greatly, so she sought out answers. She put away her anger and sought Spirit, and in the company of others who brought her information, she discovered herself.

The main thing that Mary did immediately that made all the difference was to take responsibility for what had happened to her.

She understood through studying that she had indeed planned what had happened. She did not understand why, and still cried in the middle of the night for the lost children that she was not to have, but she took responsibility for it. It wasn't long afterwards that Mary had a vision, and then she knew what her mission was. For the vision showed other mothers throughout the world reading her words and her wisdom. You see, Mary was supposed to publish information about the raising of human children, and so she did. And by the time Mary passed over again to the cave of creation, and on to the hall of celebration, she had written seven books in all. They went planetary. Tens of thousands of mothers benefited from Mary's work, her insights and her experience. In retrospect, standing on the other side Mary understood what had happened. Oh yes, she had come in with the knowledge, the "residue" of her many past lives, but she had misinterpreted it. She was not to have children, for that would have gotten in the way of her true mission! It took realizing responsibility for who she was, and the problems that she experienced, for her to turn around and see what to do with her knowledge. Hold this in your mind, for there are others for us to tell you about.

John the Abundant

Let us speak of John, the Abundant. Each one of you knows this John. John was born onto this planet with the ability to create wealth. Everything John touched made him wealth, and it was indeed his karma for it to be so. And many looked at him and said, "He must have been a fine person in a past life to have this positive karma." But they did not understand at all what his lesson was. Even as a boy John was collecting money from other children for this and for that... a service here, an act there. And by the time he was out of school, where others were just starting, John was already on his way to abundance. It went on from there, for he collected and amassed a fortune. So much wealth did John have that he did not have the ability as an individual to spend it all in his lifetime. Even so, John occupied all of his time creating more, and he became unhappy. Then he became angry. For John did not have a clear vision of his mission. It was too easy to create abundance. And so John became an irritable person, a complaining person. There were those who did not ever want to be with him, he was so angry. So the only ones who were with him were the ones who he paid well to be... which was their own karma. And so John died an unhappy man. It was only after he was on the other side that he realized what his lesson had been. He had selected one of the most difficult lessons of all, one that he was unable to work through.

Dear ones, there is scripture that speaks of this, and we wish to tell you this night what it means and what it does not mean. For the words are translated to say that, "It will be almost impossible for a wealthy man to see the gates of heaven." Let Spirit tell you what this means. It is this: it is extremely difficult for anyone with great abundance to become enlightened, and that statement stands alone without anything around it. This was John's lesson. Could he come down onto the planet, experience this kind of attribute, and still find enlightenment? For the windows of opportunity that he had to find enlightenment had passed him quickly, and he had not glanced to the left or to the right. The pursuit of his abundance occupied him totally.

Now, some have taken this scripture and extrapolated an entire scenario of poorly thought-out rules around the subject of abundance. "What Spirit really meant," they say, "was that you cannot be wealthy and have enlightenment! And," as the poor logic continues, "if you have wealth, therefore you are not enlightened. Furthermore," as the final stage of this thinking goes, "to find God, you are to give all of your wealth away" (usually to some organization ready to receive it with the purpose of helping you get rid of this spiritual burden). "Only then will you have enlightenment." These same individuals (it gets worse) have actually equated being poor with being enlightened. Believe me, dear ones, this is not the case. We ask you to see the common sense of it. We have told you before that we wish you to have abundance. In other channelings we have taken you on journeys where you opened the door to your inner spiritual life rooms, and one of them is always filled from floor to ceiling with beautiful things... gold and wealth. Now why would we show you these things, invite you to co-create your own reality, then give you a postulate that says you cannot be enlightened and have abundance? The reason is this. **You can be totally enlightened and have wealth beyond measure.** The difficult part of this attribute is simply that one who is born into the planet with the ability to create abundance easily has extremely heavy karma. Will he or will he not turn and look at his spiritual side and become enlightened? In other words, the distraction is almost insurmountable. That is the extent of it. All of you are invited into abundance, each and every one. The scripture is simply a statement of difficulty, and an admonition to be aware of it. To have enlightenment and earthly wealth requires great balance and a true sublimation of ego. These attributes don't exist together very often. When they do, you know you have met a very old soul. Blessed indeed is the one who knows God and has abundance!

Philippe the Fisherman

We wish to talk to you about Philippe the Fisherman. Now, Philippe was not on this continent, but this is indeed a real story of a real human being. All Philippe wanted to do from the time he was a child was to fish. For you see, Philippe carried into his lifetime a residue of many, many fisherman lifetimes. He was a fisherman over and over, interacting with groups of fishermen around him, and he knew it. For when he was a child, all he wanted to do was go to the seashore and mingle with the adult fishermen. He learned to tie all of the knots, and he was excellent at it. He intuitively knew about the seasons for fishing. He intuitively knew what to do and when to do it to harvest a large batch of fish. But you see, his father was a man of means, and also a man of legal training. He did not want Philippe to be a fisherman, for unknown to either of them, his father had an agreement on the other side with Philippe, and it was all part of his father's karma to fulfill this mission. The father was disturbed that Philippe wanted only to be a fisherman, for he had greater plans for him than that.

And so he removed Philippe from the seashore and moved him far inland where Philippe was enrolled in schools of legal learning. So it was that Philippe became a legal expert, and he excelled in it. In fact as he grew, he loved it. Indeed, he thought about the life of the fisherman, but instead he turned the fishing experience into a hobby. He would go to the seashore anytime he could to sail a vessel which he had purchased with his own money. There he would get to smell like a fisherman for a day or two.

As the life of Philippe continued, he was invited into the leadership court of his country, and again Philippe really excelled. For you see, he had integrity. He had spent time with fishermen! He had an affinity with nature, and the creatures of nature, and of Earth itself. Philippe carried his wise ways into his work, and he became a great leader in his country, rising to the top leadership position. The people of his land loved him. Somehow Philippe reminded them of a common fisherman, and they responded to such a personality.

So you understand that the past life residue that Philippe carried may very well have kept him at the seashore as a fisherman, had it not been for his father. For his father's mission was to raise Philippe to be a wise leader, and he had done so. Philippe's mission was to use the attributes of the fisherman and apply it to the government of his people. Together Philippe and his father had an astral plan; it was called "karma," and both humans had walked through it perfectly.

Elizabeth the Royal

Let me tell you about Elizabeth the Royal. You see, when Elizabeth was born, even as a baby she held her head high. Most of you know that this is unusual. A child has weak muscles and cannot hold his head up. But Elizabeth held her own. Oh, indeed Elizabeth was royalty, and she knew it. The only problem, dear ones, was that Elizabeth's parents were not.

Elizabeth was born into a poor group; gradually through the years this angered her, for she knew she was special. She was a princess on her way to being a queen, but nothing around her visibly agreed with that feeling. And so she irritated the other children with her countenance, and later on she irritated the other adults, for she wanted things a certain way. She carried the air of being royal in a poor family. And very much like the first story we gave you of Mary the Barren, Elizabeth's opportunity came to fruition. For a woman friend took her aside one day and explained to her the working of Spirit. And Elizabeth, looking at her own life, said, "I firmly take responsibility for the way I feel... born as a princess without the royal family. So what is my mission?" she said. Then she realized, "Maybe it is not necessary for me to have had a royal family for me to be royal."

So Elizabeth, on her own, decided she would create her own position. And everything she tried worked! The windows of opportunity flew open for Elizabeth as she moved through the leadership of her group and co-created her own reality. And in her forty-third year Elizabeth found herself respected and admired by all. Because of her talents and who she was, she had indeed created her own royalty. So once again the past life residue had served her, but not in the way that she thought it might. The alchemy is clear in this story. For Elizabeth had taken a potentially disappointing situation, and through understanding and enlightenment, turned it into an appropriate one of honor. Elizabeth the Royal – was.

Now, dear ones, from these four stories, you might ask the question, "How can I tell the difference between a past life residue and a contract or a mission? For they look the same." Mary the

Barren thought she was going to be a mother. Philippe the Fisherman thought he was born to fish, and Elizabeth thought she should have been a queen! John absolutely knew that he was born to be abundant.

Dear ones, it is very easy to know, and here are important attributes. All of the planning sessions of karma, the ones that are happening at this moment for you, are based around windows of opportunity which are action items for you individually. That is to say, they are planned in love for your enlightenment, and they face you squarely at potent times. Some windows are planted there to show you what you are not supposed to do. On the other hand, activities which you try that work well for you are obviously your missions. We invite you, if you do not know the difference between a cellular intuitive feeling and a mission, to walk directly into the challenge of finding out. Some of you have felt that you should be this or should be that. Perhaps you should go here or go there, but you're uncertain. Many of you will have to venture out in order to find out the difference between a past life residue and a karmic contract or mission, for there is often a blurry line between the two. It is this blurry line that karmically invites you to venture out to find the difference. Do not be afraid of wasting time or resources on something that seems to have failed, for it may have given you truth! It is this very action or intent of the venturing out that signals Spirit that you have decided to move into what you planned! Do you see the irony of all of this? If you sit in a heap and worry and fear what you are supposed to do, then nothing will happen. It is only when you go beyond your fear, and step into action to find out, that the "engine" of your lesson is engaged. Sometimes your action seems to result in failure, but the truth is that you have indeed found out if the feeling is residue or mission. It is the human who keeps trying the residue over and over that is the foolish one. It simply never will work.

So if Philippe had tried to be a fisherman, it would not have worked for him. There is something Philippe never found out that was hiding in his biology. He would have been sick constantly if he had proceeded with his plans to make fishing his life's work. This is another way Spirit honored him to help him find his mission. It would not have worked for him; and if it had not been for his father, he would have had a chance to look at this clearly. Instead, Philippe was successful in moving into his mission quickly because of another human at his side who had come in for that very purpose. Do you see how important humans around you might very well accelerate your mission?

There is no judgment by Spirit of whether you pass through karma or not, as you reach the other side having seemingly failed a life's test. As was in the case of John the Abundant, there was no judgment at all, not even by John. Instead John received a hero's welcome in the hall of honor just like the others. It is in the incarnation that the honor goes. There is never a time when Spirit judges whether or not the lesson was accomplished. The honor is in walking the road, not in which direction was walked.

David the Loved

We wish to tell you now, finally, about one who comes into the Earth with no karma, but only a mission. And we wish to tell you now about David, the Loved. Now, David was born with part of his brain missing. He was an intelligent child. He had all the facilities of consciousness, but the parts that were missing were the parts that controlled his growth. And so it was that the doctors knew that David would not live very long, for there was no way that he could do so with the parts missing. David's entire purpose for being was a mission. Although it was not obvious yet, it would become so. David had young parents who loved him dearly, and he surrounded himself with others who also loved him dearly.

So it was that David had an amazing life for the few years he was on the planet. There were those who took him places that a young person would never have seen. He was showered with love and given every opportunity for learning. And yet so it was in his twelfth year that he passed over. **For David's mission on this planet was to give a gift to his parents.** Oh, if you told his parents that it was a gift, they would have been insulted! There was never a worse time in their life due to the sorrow of his passing. It would not have helped the hurt of their hearts to know of David's mission. Just like it is with you, dear ones, when you know someone is passing over, it does not help at that moment to know that it is appropriate. For when the moment occurs, the hurt is there, and at that moment no amount of astral wisdom will replace the welling up of emotion.

And so David, that little one, was sorely missed. And so it was that his parents mourned him, as is appropriate for these things. But you see, David had an agreement with those parents, and his young parents had an agreement with David. David's passing presented a window of opportunity, even when they were at their lowest ebb, for the two young parents to discover a path of quickened enlightenment, a step that they took in their search for peace that they never would have taken except for David's gift. And so it was that both of those parents lived great enlightened lives and became healers, each one, administering to many over the years. So the sorrow was transmuted to joy and healing. So it was that their enlightenment was complete. And so it was that their karma was fulfilled, because of the gift of David the Loved.

For David's entire mission was to allow for the enlightenment and healing of hundreds of humans in a future that David was never to be in. His love was in his gift to his young parents, and their love was their ability to see his gift and look for what it meant. So the seeming sacrifice of the one created the joy for the many. The spiritual beauty of this is that David is eternal, and the twelve years he spent giving his gift was a only a blip on the time line of a much larger event... the elevation of the planet Earth.

We sit here in love for each one of you, and we tell you that there are those among you now who have an opportunity for a change in your life because of your appointment here. Have you ever wondered what your mission is? Why has your background been what it is? What has your training got to do with your mission? If you are hitting a brick wall, as my partner says, regarding your life, and you do not understand why, perhaps it's time that you reexamine why you have the knowledge you do. I speak now individually to at least eight of you who have this situation in your life. It is a time to sit and bask in the energy of Spirit. There will be two that go from this place tonight healed. It is one of the first times we have said this, but the intent has already been given in the last few moments, and the action is already implanted. You have done it yourself! We invite you, each and every one, to take full responsibility for the condition you find yourself in right now. For only after that will your mission be exposed. And although it may take some trial and error on your part to find out what is best for you, look for the path with the open doors. Even the doors which seem most ominous, and the doors which seem to be shut so tight, may fly open when you knock on them. Then you will know your mission.

It is with great love that we come this night to you, to give you the examples of these human lifetimes and to tell you about the human karma experience. For you see, the entity of Kryon does not have the honor that you do of selecting such a path. Therefore, you can see the awe I have, and the honor I have, when I say I LOVE YOU DEARLY! You are doing universal work, and all of your difficulties are honored. Yet we say to you that we know what you are going through, and we give special honor this night to those of you with a hurt heart. We have specific messages for you to remember that life is eternal. The passing of one human from this plane to another is only a **change of energy**! The one who has passed over has three days in the cave of creation, and during that time, he is with you strongly. Even after that time is finished, he remains with the ability to visit you. Therefore, you must know that he is not gone at all; he is just changed.

And this is what kept the parents of David the Loved going all of their lives. For when they realized his gift, they also realized that the communication of this little one never stopped. And so it is we also hope you realize that the communication of Spirit to you, dear ones, will never stop. And if you feel somehow that the Spirit of God has retreated from you, don't believe it. For it is our promise that if you ask, we will be here. If the intent is given, we will be here. As we close this channel now, we ask you to remain in silence because we are going to ask my partner (Lee) to relate to you his life karma, and what happened to him. We ask this of him so that you will understand how the voice of Kryon came about, and could have easily been missed had my partner followed his residue.

And so it is!

(Lee Carroll speaking):

Kryon wants me to tell you about the fact that all I wanted to do as a child was to be in the service... and this is Lee talking to you now. Jan (who is beside me) will verify, even to this day, that when I see uniformed men and women, I feel like I should be with them. I was placed in a military school when I was eight, and spent three years there alone as a boarder. I knew what it was like to be in the service, and yet I was never in the service. When I went on the bridge of a ship in San Diego, I recognized the chair I used to sit in, and I knew I was all Navy. I felt I had my purpose, went though Army ROTC in high school, and made plans for NROTC in later college years... just to have a career as a Navy person. But this was a past life residue, you see. And the things that Spirit did to keep me out of the Navy were amazing !

The first thing was that I had allergies. I got called during college for Vietnam to go up for a physical, and they failed me. They said, "You can't be in the service because you have allergies." Now I know why Spirit gave me allergies. Then it was later that I found out that I get seasick! (Can you see the great Navy officer leaning over the rail in the midst of battle? ... this is a cosmic joke!) Then last year (at the age of 50) I found out that I was born with one kidney. I could never have passed a complete physical for NROTC. There is simply no way I would have made it in the service of this country, and yet that's all I wanted to do!

I had lifetime after lifetime of military service. It was natural, and I sought it out again when I came in this time. Being born into my karmic group in the Navy town of San Diego was a real challenge for a guy who had a karmic Navy residue, but a spiritual mission.

So Spirit put blocks in my way to show me the difference between a past life residue and a contract. And I waited until I was in my late forties before I found my mission... always wondering if I should have been a Naval officer. And the human one that I have the agreement with is here next to me (speaking of Lee's wife, Jan Tober). She was the placeholder for me, and got me to where I am... just like Philippe's father did. So now perhaps you understand more when earlier I told you about Jan's participation in the Kryon work. It was profound. It's a karmic contract. It's a mission, and I'm glad Spirit honored me with the blocks that kept me from following a false path. As I understand tonight's message, this is common, and Spirit will honor all of us in the same way.

Thank you all for your loving response this night to the messages of Kryon.

Kryon

Kryon at The United Nations!

In November 1995, November 1996, and again in November 1998, Kryon spoke at the S.E.A.T. (Society for Enlightenment and Transformation) at the United Nations in New York City. By invitation Jan and Lee brought a time of lecture, toning, meditation and channelling to an elite group of UN delegates and guests.

Kryon Book 6, *Partnering With God* carried the first two entire transcripts of what Kryon had to say ... some of which has now been validated by the scientific community. Kryon Book 7, *Letters From Home* carries the meeting in 1998. All three of these transcripts are on the Kryon web site [www.kryon.com].

Our sincere thanks to Mohamad Ramadan in 1995, Cristine Arismendy in 1996, and Jennifer Borchers in 1998 who were presidents of that bright spot at the United Nations, for the invitation and for their work to enlighten our planet.

Chapter Eight

Ascension and Responsibility

From the writer...

Even though Kryon speaks of ascension here, I pondered if this channeling should have been in the "implant" section, since a good half of the information is regarding responsibility around the implant process. Some of the information was similar to the channeling in Hawaii (page 69) about "Becoming a New Age Human." Some of it was also similar to his comments about the "inner child" on page 133, but the message really stands alone when you add the story on the end.

Kryon Book Two, *Don't Think Like a Human*, introduced us to the individual called "WO." The parable here has Wo on an island trying to co-create his own reality, and his lessons around what happened to him.

Kryon wants us to understand that asking for the implant is like asking for a new tool box. This information was first given by Kryon on page 131 in a brief response to the letter from Laura Grimshaw. This channel elaborates on the issue that if we take the box and sit on it, we have the gift, but there is no action around it. If we take the tools out and start learning how to use them, there is wonderful action and results. Within the learning process, however, there are still lessons.

What follows is a combination of two channelings from two areas of the country. I combined them because they were very similar. It doesn't happen often, but sometimes Kryon will give the same message with slightly different words to two groups of people very far apart. That was the case here.

Kryon

"Ascension and Responsibility"
Channeled in
Carlsbad, California
and
Vancouver, Canada

Edited from two
Kryon seminars

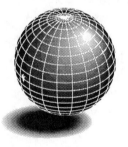

The Kryon Writings, Inc.

PMB 422
1155 Camino Del Mar
Del Mar, California 92014
[www.kryonqtly.com]

"Ascension and Responsibility"
Live Channel
Canada and California

These live channelings have been edited with additional words and thoughts to allow clarification and better understanding of the written word.

G reetings, dear ones; I am Kryon of magnetic service. Oh, and if the energy in this room could be visualized, you would be amazed, for there are colors abounding which are beyond your sight as each one of you gets used to hearing the voice of my partner translating this message of love to you. We are going to take a moment to fill this room with other entities that support you. As this intensifies, we tell you that you are loved dearly, and that we come here in this position of love to wash your feet. Each one of you this night has an appointment with Spirit in your chair. You see, many of you have been brought here on purpose to sit in the energy for a life-changing event. If you find yourself here under unusual circumstances, you are indeed a candidate for this condition.

The energy transmitted this night (in the third language) for your Merkabah is the energy that you need to continue your work, your life and your contract in a much higher plane than ever before. And oh, dear ones, it matters not the age that you are in your biology, for some of you are seemingly at the beginning of your lives and some of you are seemingly in the twilight years. This is all an illusion, I assure you. Each of you is eternal! Some of you are keenly aware of how many biological beings you have been, and some of you are not aware at all. Spirit fills this room with an intensity that is even higher than the last time humans formed around the Kryon. Some of you will experience physical changes, for you see, that's why you're here. We know who you are, and we know you each by a name that even you are not aware of. For it is you who have chosen to come here, and to walk this planet in biology – to suffer some of the tests and the hurts and the wounds and the joys. Oh, dear ones, not even the Kryon has done this. Is it any wonder we love you so?

For this there are gifts, and this night they are dispensed. So we invite those of you on the edge of healing to go ahead and give yourself permission. We invite those of you on the cusp of something new and different and bold to go ahead and give yourself permission. You see, the tools are in front of you and the New Age supports you in this – and the Love of Spirit is yours. You own it, for you are one of us! Each and every human being who hears or reads this voice now – regardless of when you are hearing it, it is in the now. For it is for you – your pair of ears (and eyes) – and for your heart as you sit there. Oh, believe me, we know who you are, and we know why you're here. We are ready to hug you and hold you and say, "Isn't it a grand thing that you find yourself in this New Age?" You knew you would be here. **You stood in line to be here!** You made an agreement, so it is a grand time for each of you.

Ascension

Tonight we wish to speak of something that we have not spoken of much in the past. This information is given in love to you, for it is about something that you have heard about that is stirring, and that is being published. There are specialists regarding this subject. And we talk now about **ascension**.

For you to understand fully what is meant by the new paradigm of ascension, we must speak briefly again of the tools of Spirit in response to what you have done on this planet. Now, some of you were totally aware of what you called the event of the 11:11 and its meaning. But briefly in review, this was where the code was passed to you and to your biology – to your very cellular level that said, "Permission is given to you as human beings to hold the entire vibration of your entity and to begin the steps of this." And the code that was passed on was magnetic, and the code that was passed on at this time was given to all humanity at once. That is the way Spirit treats this planet as the planet of **honor**! For all of you are seen equally in love.

Then on the 12:12 an amazing thing happened. For as we spoke before, some of you were there to hear my words. We spoke of the fact that on the 12:12 permission was given for the place-holders of this planet to leave. And so started the process where the planet was truly turned over to humanity. Now, let me explain this. The energy balance of the planet has always remained the same, but the vibration level has not. They are different and totally independent. But the energy level must remain the same for the workings of the grid to operate. So there were placeholders who held the energy as humanity grew, and more and more human beings arrived. But even with five billion humans on the planet, there still had to be placeholders – the great master placeholders that have been here since the founding of the planet. For they have had to remain to hold the correct energy. The 12:12 was a grand time, for it gave permission for them to leave, and turn the energy balance over to humanity. You see it was time for humans to have "the torch." The 11:11 gave them permission to hold the energy, and so it was that they did. So it was also in the passing of this torch and in the months that followed the 12:12, we called for at least 144,000 human beings to take the ascension status. Now the ascension status is the permission given for a human being to hold the **entire** energy of his vibration while walking this planet with the biology that he has. This is a very difficult thing to do, and because most of you on your continent were not prepared to do this, it may not surprise you to know that of the 144,000 that took this challenge, most of them did so from a continent which was not yours. This has no meaning whatsoever to your enlightenment, nor is it any measure of judgment. It simply is a fact. For the humans who did it were trained and knew how. They understood the mechanics of it, and therefore they were ready.

What is this, then, that you call ascension status? Permission has been given, but what does it mean? Here is the answer to this: in a very simplistic way, we say whereas the word ascension in the past has meant "someone who passes on and raises into heaven," it now means something totally different. It is an enlightenment vibration measurement where the biological human is able to hold the entire vibration and energy of his entity!

Now, this cannot happen all at once, and it is not for everyone. We tell you this with great caution. We say, "Those of you who elect to do this must be ready." It is a difficult path. It is one that is often done alone, with many steps over much time, and we do not call all of you to do it. Hardly! But we would like all of you to know about it, for it is a marvelous new gift.

The steps of ascension have been outlined and have been studied and are here for you. The specialists who have channeled this information have made it available even at this time for you to read about it. The process is complex, and each one of you may choose to do it if you wish. You may someday find yourself only at the third or fourth stage – unable to continue. But we say to you there is no judgment around this. There is no failure around this. We invite you to start the steps and see how far you would like to go. For each step raises your vibration, and raises the vibration of the planet. It is a wonderful path to start, and you will find your own level. If you only go for the level of the three, relax, for it is where you belong. If some of you choose to go the entire way, we say it is a grand journey indeed!

What are the attributes, you might ask, of an ascended one? Oh, let me tell you. You will have no problem in identifying a person who is in ascension status. Some of you already know of the Avatar who is not on this continent. There is an example of ascension status. Does that surprise you? Are you personally ready for this? This is what it's all about: permission to contain your full entity. Now, if you were to do such a thing right now, you would simply burn up, for the vibratory level of your biology is far, far lower than this new status calls for. That is why the study is necessary, and the steps are necessary; and the time is necessary, and the dedication. For all of those things use the mechanics of your cellular body, using the tools that were given to you on the 11:11 – permission to rejuvenate, permission to grow.

If you would have any kind of healthy exercise regarding your biology, we say to you that there is an area you have ignored. It is the organ behind the breast plate you call the thymus. It is the seat of the rejuvenation process. Co-create the health from this. Do not be shocked if it grows, for this is part of the secret of ascension. Your biology must cooperate entirely in this process. Now, some of you have heard about the Merkabah. And you might say, "What is this thing we call the Merkabah?" Now, this is your word; it is not ours. But suffice to say that what we are speaking of is what we call the "energy shell." It is that which holds your entire energy together. It is like the skin of your entity, but oh, it's so much more.

You have only seen the Merkabah in history a few times. You are starting to see it more now, and confusing it with ships from space. For it was Elijah who claimed his Merkabah in the field; it glowed, and you saw the wheels within the wheels. You saw the colors, and you saw the magnificence when he ascended. This was the Merkabah that was seen. Each one of you, when you are not here, has a glorious look to you, with colors and vibrations and sounds and shapes all intertwined in the Merkabah, things which you could not possibly see or hear with your biology now. For there is so much dimension to the Merkabah, I cannot begin to tell you what it contains. Now, in the past we have told you that the Merkabah has your color stripes, those things which tell the other entities of the universe, when they meet you, where you have been and what you have done. And we have told you about the great hall of honor where you received the new colors for being a human on the planet Earth. For it is a wonderful journey that you take. All of you sitting here this night (and reading this) have many stripes from being here so many times. And the great irony is that, although you would come into this room only one time and see these faces of those whom you pretend not to know, at one time they were all your relatives! They are part of your karmic group – brothers, sisters, mothers, fathers: so much has happened between you, and yet you pass as strangers. It is such a wonderful testament to the veil that is here keeping you from seeing the truth, for to truly know these things would cause you to leave.

Oh, dear ones, we honor you for this! Walking the planet in lesson with this veil of not knowing who you are. As we look at you and say to those around us, "They volunteered for this," we love you dearly for it. And so it is that the Merkabah shouts a language that all entities hear, see, feel and experience. So the Merkabah is not just your shell, dear ones; it is your language as well. The Merkabah is the energy which allows you to move from place to place. When you move from one place in the universe to another, it is almost instant, but your Merkabah changes shape to do it. And although we will not get into the science of this, we tell you that it has been channeled before. Look for it, for your Merkabah, therefore, is a shape shifter! The shapes that are present in the Merkabah are pure – total– science. And this, dear ones, is a great humorous irony: that your society has chosen to separate the spiritual from the physical, and from the ones who work on your mathematics, and the ones who work on your geometry and your physics.

If you could see the Merkabah, you would understand totally that the relationship is complete and married, for the Merkabah is made of geometry, and it shouts to you your base-12 system. It says that all the shapes are mathematically divisible by six, that there is purpose for this – and yet you still have not seen it. And so we speak of the Merkabah as something grand and glorious. It is owned by you and each one of you has it. But it will not appear on this planet, for to have it would vaporize your biology. The energy is simply too great. And so short of claiming the Merkabah, you can still work on it, for it still exists in the astral. Part of the steps of being in ascension are to work on it and marry it into your biology.

So we have said enough at this moment, except to say that again it is not for all of you to take these steps. You are honored for all of your processes, and whatever steps you take are the ones you're to be in. Some of you may ask, "How do I know whether I should do it?" And we say to you, you should eliminate all thoughts of what Spirit expects of you, and replace them with the thoughts of what you are to do for you. You see, you are a piece of God, and your contract sits there in front of you; the words scribed by your own pen say, "This is why I'm here." Look for that contract. Co-create your contract and ask for it to be brought in. It is so intuitive, you will know what it is. We will have more on this soon.

Oh, there is healing even now this night, and some of you are feeling the heat of it. And we say to you, "Do not fear this," for the heat speaks of love and light. Did we tell you that in the subject of light, the Merkabah carries it's own? That wherever the Merkabah is, there is light? This makes you creatures of light! Accept it. If there is heat here now, do not fear it, for it is the love of God in your biology.

Responsibility

And now we take you to the subject of the responsibility you have as human beings when you take the implant. We have wished to speak to you of these things many times, but now the vibration is correct to do so. My partner has explained the implant to you in these channelings and writings, and it is so. All of the things that were mentioned are so. But you must realize this: again we say to you that the implant is your "tool set." Those of you who have chosen to take the gifts of Spirit have taken the implant. Those of you who have said, "I don't know what is going to happen from now on, but whatever is for me, God, I accept it," have taken the implant. For you have called on the gift, and it is in front of you. Now you must use it.

Let me itemize what your actions should be. To take the implant and stand waiting for Spirit to do something is not proper. for nothing will happen in your life. You will sit with the tools in the drawer, and the drawer will stay closed. It is time to open it! Use the tools and do the following things.

1. First, again we mention your biology. We have spoken of the ascension status and the fact that your biology must be raised to match your consciousness. You see, it's not automatic for this to be so. So the first action item is this: start incorporating your biology with your mind. Now, all of you have your senses located in your head. That is where you see, and that is where you hear. That is where you communicate and smell and taste. It is where all of the comfort and pleasure centers are. So, dear ones, your spirituality seems to be there as well. And although we speak of the heart many times, it is your head and your brain which feels that consciousness which you call enlightenment.

Many of you look down at your bodies and your biology, and you look at the parts and you say things like, "My hand hurts; I wish it would get better. My leg is doing this or that." Now, we have already put my partner through this, and he speaks to you now through the translations of Kryon with knowledge of this. For it is time that you incorporate your biology to your enlightenment! When you speak of your body, speak of it as "WE." For the biology of your toe and the cells there must know of your conscious enlightened decisions.

Also in this new age we again tell you that concerning the items you ingest, or the energy work you do... that you must greet these things before they enter your biology. What this means, dear ones, is that you must have ceremony regarding these things, even if it's short. This may seem odd to you, but it is the truth. For the things that you put at your cellular level, and into the "We-ness" of your biology, have to be greeted. You have to give your biology per-mission for them to work! For if you ask for healing and you use substances and energy for that, the substances and the energy have no idea where they're going or what they're supposed to do. If you greet them in advance, you are speaking to them. There will be a marriage and a handshake, and an agreement in love. Oh, these things sound very strange to some of you, but so it is that truth has a way of settling in later when the results are seen to be accurate. So the first step is to marry your biology with your spirit, and to consider your biology as part of your mind. See all of the parts as one, for this is the only way the vibrations can increase to match the tools of the implant.

2. The next one, perhaps one of the most important, is what you might call the psyche, but it is what we call your "attitude of peace." Let me explain. So many of you have said, "I have taken the implant, and I have heard you speak of the peace that it can bring, and the changes in the way my life goes. There are those things around me which cause me discomfort. There are things

around me which poke and prod me, and they cause reaction. But I am not peaceful." And we say to you that this is what you must change: peace is a natural occurring event with the implant, and this peace is what your biology is going to eventually interpret as health. Now, how do you claim this peace? We say to you that the key to peace is in your remembrance of the infant. Oh, dear ones, there is so much to be said for this!

When you were a child, perhaps you can recall the fact that there were very few worries. The things that you considered when you were a child were on a day-by-day basis. They were items that were going to happen in the next hour, and the things to look forward to. Do you remember the comfort of knowing that there was no problem too great for mother to solve? For mother could do anything; all things were taken care of. There was never a question about where you would sleep or what you would eat, for on this continent so many of you grew up in this kind of peaceful environment. And so we say to you that it is the consciousness and the attitude of the infant that is the key to peace. It is the discovery of the inner kid within each one of you that is the key to your real peace.

You might say, "That's good information, but how do I get it?" We say to you that you co-create it! If you want to be in touch with this inner child, you may have it instantly, but for those of you who still do not know how, we say to you that there are facilitators walking this planet who have come here just exactly for that purpose. For they're here in love to show you the path to the infant within – to help you wade through those angers and fears and frustrations and get right down to it. So we support these who are here dedicated for this purpose on this planet at this time. Have you realized there are no accidents as to why so many are facilitating this now? They are here as the "first wave," as my partner has called it, to facilitate humanity. The infant within – seek it, and watch what happens with the peace in your life. For true peace is a state you're in where those things which bothered you in the past will not bother you now. The individuals who had karma with you who were able to "push a button" and cause a reaction, will now have that button completely disengaged! And just like the parable of the tar pit that has been channeled to you before (Kryon Book II), you will find that those around you will start changing with your own peace level. For when the karma is disengaged from those around, they will simply stop trying to reengage it. Many of them will pass out of your life, and you will wonder, how is this possible? We say again to you that it is because of the change of the one, that affects the many. **So if there were ever an evangelical approach to this new age, it would be in changing yourself...** Co-creating for yourself. Letting those around you observe you and change accordingly.

3. The next attribute of action is indeed co-creation. And we say to you that it is your duty. It is the duty of your contract with yourself to begin co-creating what you need in your life. So many of you would say, "What is it? I have no idea what I'm supposed to do." We say what you're supposed to do is what you agreed to do. It is your passion! It is your contract. It is your intuition. You already know of it, but you say, "I'm not aware of it." We say all right, you have the power to co-create, so do the following. Verbalize daily: "In the name of Spirit, I co-create the ability to be in my contract no matter what it is. I co-create in the name of Spirit to find the sweet spot which is that place on this planet that I agreed to be in." That is the best beginning.

Now, dear ones, we've told you in the past that the way things work in the New Age are different than they used to be. So many of you are used to planning for the future. So many of you say, "I know I'm walking down this path, but I know there's going to be a fork in the road. And when there's a fork, I want to know which way to turn." So some of you this day will see the fork approaching, and instead of walking up to the fork and reading the road signs which Spirit has given you, you stop! You sit down and you say, "I'm not going to proceed unless I know what the signs say... so I can plan for it." That's where faith comes in now, doesn't it? And so we say to you that you are to walk up to the fork in total peace, co-creating all the way so that you will know when you get there the road signs indeed are posted. Then the signs will say, "We know who you are! Turn right here," and the proper way will literally glow for you so that you will not miss it. It is the co-creation that gives the energy to the sign posts! Use this gift!

4. The next attribute is that we invite you to discover the new knowledge. Now, the new knowledge may not come to you through a channel or a book; it may come seemingly right out of your mind. For those of you who are facilitating the healing of humans, we say to you, "You are poised and ready for this new knowledge in your new healing methods." But you might say, "Well, what are they?" We say, "You'll know when you get them." No matter what your specialty is, dear ones, we tell you that there are new methods that are going to give you greatly enhanced results. Try them. No matter how bizarre they may seem, try them. For you will find that even some of the greatest masters who have taught for hundreds of years did not have this knowledge. Then when you receive these methods and have evidence of the results, we invite you to tell the others, and not hold it for yourself. It is not something that is only for you. You may come in at this time with the sole purpose of having this new knowledge in a specific area and publishing it for all humanity! You never know.

So we ask you and invite you to claim the new knowledge. How can you do that? It's simple. "I co-create in the name of Spirit for the new knowledge to come to me, that I might have it in pure love, and use it for humanity." You have co-created it again.

Wo and The Big Wind

So these are the action items. But we have one more thing to give you this night, and it has to do with being in the right place at the right time. For many of you have felt that being in the right place at the right time means completely escaping all things that might happen around you that seem negative. We say to you, dear ones, that you are misinformed. Oh, but there is so much love that goes into this! Listen.

We have spoken before of the individual entity whom we call Wo. Now, Wo is a name we give to this human being walking on the planet. Wo isn't meant to represent a male or a female, for when you are not here you are neither. But for the purpose of this story, and to make it easy to tell for my partner, Wo will be a male. And the title of this story and this journey is "Wo and The Big Wind."

Now, Wo was an enlightened individual. He lived on a very small island with other people. Wo lived a good life, for he was indeed on the path. We would call Wo a warrior of the light, for Wo indeed meditated and followed Spirit. He had fine children whom he taught the essence of Spirit through his love. Wo was greatly loved by his neighbors, for they recognized that he was a good man. And so we find Wo living on the island, and daily Wo would say, "Oh Spirit, I love you. I want so much to be in my contract – the right place at the right time. That's what I want."

As Wo moved forward in his life, year after year, he would daily go down to the beach, and with the sound of the surf crashing in his ears, he would get as close to the water as he could and there he would sit. Wo would say, "Oh Spirit, put me right where I belong. I don't care if it takes me away from here. I want to be in my sweet spot." Now you see, Wo was doing this correctly, and he was greatly honored for this. Wo would also say, "And in this new age, Oh dear Spirit, there is something I would really like as a gift. I know there are some who never get this, but if it's appropriate, let me see my guides! Even just once." So now you know the inner workings of Wo's life and his mind. This is who Wo was.

A storm approached this island that had great ferocity. Wo was frightened, for it appeared as though the storm was going to pass right through his home. In hundreds of years there had never been a storm like this one, for it was great indeed. And as it approached, there were many who left the island. But Wo remained, knowing full well that he would be in the right place at the right time, just as he had co-created. Any minute Wo expected miraculously for the wind to change course. But, you see, it didn't. Instead it got worse and worse. And so residents were sequestered in their homes and told, "Do not go out. You will be harmed if you do."

So the folks stayed in their houses and they watched the winds come and the waters rise. They saw pieces of their homes start to disintegrate, and they were very afraid. But Wo was silent. He didn't talk to Spirit anymore. You see, Wo was angry. In fact he was mad, for you see, Wo felt that he had been betrayed. "How many years do I have to ask for one thing, and when the time comes I don't get it?" said Wo. And the winds grew stronger and Wo grew angrier. Then the power failed. Wo heard the trucks coming through the street to pick up the people. They announced, "You're not safe. Get in these trucks while you can. We're going to take you to the school where the building is solid. There you will have a safe shelter."

And so it was that the large trucks went gathering all of the people of the island, taking them to the various schools and churches. Wo ended up in one of the largest schools that was near his home. He walked in with so many other neighbors, and he looked at each one. He looked at faces that were blank and fearful, but in Wo's eyes there was only anger at God. As they crouched in the basement where they thought it was safe, indeed the power failed there too... and they were in the dark. Out came the candles, but then the water started coming in, and the winds started tearing at the very fiber of the school building. They started hearing the groaning of the cement and of the wood. They huddled in the dark terrified – making no sounds at all.

Then Wo came to an astonishing conclusion. He realized he was not afraid. He was very angry, but he was not afraid. He looked around and saw those huddled down the hallways in ankle-deep water, freezing without any heat or candlelight. He also saw their terror. For many that night felt that the entire group was going to die. How could it not be so, for they were told the eye of the storm was not even upon them, and that they were headed for something even worse. If the school disintegrated, they would surely be at the mercy of these elements of wind and rain.

And so Wo stood from the place where he had been seated in anger. He hugged his family and said, "There's work here. You will be safe." And he looked into the eyes of his children and he said, "Look, there is no fear in my eyes, because I have been promised we are going to be safe." Then Wo left and began going from neighbor to neighbor, and from group to group. Wo told them of his love for Spirit, and he told them that Spirit had never failed him. He told them that they would be safe, and he imparted to them the love that can only come from an enlightened human being! As he left each group, he saw that the terror had also left, and like a black cloud had dissipated, they were left with hope. Some of the groups started songs, so instead of sheer terror and the silence thereof, it was replaced by the sound of singing. Some of the groups started laughing by telling humorous stories of their lives, and the fear diminished. The terror left.

Wo, as he made his way from group to group, did his work that night. And like some kind of miracle, the eye of the storm never arrived. Instead the storm reversed itself, and went on its way, slowly diminishing instead of intensifying. So just about the time Wo's work was done, the storm had abated enough that they got the word to return to their homes in the very trucks that had brought them to the school. The sun was coming out, and Wo realized they had been there all night. As they walked outside, the winds had almost totally gone. How quickly it retreated! The birds were singing and the sun came out, and the folks made their way back to their homes. Oh, and some of them had great sorrow that their homes were destroyed. And oh yes, Wo was among all of his neighbors seeing that his roof was gone, and the water had come in and ruined so many things.

So it was in the weeks that followed the rebuilding began, and it went smoothly. Slowly on the island, a story began unfolding. You see, there were news reports and stories of what happened that night in the school. People were saying, "There was this man and his associates that came to us at the worst moments in the dark. They told us about how we were safe, and they gave us hope. They shone in the darkness with love and peacefulness. They brought hope to our terrified consciousness, and they also brought humor. They gave us song, and it changed us that night, for we were no longer afraid. Our children responded first, for we saw in the eyes of the children the fact that they were no longer terrified, and then we relaxed. The man's name was Wo." Group after group reported this, and embarrassingly to Wo, they asked him to come to a ceremony where he would be honored. And so begrudgingly Wo went to the ceremony and heard the testimony of the neighbors of how he and his associates had helped that night.

After the ceremony, Wo went to the beach, where he sat down next to the water. Then Wo realized what "being in the right place at the right time" meant. **He realized that all of his prayers and all of his co-creative ability as a human being in the New Age had come to fruition.** You see, Wo had prayed to be in the right place in the right time, and that's exactly where he was!

He realized that his prayers had been answered one hundred percent. Then Wo wept, for he realized that one hundred percent co-creation meant that his guides had also been seen that night. Every group of neighbors had seen three: Wo and his "two associates." Wo knew that he had gone into the darkness alone to help his neighbors that night – so he thought.

So although Wo was not aware of it, his guides had been seen clearly that night. In the candlelight his neighbors had described them, and so through the voices of those he helped, Wo saw his guides! Oh, it's true that he had lost his home, and it's true that some wood had been destroyed, but the contract that he had agreed to before he came had been accomplished, and everything paled in comparison to that. All of the co-creative prayers had centered around being in the right place at the right time. Wo realized that Spirit had honored him with a complete, full miracle of co-creation. It changed his life, for he discovered his passion – that of being able to bring peace to the lives of others.

And from that time forward, Wo knew what it meant to co-create and pray for his contract. He knew that it did not mean that he would be spared all of the tests. It did not mean that he would not be present when the earth shook. It meant that he would be in his sweet spot and he would be in total peace when these things took place. And that he would be available for facilitation of other human beings when these things took place.

So as we now return to this group of humans who sit in front of Spirit (and the eyes that read this page), we tell you that we love you dearly, and that you have work in this area of co-creating your contract. For when things appear to be dark, it's only a perception of darkness. Instead of anger, you should look at the overview and see the love that has gone into the event. When some apparent negative things seem to be happening in your life, look at them in the overview, for they may be only temporary things to steer you to the right spot at the right time, things that you helped set up within your contract. Oh, this is why we call it "work," dear ones. For sometimes it is not easy, and it might seem that what is being asked of you is too difficult. You will discover, as Wo did, just the opposite. For there is no sweeter spot than that which is your passion, and your contract!

So finally we say to you that this night, in this energy, Spirit has done a great deal. Oh, there have been stories told and information presented, but what this night was about was the energy transmitted to your heart and to your mind. Each of you by name is loved dearly. Go from this place knowing that you sat in front of Spirit. Go from this place knowing tonight that what you consider God is part of who you are! Know that if you could qualify what truly happened tonight, you would say that "a piece of home visited you tonight." That is the feeling that each one of you has when you sit in this energy.

Dear ones, when we finally see each other – and I will see you and your Merkabah – I will honor you with your new colors. You will remember this night when I told you we would see each other again... hard to believe as you walk around this planet in the biology that you have, but true. All of the things that have been brought to you this night are true. Many of you will discover your truths with results, as your lives move forward. You have permission and enablement to say no to the evil which is around you. Never again does it have to be part of your life. Leave this place enabled! Leave this place with joy! Know that Spirit says to you that you are in a new age and things are getting better, not worse. Expect it. Live it. Co-create it. And the planet will vibrate like it never has before. Oh, we love you so much for this!

And so it is.

Kryon

Scientists seek mystery source of high-energy rays

THE HUNTSVILLE TIMES
May 3 1995
by Cliff Edwards
The Associated Press

CHICAGO – It's a classic whodunit, with cosmic proportions. Something – or someone – out there is hurling incredibly energetic particles around the universe. Scientists and engineers have gathered in Chicago this week to develop a plan to track these "ultra-high-energy cosmic rays" back to their source.

"This is totally inexplicable," said Nobel laureate James Cronin, a physicist from the University of Chicago. "We've learned so much about the sky and about the cosmos, but this is a puzzle. ..."

The particles striking Earth have 100 million times the energy produced by the world's most powerful particle accelerator, at Fermilab in the Chicago suburb of Batavia.

Scientists know of no source – not supernovae, not black holes – that can produce such energies. They believe they come from outside the galaxy.

Additional verification of Kryon's 1994 predictions

(entire article not shown)

Please see page 243

Chapter Nine

Predictions, Validations and Skeptics

"I am Kryon of magnetic service. I have created the magnetic grid system of your planet. The creation of your grid system took eons of Earth time. It was balanced and re-balanced to match the physical vibrations of your evolving planet. During the time I was initially here, what you now perceive as positive and negative Earth polarity was altered many times. Your science can prove this; look for soil strata that will show multiple flips of north and south polarity of the Earth during its development.".

Page 21

Kryon Book One
The End Times
October 1992

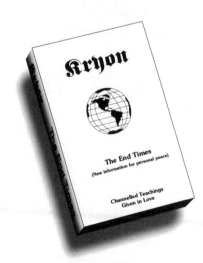

When Earth's Magnetic Field Went Wild

Had any mariners been around 16 million years ago, they might have been in for quite a shock if they tried to navigate by compass. That's because something very strange was happening to Earth's magnetic field.

Nobody was around back then to note the event. But a record nevertheless exists, and a team of researchers led by Robert Coe of the University of California at Santa Cruz has succeeded in reading it. The record consists of tiny magnetic particles in lava that once poured from Steens Mountain in Oregon. As the lava cooled, the particles aligned themselves like compass needles with Earth's magnetic field. By studying the alignment of the particles, the scientists have determined that the field was inexplicably shifting as much as 6 degrees per day – a far higher rate of change than scientist have thought possible. ...

Coe and other researchers proposed this theory about ten years ago. But scientists generally dismissed those earlier findings, thinking the huge field shifts too big to be true. The new study contains powerful evidence to refute the critics. ...

by Tom Yulsman

Earth Magazine
August 1995

"If you are awash in lost continents and channeling and UFOs, you may not have intellectual room for the findings of science."

Carl Sagan
(famous scientist)

"Those who decide in advance what possibilities cannot be included in research, do logical science an injustice."

Lee Carroll
(not so famous nonscientist)

"Ignoring astral evidence in the pursuit of scientific solutions is to decide not to seek the whole truth."

Kryon
(master scientist)

Predictions, Validations and Skeptics
Chapter Eight

From the writer...

This chapter is mine, and is one of the few that will not feature actual channels from Kryon. The reason is that I wish to show what is taking place regarding the validations coming from the Kryon work, and also discuss some of the logic behind our current skeptical thinking.

One of the things about being a channel is that it often brings out the skeptics to comment on your work. With the success of the Kryon material world wide, I knew I would be the target for many comments and criticisms by logical mainstream folks (not to mention the new age folks)! Then I stopped to realize that **I myself was one of those logical mainstream folks!** "Kryon, give me something that validates some of this weird stuff," I asked. "And could you make it in this century please?" My thinking was that if I could get a stream of validations going from the scientific community on some of the wildest Kryon predictions, I would be a very happy logical mainstream guy!

I also knew that ironically it might help convince some of the new age skeptics who have clung to the old energy paradigms and were very wary of the "new channeling guy on the block." Actually my heaviest flack has come mainly from old energy metaphysical workers who have been extremely comfortable in the way things used to be. The implant, co-creation, self-healing, and many of the new gifts of Spirit have been difficult to accept, since the older metaphysical concepts have been valid for so long. Some metaphysicians, along with many Christians have decided Kryon is from the dark side, and fear these changes (take a look at page 184). It would be easy to dismiss the Kryon work as just another "flash in the pan" of popular new age belief. I do not judge these old energy workers, and gladly join in with empathy for how it must feel to be in their shoes.

Scientific validations, therefore, would be an instrument of confirmation to both groups of people, the non-metaphysical ones and the skeptical new age ones. Funny, isn't it, how much of an impact our non-enlightened scientific community has on enlightened workers. The reason for this is that we all respect the intelligence of the leading edge scientific community of this planet. And as I spoke previously, many in this community have written to me covertly to encourage the work! They are just as hungry for good answers that make sense as we are.

In August, and again in December of 1993, Kryon spoke of scientists being able to "see" the master guides arriving from all over the universe to facilitate the new energy of the planet (a pretty weird prediction). This prediction was given as a direct answer to a question put to Kryon. As described in Kryon Book Two (*Kryon – Don't Think Like a Human,* page 67), the actual quote of the transcribed question and prediction is again shown here:

Question: With all this Universal activity, why can't our scientists see something happening? Is it all too far beyond our senses?

Answer: I will never give you information that will expose the duality, or raise questions for the Earth scientists to ponder that would risk the new level of learning that you are in; however, I can tell you that master entities leave a residue when arriving. **Look for short, highly intense, unexplainable gamma ray activity.**

As shown in Kryon Book Two, in February of 1994 two articles hailed the discovery of these cosmic gamma rays in a fashion that read as if Kryon had written it for his own publicity! Science News, Vol 14, said, *"Gamma-ray bursts: a distant stretch? These flashes of radiation rank among the most mysterious phenomena in the universe. No one has found the sources of the bursts..."* The Grand Rapids Press, Feb 15, said, *"Los Alamos National Laboratory's $17 million Alexis satellite has recorded about 100 of the bursts, 'the likes of which have never been described in scientific literature.'"* This validation took about 6 months from the point of the original Kryon channel (see page 228 of Kryon Book Two *Don't Think Like a Human,* for the entire text of the articles). It was the beginning of exactly what I had asked for in the validation stream of Kryon predictions. I am told that seldom in the history of published channeled works does this happen with such clarity as was the case here. Are the cosmic rays still happening? Check out page 236.

On February 10, 1994, Kryon sat within a familiar setting in Del Mar and gave out startling information, which you can read in full on page 185 of *Kryon Book Two.* Before I continue regarding this information, I wish to relate to each of you how seriously I take my mission of publishing this channeled work. When I sit at my keyboard channeling a Kryon book, I look for a certain "feeling" to know that I am deep in integrity of translation before I will consider letting you read it. This is actually a harder process than in live channel, since in a live channel I usually have over 200 people's energy in the room to supply the instant link for this. (Kryon loves to speak to groups of Humans, and the energy is always high due to the love transmitted and the honor present. Believe it or not, Kryon always approaches a live channel as a human would approach a meeting with a group of celebrities!)

It's important for me to know that what I am translating isn't tainted with something I have wondered about, or postulated within my intellect, or a reflection of something someone told me in some past, hazy conversation. When I channel at the keyboard, there is time to reflect on this and examine all of it. Sometimes it takes longer due to this, but the information is very clean and precise. In live channel, however, Kryon knows that there is no time to "think it over;" therefore he often chooses these times to offer information of emotional value, and revelations for our time. It comes through very fast, and is recorded for transcription. I can't second guess anything, and Kryon knows and respects my process. Therefore some of the most "gee whiz" stuff has come from the live work. (This happened again in this book with the Sedona channel in the next chapter.)

On this February night all seemed normal as I started the channel. The love feelings were present, and the crowd was respectful and receptive (as always). Then Kryon began his story of why he arrived in our solar system three years prior to my involvement, and spent time in the area of the orbital track that Jupiter makes around the sun. Then he started giving the message about MYRVA, the death rock on its way to terminate Earth!

My heart was in my throat. Kryon is not a gloom and doom channel, to say the least. He always features love and honor, and a good news approach for what we have accomplished for the planet. His whole reason for being here is to marry his work with what we have done. So when this message began I wondered if we had changed something since the harmonic convergence (which we have the ability to do). Kryon knew what was going on in my mind, so he gave me an incredible "wink" of emotion to know that what was coming was going to be some of the best news I had ever translated. He was right.

He went on to tell how his job in the new energy was to break this space rock he called MYRVA into pieces, thereby deactivating its potential to terminate us. This was a similar astronomical phenomenon as the Shoemaker/Levi 9 event (but Kryon said that

MYRVA was not Shoemaker/Levi 9). Evidently MYRVA was all part of the termination scheme that we had agreed on in that great elusive planning session we keep being told about (that we can't remember in all appropriateness). Kryon's actual words were:

> "I sit in front of you, rejoicing in the fact that MYRVA is now in pieces! There is protocol and precedent to what happened to MYRVA, for your scientists have seen it before."

My heart soared with the punch of the emotion that Kryon gave with this message, and I was almost unable to continue. No one in the room truly got what I did that night, for the news wasn't about a rock in space... it was about the incredible job we had done to allow for its destruction, and the honor that went with it for us. The news wasn't that Kryon had done something... but that we had!

Analyzing this message scientifically, Kryon was saying that MYRVA was indeed still in the orbit that Jupiter takes around the Sun. In addition it is now in pieces, with a scenario similar to what we saw with Shoemaker/Levi 9. In fact, I am convinced that we got to see Shoemaker/Levi 9 so that we would have a first-hand understanding of the kind of natural process that Kryon put into place regarding MYRVA. If we had not seen Shoemaker/Levi 9, the breaking up of MYRVA would have just been another "woo woo" mystery to the scientists on how Kryon was able to do such a thing. Now we have seen it in real time, and it is an accepted fact how a comet or asteroid can break up with natural gravitational forces... and we got to see it right in the area where Kryon said he was!

I feel so honored that seven months later the article on the next page appeared in the *San Jose Mercury News*. They picked it up from *Reuters*, a European news service. I feel honored since the timing allows me to share this with you in the pages of this book (and not have to wait another year until the next Kryon Book).

Take a look at what the scientists say in the article below. On a point-by-point basis here are the facts: (1) Scientists found a comet on the way that some believe will threaten Earth. (2) After it was discovered, they noticed that it was in pieces! (in five pieces – the numerological number of change). (3) The influence of **Jupiter** would direct the eventual trajectory, and (4) Current trajectories show that the pieces should avoid an impact with the Earth! Did Kryon write his own article again? I think so (see below).

Not only was it again wonderful to see the validation of a Kryon prediction, but the simple numerology computation for **MYRVA** and the scientific name, **Machholz-2,** were identical! Both names in English work out to a simple numerology of 7, which is a spiritual number.

The MYRVA Article

San Jose Mercury News   *Sunday, September 11, 1994*

Destination Earth?

Newly found comet fragments bear watching, observers say

Reuters

LONDON — Astronomers are carefully observing fragments from a recently discovered comet that some believe could potentially threaten Earth, Britain's Sunday Telegraph reported.

The new comet, known as **Machholz-2,** was discovered last month by an American astronomer as it raced toward the sun, but as other observers turned their telescopes toward the object they found that comet had broken up, just like comet Shoemaker-Levy 9, which hit Jupiter in July.

By Saturday, five fragments had been seen — all on a path that would bring them within the orbit of Earth.

Information from observatories so far suggests that if the fragments continue on their current trajectories they should avoid an impact with Earth, but astronomers said it was extremely hard to predict their long-term behavior.

Duncan Steel of the Anglo-Australian Observatory told the Telegraph that the influence of Jupiter would dominate their orbital behavior.

"It's most likely that Jupiter will pick up the objects and throw them out of the solar system again. As far as we can tell, they should not hit the Earth in the next 100 years," he said, but added, "we might be wrong."

"It could happen in the next few decades. What we need are more observations so that we can get a more accurate orbit."

Computers

Now I would like to mention some of the items that Kryon gave us specifically in Book Two's science chapter that have begun appearing. This chapter featured several questions asked which resulted in answers that were advice from Kryon. I don't count these as predictions, but rather simple common sense cosmic advice whose time has arrived. Still it's remarkable that within a year after the channeling some of the things are in the news!

On page 222 Kryon was asked about our computers. Again, here it is reprinted for your reference. Channeled in July of 1994.

Question: I am interested in computers. Where is the technology going? Are we on the right path to creating machines that will help us?

Answer: ... in regard to computer technology, you are missing the most obvious thing imaginable! When you see the Earth's most amazing computer operating in biological beings all around you, why haven't you emulated it? ... The electrochemical computing machine is the way of the universe. It is the way of your own biology and your own brain. When will you start investigating merging the two together?

I don't regularly peruse science magazines, so it's common that readers send me articles in which Kryon's projections have been seen. This was the case in the MYRVA article, and also in the one on the next page. In March of 1995, the following article appeared in <u>Scientific American</u>.

SCIENTIFIC AMERICAN
MARCH 1995

Protein-Based Computers

Devices fabricated from biological molecules promise compact size and faster data storage. They lend themselves to use in parallel-processing computers, three-dimensional memories and neural networks.

by Robert R. Birge

The world's most advanced supercomputer does not require a single semiconductor chip. The human brain consists of organic molecules that combine to form a highly sophisticated network able to calculate perceive, manipulate, self-repair, think and feel. Digital computers can certainly perform calculations much faster and more precisely than humans can, but even simple organisms are superior to computers in the other five domains. Computer designers may never be able to make machines having all the faculties of a natural brain, but many of us think we can exploit some special properties of biological molecules, particularly proteins, to build computer components that are smaller, faster and more powerful than any electronic devices on the drawing boards thus far.

Although no computer components made entirely or partly from proteins are on the market yet, ongoing international research efforts are making exciting headway. It seems reasonable to predict that hybrid technology combining semiconductor chips and biological molecules will move from the realm of science fiction to commercial application fairly soon.

Soviet scientists were the first to recognize and develop the potential of bacteriorhodopsin for computing as part of what came to be called Project Rhodopsin. Yuri A. Ovchinnikov obtained a good deal of funding for such research because he had the ear of Soviet military leaders and was able to convince them that by exploring bioelectrics, Soviet science could leapfrog the West in computer technology. Many aspects of this ambitious project are still considered military secrets and may never be revealed.

...Entire aritcle not shown

In fairness to Mr. Birge, the author of this fine article, it was about ten times the length of what I have shown here. It went on to illustrate the mechanics of this new technology, and describe the fact that we may very well be close to creating artificial intelligence at a high level. I feel that this is exactly what Kryon was speaking about.

Nuclear Waste

On the top of my "wish list" regarding Kryon predictions and projections is our ability to eliminate nuclear waste. Kryon spoke of it in Book One, and again in Book Two in response to a science chapter question.

Question: In previous writings you said that our nuclear waste was one of the biggest dangers we currently have. The stuff seems indestructible, and it is volatile forever! What can we do about it?

Answer: The real answer should be obvious. It must be neutralized. I spoke of this in earlier channels, but now I will expand on it. There are many ways of neutralizing this waste, but the one which is currently within your technology is simple and available now. You should immediately turn to Earth biology! Look for the micro organisms you already know about that can devour these active substances, and make them harmless. Develop them using your science to increase their number and efficiency, and let them eat your waste!

I am pleased to report that this seemingly miraculous solution to the Earth's waste is being worked on in exactly this way! I understand that there are several active, leading edge companies that are developing micro organisms for all kinds of waste on the planet. They call this technology "Bio Remediation." Basically it is converting toxic contaminated substances using specifically bred microbes, used with oxygen. This has had the result already of converting contaminated soil from heavy soil abuse to fertile soil with no dangerous chemical residual effects. It also is beginning to be used very effectively on oil spills and other man-made disasters. This is a great concept and is very aggressive in its approach. Naturally these companies are going up against giant chemical companies that have been in business for decades, so there is a large marketing battle looming in their future.

What really got me excited, however, was an article in *Science News* volume 150, page 42 in July of 1996. It seems that DuPont and Exxon are experimenting with certain plants in ponds close to the 1986 Chernobyl nuclear disaster to clean up radionuclides cesium 137 and strontium 90! That's right... specially bred plants are cleaning up nuclear waste in water. Here is a quote: "*We are testing a variety of plants to see if they can do some of the dirty work of cleaning up such pollutants as radioactive material, lead, selenium and oil.*" It seems to be happening the way Kryon suggested.

By the way, some of you were interested to know what the town was whose name began with "H" that Kryon spoke about in Book Two. This town was mentioned by Kryon as being a prime site for potential nuclear waste instability. Subsequent to the publishing of Book Two, we believe that we have identified this town in the northwest area of the U.S. It is Hanford in the state of Washington.

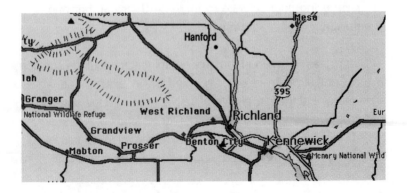

The Photon Belt

The book, *You are Becoming a Galactic Human,* by Virginia Essene and Sheldon Nidle, was on the best seller list of distributors for months (and at the writing of this book, it still is)! It deserves to be there, and everywhere we go in seminars we advise anyone who is interested to go get it, for it can provoke much thought.

We have discussed some of the book's subject in our seminars point by point. I feel there is some commonality between the Kryon material and Sheldon's work. (1) *Galactic Human (GH)* speaks of a group coming to prepare the grids (the time lords). I believe this is the Kryon group. (2) *GH* does not foresee a physical Earth polar shift (the basic message of Kryon). (3) Both books speak about a brand new path for the planet. (4) Both books admonish us not to trust what the Zeta tell us. (5) There is even mention of the Gamma rays in *GH* (that in Kryon Book Two are validated by science). (5) Regardless of the potential of frightening things in the future, Sheldon and Virginia treat the information as basic good news for all of us.

The fact remains, however, that Kryon never mentioned the **photon belt** or the long day/night scenarios that were discussed as coming in 1996/7 according to *GH*. Kryon also speaks of the grids being vital to us... and *GH* has them being taken away (but a bubble of protection replacing them while this happens). Kryon also has nothing but positive things to say about our seed biology Pleiadians, whereas there is some negative news in *GH* about them.

Repeatedly, Kryon speaks of the fact that we are currently writing our own future. He tells us that there is no psychic, sooth sayer, or channel who can peg a date to a specific event accurately coming up in this new age. This is because of the prime issue that Kryon often brings up: **Our future is a moving target!** When you examine many new age prophets, plus the old energy one of over 400 years ago, they have something in common today – the predictions haven't happed! We are years behind everything from the Christian Revelation predictions, to Nostradamus, to the Hoppi Indian nation map. Something is happening that is voiding out, or greatly delaying these predictions. In 1989 when Kryon arrived, we didn't have the proof we do now that we are truly in a New Age. Now we do.

The entire work of Kryon is centered around the fact that we changed our future, and he is here to adjust the grid because of it. Within the scope of all this we find that our future continues to shift as we increase the vibration of the planet. Unknown to us in 1995 (when this book was originally written), some attributes of the physical planet Earth itself are now changing. The Schumann resonance, a measurement of the standing wave within the current between the bottom of the ionosphere and the surface of the Earth, has been consistent at approximately 7.25Hz to 7.8Hz for eons. It has been so consistent that even some scientific instruments are calibrated to it. Gregg Braden, noted author of *Awakening to Zero Point*,* indicates that this resonance is currently (as of 5/97) being measured at 10Hz to 11Hz! The earth is not only changing its spiritual attribute as a result of our work, but also physically changing its vibration, and science is showing it in these areas. Did anyone notice the weather changes that in 1989 Kryon told us would eventually take place? They are now here! All this activity is a strong reaction to the fact that consciousness changes physics... a phrase that Kryon is often heard to say. By our work, we are changing not only the face of our planet, but our future as well.

I believe that before the ink was dry on *GH*, we had again changed our future so that the photon belt experience as predicted by Sheldon was invalid. He didn't 'see' it wrong... the scenario just changed in the time it took to publish the book. This will be a very common thing, and it's going to frustrate those channels who don't understand the new paradigm.

* LL Productions 1-800-243-1438

There are still "doom and gloom" New Age prophets that don't get it. Their maps of seeming Earth demise didn't happen when they predicted, so they simply issued new ones with updated doom and gloom dates. When those dates go by and the planet doesn't tilt on its axis, or California doesn't submerge, I guess they will again issue them... and again. Such is the attraction of the sensational.

I don't think Sheldon and Virginia are here as predictors of doom. They are here with important information that is valuable. I feel the timetable of the photon belt was not the issue. It represented only four pages in the entire *GH* book. The information has now mutated into something entirely different due to our vibration changes. The timing didn't fit the mold that was foretold and Kryon has basically said it will be a non-issue, but again, that does not void the work of *GH*.

This is not a time for channels to be at odds with one another. This is a testing time of ego sublimation and openness of spirit. I welcome the information in *GH* because I believe it is good news. The bottom line of the message of *GH* and Kryon is that our Earth changes and position in the galaxy are good news for the planet. That's good enough for me.

> *The Schumann resonances are quasi standing electromagnetic waves that exist in the cavity between the surface of the Earth and the inner edge of the ionosphere 55 kilometers up. The standing waves represent several frequencies between 6Hz and 50Hz, with the fundamental being 7.8 and a daily variation of about +/- 0.5 Hz. For more information on the Schumann resonance, see <u>Handbook of Atmospheric Electrodynamics, Vol. I</u> chapter 11 by Hans Volland - 1995 - published by the CRC Press.*

The Shumann Resonance

Skeptic Logic

I now wish to take a page or two to address an issue that has had me baffled for some time. It refers to the seeming lack of good intelligent logic regarding any skeptic's approach to the paranormal and metaphysical.

Almost all of you know by now that I consider myself skeptical. I still do, and yet my approach to almost any puzzle is far different than most of the "experts" that I have observed. If someone suddenly appeared on my porch acting excited, stating that he had just seen eighteen little 4-foot-tall purple men get out of a flying saucer in a field outside... and they all looked exactly like Elvis, I would be skeptical (to say the least).

But my actual brain function would say, "Boy does this sound stupid; I think I'll go see for myself." So suppose the guy takes me to the spot where he said he saw all of this. I look around and find nothing at all. No marks where a saucer might have landed, no tiny Elvis footprints, and most of all no other witnesses. Then my brain would say, "I guess this guy is nuts," and I would go back to my house (to watch *The X Files*).

If, however, later I found out that at that same moment many unrelated other people had also seen the same thing in many other fields, I would be very interested indeed. At that time my brain would probably say, "The correlation factor of this bizarre event is too great to be ignored, so I will investigate." My belief factor would go up immensely, and I would want very much to take a real good look at this phenomena.

I have always approached logic puzzles in this fashion. Those who decide in advance what possibilities cannot be included in research do logical science an injustice. What I am saying here is that I believe it is necessary for logic to remain open to all possibilities, no matter how bizarre... especially if there is any evidence to support it (like multiple witnesses, for example).

Unfortunately many of the skeptics who are in the forefront these days have decided, in advance of any research, the following items: "There is no such thing as psychic power ('cause we can't measure it)." "There are no such things as flying saucers ('cause we haven't been given proof of any)." "There is no place for religion in science (since we all know better now, don't we?)."

Looking down their noses at the paranormal, scientists wink at each other as they totally discount any possibilities of real science in the hodge-podge of spooky stuff that has become commonplace. Kryon says that to ignore astral evidence in the pursuit of scientific solutions is to decide not to seek the truth! In my opinion, a real scientist will try to sort out the real from the unreal, and delve into the things that truly contain correlation factors that can't be ignored. Perhaps it's sorting out the Elvis sightings from the near death experiences that's difficult for the serious scientist. To them they are both too spooky, and therefore are lumped into one kind of event. To me, from what I have investigated, one is simple fun, and one is very real and has scientific attributes.

An article in the May 15, 1995 issue of Time Magazine, called Weird Science, commented on the amazing growth of paranormal shows on prime time television. The article came from exactly this flawed approach. The bias was obviously that since none of these things could be real, how come the American public is so gullible? According to Time: "Despite the nonsense that prevails on these shows, several of them make a pretense of objectivity by including rebuttals by scientists and skeptics. But any reasoned responses are generally lost in a barrage of fanciful fiction."

Of course from the perspective of those involved in broadcast (like myself), we understand that economics drive the prime time television schedule. Arbitron ratings and "areas of dominant influence" are the real language of why these shows are on the air, and in plain English it's because **people are watching them by the millions**. Again Time says: "*As a group, these shows are a celebration of the nonexistent, a feast for the eyes and ears of the gullible.*" Time has just insulted most Americans on the continent. I personally believe that humans are very interested in what intuitively they already know at the cellular level, and four prime time television specials on Angels in 1994 and 1995 isn't a coincidence in this, the new age. Where did the rules of the scientific approach go in regard to these facts?

For years there has been a gentleman who calls himself "The Amazing Randy," who specializes in debunking the paranormal. Now, you probably think I would be in a group that would not like him for this action (since I am now a channel). Actually I respect him greatly. Within his process (what he believes), he has set out to help people. He firmly believes that paranormal activities are nothing but shams on gullible people, and so he has successfully given his life to showing audiences this very thing. It's theatrical in the way he does it, but that just gives him a better platform to help more people from being taken in by dishonest individuals who take money posing as psychics, seance givers and spoon benders.

Now, Randy's entire premise is that psychics, seance givers and spoon benders are all fakes. So Randy sets out to prove it by showing audiences nationwide that he can do the same thing with illusions, as a theatrical magician would. And he does! He bends spoons, gives amazing profound answers to individuals (like a psychic would) and creates seance-like effects... all with illusion. It's a great show.

I tell you this to point out an enormous flaw in the thinking of humans regarding this kind of "proof." Let me ask you this. If David Copperfield could give you an illusion of the parting of the Red Sea (and I bet he could), would that prove to you conclusively that therefore God did not part the Red Sea? Of course not. Then why does everyone think that because an illusionist can make an illusion of an event, therefore the **real** event could not have happened? It doesn't make sense (Kryon speaks of this later as well).

Naturally the inference from Randy's point of view is that all others were doing an illusion just like him, so in his mind it is indeed proof. Since Randy can't comment on these pages, I again want to tell you that I believe that in his travels he probably has indeed saved many people from unscrupulous activities by those posing as real new age workers, who were out to just "make a buck." So look at his activities in a light of love, and you will see his mission is truly humanitarian. Again, I honor this. If I hadn't turned out to be a channel, I might have joined his ranks!

Conclusion:

I grew up in the late 50's and 60's in what I thought was a very sophisticated, scientific era. After all, we had big fast cars (with neat tail fins), satellites spinning around the Earth, nuclear power, the Beatles, and some of the most advanced scientific inventions right in our homes (like big stereos and color TV). I poke fun at it now, but truly it was hardly the dark ages. NASA was growing; we were putting men in space, and it seemed like a very technical time.

Now, during this time in the early 60's there were a group of people who were very strange indeed (according to the scientists). These people were proponents of a theory that was laughable! They observed the mapping of the continents on Earth (from 60's satellite photos) and put forward the idea that all of today's continents were once part of one land mass, and that somehow the big mass had broken up and "drifted" apart. "Just look at the outlines," one of them would say. "They fit each other like a puzzle!"

Again, scientists winked at each other and walked the other way, knowing that continents don't drift. They did this instead of giving some credibility to a strong correlation of observable evidence that suggested something like this could actually have happened. The continental drift group were not believed, since to the scientists of that day there was no observable mechanics that could even begin to explain such a thing. Therefore it was nonsense. Again we see how biased our modern science community is to anything for which it doesn't have a proven mechanism.

Thanks to men like Dr. Robert Ballard (who spent lots of research time in La Jolla, close to my city), the mechanics of plate tectonics were discovered deep under the ocean, and the theory of continental drift became scientific fact almost overnight.

I give you this story to show you that in our modern times there is evidence of this same flawed thinking in a non-metaphysical venue in my lifetime. I guess you don't have to believe in pyramid power to be shunned by the scientists after all!

My contention is that much of today's paranormal is tomorrow's fact. I'm just disappointed that very intelligent men and women won't consider this seriously, and try to sort out the facts from the ridiculous. It would only take a few to come forward and say "It really looks dumb, but we are scientists, and in honor of the scientific method, **we should consider all things which have observable correlating attributes... no matter how bizzare.**" If Kryon is right, this would result in a search for the whole truth. Doesn't that goal line up with the entire idea of science research on the planet?

Chapter Ten

Science

Science
Chapter Nine

From the writer...

Here we go again delving into areas that have brought more reactions from the Kryon writings than any other subject. The last chapter dealt with the results of scientific predictions in Kryon Book Two. You can see that both the metaphysical community and the scientific community are interested in what goes on here.

I have to laugh, since I get an overview of thoughts from all over concerning the issues of Kryon. Although confidential, I can tell you that I have received letters from a rocket scientist, physicist, many medical doctors, and a geologist or two who secretly tell me to "keep going; we need these ideas exposed." They all are closet metaphysicians who can't tell their science colleagues about how they really believe, since it would actually destroy their credibility with the science community. I can picture these men and women at work, with the Kryon book sandwiched among technical papers (covers torn off, of course) like a school boy hiding his first girlie magazine from a teacher in school. Then I stopped laughing, realizing that was exactly what I did with the first book at my own workplace for a year! Oh well, humans are very predictable... and I'm glad I'm one.

This chapter is divided into three distinct sections. The first section is where Kryon will answer specific questions from readers regarding science ideas generated in past channeling. Next we will have a wonderfully scientific channeling that occurred in Sedona, Arizona before 200 seminar attendees. During this channeling Kryon had some startling things to say about mathematics in general. About a week after the event I got a seemingly unrelated letter from a mathematician who was interested in some of the numerology numbers in book one. I thought to myself, "What a coincidence (ha ha) that I suddenly have the ear of a mainstream math person!" So I took the opportunity to correspond with him and ask him about the math items Kryon spoke about. His reaction may surprise you... and I felt it important enough to invite him to write an article for this book! I'll tell you more about that when that section is presented later. The third section is therefore his article.

For those of you (like me) who use math mainly at the grocery stores and restaurants (and use your fingers under the table to calculate the waiter's tip), don't be scared if you look ahead in the book to the math article in this chapter (or the 9944 math appendix) and see a bunch of arithmetic and algebra. Much of this is actually in plain English, and you can get the point without bringing out your scientific calculator (or your fingers).

For those of you (like some of my friends) who consider math a second language (the one they would rather speak), then you may devour these sections with calculator in hand – extra batteries in each pocket – drooling on each page with numerical excitement. You can also write to receive even more numbers and "proofs" if you desire. There's even some breakthough stuff. Look for it.

Why include articles written by others in the Kryon book? Because I have reached the point where mainstream validation is critical to the credibility of this work. In the past I have had to wait months and months for published confirmations (as you have seen in the last chapter), but in the case of the Sedona channeled math question, I had the opportunity to immediately get comment and publish it in the same book from very credible sources. This brings the validity to you within the same book as the channeling – no waiting. I like that. It also brings the Kryon work into the hands of non-metaphysical scientists to examine, since it contains a full argument on some of the principles presented. This wouldn't necessarily be the case if I did not have these extra pages from those invited to comment.

The first three questions are from a world-class astrologer. "Why," you might ask, "did you put astrology in the science section?" The answer is that Kryon tells us over and over that astrology is very high science! It deals with magnetic imprints at birth, and the workings of magnetic influences while you are alive on the planet. It is an exacting science, and its rules are just as valid and interesting as geometry. Convincing a scientifically minded person of this is difficult, since the science of astrology has been grouped into the same area as reading tea leaves and speaking to the dead in seance. The facts are that the mechanics of astrology are wonderfully complete, and scientifically based (but not yet proven to our Earth's science community), to let people know how they are doing in general. There is no science other than medicine that affects the human body so directly. If you want to hear Kryon's words on the subject, keep reading.

Question: Book one says a three degree correction would be necessary after January of 1992. I take that to mean that three degrees should be added to all transiting planets and to astronomical phenomena that impacts astrological readings; i.e., eclipses, new and full moons, and stationing planets. But my own logic tells me that this should apply to the table of houses in regards to setting up birth and event charts from that date also, probably by the same three degrees. Is this correct? Also, I use the declinations of the planets, since they are so telling. Would the same correction also apply here?

Martha E. Ramsey
Phoenix Arizona

Answer: Dear one, you are among many who have asked about the science of magnetics regarding the disposition measurement of individuals within the influence of your solar system magnetics. The answers you seek for your science are just as critical as the answers sought by those looking to change small particle magnetics. The appropriateness of specific answers from the Kryon to these questions are limited and tempered, since we ask you to find these solutions in a human fashion. Just as Kryon will not tell you the answers on how to exactly create a massless condition, I also will not disclose the exactness of what you seek for your charts either. Although this may seem like side-stepping the question to some, it is an honoring of Spirit to you. Kryon doesn't care how humans feel about the credibility of Spirit. The loving truth remains, regardless of all comments from humans. It is up to you to discover the exact answers as your karmic setup, and your new gift.

I will tell you this, however. I asked my partner to include some of the questions from scientists like yourself who have studied hard and who help humans daily with knowledge and insight. The approach you are taking features some very high insight as to the changes and are generally correct. I will also tell you at this time that there are still poor human assumptions around the interpretation of the original channeling regarding the three degree shift. In your astrological science, three degrees is a tremendous change and would change attributes dramatically for you. Many have assumed that the entire wheel has moved three degrees. Instead, start thinking in a non-linear way. The total change is three degrees. This is spread out in the shape of the twelve houses, for the houses have changed incrementally to total three degrees, not spread equally. To some houses there has been no change at all. Most of you have yet to discover this, but those who read this will think to themselves, "What area of this science is affected by the timing of the Kryon's arrival? What is the magnetic attribute of this new age?"

These puzzles are hints at what houses are being affected the greatest. To many, this information will only confuse. Start experimenting with overlays and use your intuition regarding what the changes might be. Use logic and common sense as your guide and you will be rewarded. When you feel you are accurate about what the new age changes are bringing to your measurements, then publish the information!

Question: What about reading for someone who has requested the implant? I got the impression that the implant would negate the imprint that the chart represents, but the wording seems to indicate the erasure of the chart was a choice, that it could still be used as a timing device if the person so wished, with the correction taken into consideration via transits. Is this correct?

Martha E. Ramsey
Phoenix, Arizona

Answer: In the Kryon analogy (given in prior channelings), a fern is born into existence with a predisposition of certain positive attributes regarding water, shade, climate and seasonal preferences. If you are a fern, you will be far happier in certain places than in others. In addition, there will be certain seasons of time that will favor your growth, and certain ones that you should move slowly within. For humans it is the same. The magnetic imprint will give you certain predispositions of preference, and there will be magnetic conditions that will favor your growth and some that will ask you to go slowly. In addition for the human (not the fern), you have wonderful hints regarding your life contract, for the magnetic disposition of your solar system is allied to you for your entire lifetime, and gives marvelous hints over the years to assist you with your plans.

When you take the implant, you become a miracle fern! Suddenly direct sunlight no longer hurts you. Although you still prefer shade, you now have no fear of sunlight. In times that were previously "go slow" times, you now have the ability to whisk past other ferns who are huddled together in a time of hibernation. For the human this means the following: Astrological magnetic imprints are with you for life, just like your face. You may continue to consult the science for timing issues, and still follow the advice of the magnetics. However, the implant gives you the ability to void the attributes that in the past have slowed you down. Do you dare make complex plans or travel during days when your personal chart indicated it wouldn't be wise? The answer is yes! Feel the freedom to voyage out when previously you were told it wouldn't be a good idea. In times where you might be introspective, you may actually feel outgoing! Such are the changes that are possible when you have control of your imprint via the implant.

Now, this is important: a planetary condition such as a retrograde is planet-wide. Although you personally may no longer have the same kind of admonitions within this time, those around you still will. Use this advice when you decide to create partnerships or do business. Although you personally may be fine, these actions require more than just yourself. Therefore, it might be better to slow down and honor the alignment for those around you during these times, for they are still affected. The only exception would be business or partnership with another who had the implant (a wonderful thing indeed).

Question: If the imprint is voided via the implant, and the chart canceled in effect, what is the system of astrology that might take the place of the current system? Are there any suggestions as to the course this would take and the changes in application that would need to be made? As an astrological instructor, I would like to begin working with this information with my serious students. I want very much to do what is correct for myself and the science I love so much.

Martha E. Ramsey
Phoenix, Arizona

Answer: It is important that you don't throw away your personal astrological science. As indicated, even with the implant your system is a wonderful guidepost for your lifetime. It also gives marvelous hints about what others may do around you (important information indeed for those who wish to know when the best times are for nurturing and healing others). Find out what the changes are and stay with the system. It will continue to serve you for the lifetime of the planet, just as your universally corrected mathematics will.

You do raise a marvelously insightful question, however, and I will allude to an area that I have not spoken of yet. Your galaxy is also very magnetic. You already know that there are forces which control where your solar system and your planet are in respect to the center of your galaxy. Would it therefore not be reasonable that there is also a *galactic astrology chart*? How is the planet doing in regard to galaxy magnetics? If you had known of these things years ago, you would have easily foreseen the new age you are in now. In addition you would have seen (on your galaxy astrology chart) that your solar system is entering areas where it has never been before. "What awaits you there?" you might ask. My answer is for those who worry about the new area and for those who worry about new neighbors. ***Take care of your individual spirit and all else will fall into place.*** There is potential for fear in these issues. Changes will happen, but your place on this planet is a birthright and is honored by God.

Begin the investigation and study of galaxy astrology. You will indeed be the pioneers.

Question: (Referring to the Temple of Rejuvenation explained in Kryon Book Two). *In regard to the three year program of refreshment and rejuvenation, what aspects of the program were there, if any, that did not require the technology of the Temple that conceivably could be implemented now? Also, why did it take* three years? Did the processes taking place in the Temple require periodic visits as opposed to one grand process at the end of the program?

Greg Ehmka
Akron, New York

Answer: The actual "program" is less than a day. The results of the program lasted only three years, and then a revisit was necessary. Although the technology exists now to duplicate the Temple, the knowledge of biology does not. It may be some time before you decide to build this device, and there are other more advanced rejuvenation possibilities that make the Temple of Rejuvenation seem like a dinosaur to you! Dear ones there is a great deal of information hiding in the information given regarding the Temple of Rejuvenation.

The first question all of you should ask is, "Why do humans need rejuvenating at all?" Your bodies are designed to rejuvenate themselves! Why isn't the biology more efficient to rejuvenate 100% of what is lost? What is the process?

The real answer is spiritual. Your biology in this cosmic energy is flawed, and therefore creates death. It wasn't actually designed this way, but became this way over time, thereby allowing the birth-death-birth-death attribute that has become the important "engine of karma" and has allowed you to raise the vibration of the planet. Long before any human of any kind set foot on this planet, the biological energy ratio was less than 100%, meaning that all biology was destined to only last a short time, then be renewed by reincarnation.

The science answer may surprise you, for the machinery of the body reacts to an energy quotient of the cosmos. As that energy reduced over eons of time within your universe, those internal machines became less efficient (with less energy present). It is therefore no accident that your planet and your biology was set up at a time when this energy quotient was inefficient. Otherwise you would all live forever, and the karmic work that is the work of the entire planet would never be able to be done.

Now, the exciting news is this: the tools have always existed to give your individual biology that extra 10% "push" to allow for true rejuvenation. True rejuvenation is 100% internal body rejuvenation, where the biology actually is able to keep up totally with all loss due to human living. In the days of Atlantis and Lemuria the "push" was done with magnetics. Those in that day understood the magnetics of Earth and the human body. They were able to give the biology an outside "tune-up" to allow the magnetic DNA structure around the biological one to operate at full potential for at least three years without deterioration. During that time the biology kept up with the deterioration, and the immune system was 100% effective. As the magnetics of the DNA slowly returned to reflect the current energy quotient of the cosmos, aging again set in and another trip to the Temple was in order. This pure science healing was wrapped in ceremony and kept close to those with power. As previously channeled, however, this culture also misused its knowledge; and although some of the elite lived exceptionally long lives (not everyone got to use the machine due to political power struggles), their entire culture died dramatically.

What you should know is that the entire channeling regarding the Temple was to give you insight into what is actually going on inside you. The information for your health science is this: there are at least three ways to accomplish total and complete rejuvenation potential for humans in this time that is well within your capacity to produce. One is magnetic, one is biological and one is spiritual. Does it surprise you that again you have the team of physical, biological and mental (spiritual)?

(1) The magnetic method deals with the Temple of Rejuvenation (as channeled in Kryon Book Two). The science of your time will allow you to recreate this temple at a fraction of its original size if you wish. Those who have worked with this information already have recognized this fact. (2) The biological method is just now being discovered, and uses live essence medicines. It will cause great controversy within your medical community. The controversy will be around the fact that the information will challenge the very basics of how the human body works at the cellular level. (3) The spiritual method is ascension technology, which many of you are working on daily.

This information is given in love at a time when we wish you to start the New Age on Earth. As we have said in the past, we want you to remain and do the work of enlightened humans. All who use these methods will eventually raise the consciousness of the planet, thereby helping the whole. You are honored for your work to remain here!

Question: In creating the "massless" condition (Kryon Book Two), is it sufficient to move only the electrons out of synch with our time frame or must the atomic nucleus be moved out of synch also?

Greg Ehmka
Akron, New York

Answer: All parts change vibration. The change in vibration changes the distances between the parts. Here is a question for you. What do you think happens to your sacred geometric calculations when you have a higher vibratory rate? Do they remain the same? Do the mathematical numerical tools that give you distance solutions hold true? I give you these questions in love. It is typical of the Kryon work with humans that you may come away with more questions than the ones you brought.

Question: Does dark matter exist in space? Our science is finding that unless they allow for something like this, the gravity related observations on seen matter don't add up.

> The Writer
> Del Mar, California

Answer: What you call dark matter isn't. Know this. You already know that gravity and light are related. What you do not yet know are the exact attributes of light. When light is synchronous, you are able to see it with your eyes and measure its luminosity with your instruments. This is when the waves all align with each other in a synchronous manner. When light is asynchronous, the waves align in such a manner that they cancel each other out. What we are saying is this. There is regular (seen) matter that is totally hidden from you due to the fact that the light traveling from it is asynchronous. This asychronicity is caused by intense gravity that is either near the matter or in the path the light takes to your eyes.

Here is a question for you: what part does light play in your own personal biology? The answer, when known, will astound you.

Question: Density is measured as mass per unit of volume. There is an atomic density which is the mass of protons and neutrons in proportion to the volume they occupy. There is an atomic density which adds in the electrons and is in proportion to the volume that the atom occupies. Then there is gross matter density. That is, a piece of iron is denser than a piece of wood, which means that if they weigh the same, the iron has less volume (is smaller). Does altering the mass attributes mean changing these proportions by electromagnetic means only? If so, is the desired "massless" state one in which the volume remains the same, the particle of particles "disappear" due to being moved out of synch time-wise, and the density therefore reduces to zero or less?

Greg Ehmka
Akron, New York

Answer: Your density measurements must change when the vibration of the parts change. The electromagnetic engine is what creates a vibratory change. The mathematics that revolve around density are relative to the vibration levels of the parts. The vibration levels change the time frame. It is therefore possible to have an object in front of you that is an apple, but its atomic parts are vibrating extremely fast. The speed of the vibration creates a time shift for the apple, so it is not entirely in your time frame. Its mass is not relative to an apple in your vibratory level (time frame), and it might weigh as much as a flea. If you kept this apple in front of you for a long time, you would also discover that it is aging far slower than a normal apple. In fact, it might even outlast you!

In the atomic world the space between parts is enormous. Those of you who work in this area already know that most of matter is actually space between the parts! Therefore it is possible to have a vibratory rate which is extremely fast, where the distance between the parts has been adjusted, but where the actual physical dimensions of the overall object remains the same. There is a tremendous variance possible within the atomic parts before the overall object changes its shape. This is the massless condition we describe for you.

Here is another question for you: what happened to the time frame of the individual in the great theoretical time puzzle that your scientist Einstein presented to you? This puzzle was about the space traveler who was traveling away from Earth at close to the speed of light. What do you think was happening to him atomically? Many felt that he would become very large (but I am telling you the expected increase in size is only an increase in the distance between the parts). Let me add to this puzzle. What do you think he weighed while he was traveling that fast?

Question: Is the biological danger of the "massless" condition due to the ionization of nearby atoms that I understood you to indicate would occur? If so, does this mean that the "massless" condition has the ability to ionize normal biological materials like molecules of combinations of Carbon, Hydrogen, Oxygen and Nitrogen, and therefore may ionize air and /or water?

Greg Ehmka
Akron, New York

Answer: I mentioned to you that a clue to an object in a different time frame than your own was that atoms directly involved between time frames would have a different number of electrons. Biology within this area would indeed be destroyed. You are now asking about an area that you have seen before in regard to humans. Any kind of material that is in this zone where one time frame meets another will be affected. The atoms don't care what kind of molecules they make up. They all react the same.

The danger, however, to the occupants of a massless driven vehicle is within the mechanics of the engine itself, for it creates a situation that would greatly harm biology. Shielding is therefore very important to those traveling inside.

Question: What do you mean, "We have seen this before in humans?"

The writer
Del Mar, California

Answer: In all your questions regarding magnetics and massless conditions you have never asked about what happened in your year 1943. You tried to create a massless condition with coarse equipment and little understanding of what you were doing. In the process you actually did indeed create an unstable massless condition for a moment. Its instability created a situation where instead of a true massless condition, you received one where the time frame changed but the parts within the sphere of the time change did not have the fine-tuned synchronicity needed for a massless object. The result was an actual distance displacement of the object instead of a true massless condition. Indeed humans were involved on the large object, and their biology was damaged greatly.

Your experiment was done in an atmosphere of desperation, and your goal was flawed. For your math told you there might be a possibility of invisibility, and that was your goal. This was again because you did not understand that just because the distance between the parts change, it doesn't necessarily mean that the overall size will dramatically change (or that it might vanish). Although this may seem like a paradox to you, the internal mechanics of small particle behavior supports this. The change is measurable, but very small, much like what happens with heat and chill.

The reason that you felt the object would vanish was that you were able to simulate a "vanishing" in the laboratory with smaller objects. This observation was not consistent, however, so you again were in desperation to try this experiment on a larger object. The "vanishing" was an illusion and was due to a distance displacement rather than an "in place" vanishing. Here is the question from me: Since the object was transported instead of vanishing, does this give you a clue to long distance travel using magnetics and the vibratory rate of matter? Only one human on the planet has ever captured a true massless condition, and even this was a coarse one and lasted only for a few moments that were uncontrollable in scope.

Question: Who was the human?

> The writer
> Del Mar, California

Answer: The inventor of your multi-phase electric current, born in the land you now call Yugoslavia.

From the writer...

What follows is the channeling from the March meeting in 1995 in Sedona, Arizona where Kryon began speaking about science and math. Every time this happens I get nervous. I'm a businessman, and when I get letters asking about small particle physics, I want to hide in a closet (since I really don't understand any of it). My small particle behavior knowledge is limited to the ones in my socks when I walk on the beach. The title "The Sedona Surprise" is because Kryon decided to speak of many scientific principles that we hold dear that he says are wrong! I gulped hard knowing the mail I would receive. Thankfully before this book was finished we had reams of work done by knowledgeable mathematicians commenting on what he said. You will find some of this coming up, and also in the two appendices of this book.

Right before the transcription I include a letter received in May (as I was writing this book) from Eléna Johnson. This letter exemplifies some of the miracles of timing that Spirit has brought to many of those who end up in front of me for a Kryon seminar. Typical of the Kryon meetings, this simple gathering of two hundred people in Sedona brought folks from seven or eight surrounding states, and four foreign countries. A raise of hands during the meeting confirmed it.

Eléna had her own amazing story, and I include it right before the actual Sedona transcription.

May 18, 1995

Dear Jan and Lee:

My name is Eléna, and I want to express my gratitude for you and your work in bringing through the Kryon (group). Here is my story. Since around November 1994 I felt an urge to go to Arizona. In January of 1995 my urge turned to urgency, and I knew that Sedona would be a good place to start.

To be brief, this represented a complete upheaval in my life. Should I quit my job? Should I move? Maybe a vacation... should, should. I requested and received a two month leave of absence, and picked a day to leave, March 15th. I arrived in Sedona on March 17th, knowing I had a place to stay for the next ten days. I woke up very agitated on Saturday March 18th wondering "Why am I here? I'm crazy for making this trip," and much more.

Blaming my emotional state on the energy in Sedona, I took a trip to Jerome (a few miles east) to get away from the vortices and to regroup. I did (regroup). I decided life was okay after all and wouldn't it be nice to finish reading my blue Kryon book and have a picnic, maybe at the airport vortex. I drove back to Sedona, got my picnic and headed to the airport summit, when I saw a white box with glitter lettering and an arrow that said "KRYON." I was turning that way and I thought, how weird! Here I am going to read my book and here is a Kryon sign. Oh well, I stopped at the lookout to take a picture.

I continued on, looking for signs of where the vortex might be, when I saw another box with glitter lettering, "KRYON!" ... and parked cars spilled out onto the road. I said out loud, "Okay, universe, what is going on?" I thought, well if this is where I'm supposed to be, then there will be a parking spot up front for me. There was.

I walked to the side door wondering what was going on. I talked to a woman and asked her, and she said that "Lee Carroll was here giving a question and answer talk, and then at 7pm there would be a live channeling session with Kryon." That blew my mind!!! "... and he only started five minutes ago, so you are right on time!!" I asked her how much... "Fifty dollars." I just happened to have $50 on me and gave it to her while I was laughing and crying and telling her my story. She told me I had agreed to be there and it was exactly as it should be (or something like that.) There were two other women who had stories of trust and faith that afternoon and we all shared our stories.

That was a most impactful day in my life (the events of the day), and I really want to thank you both again for your sharing and work with Kryon.

Eléna Johnson
Gresham, Oregon

Kryon

"The Sedona Surprise"
Channel of March 18, 1995

Sedona, Arizona
Kryon Seminar

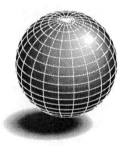

The Kryon Writings, Inc.

PMB 422
1155 Camino Del Mar
Del Mar, California 92014
[www.kryonqtly.com]

"The Sedona Surprise"
Live Channel
Sedona, Arizona - March 1995

This live channel has been edited with additional words and thoughts to allow for clarification and better understanding for the written word.

Greetings! I am Kryon of magnetic service! And so the pause before this greeting was for you, my partner, was it not, for you know that I can hardly wait to speak to these who are before you now. Oh, Dear Ones, some of you sit in such non-belief! And we honor you and we love you nevertheless. For it is difficult for you to believe that such a thing could be as this... messages from beyond the veil, messages from God. The duality is strong among you, and it keeps you from seeing the God-self that each of you has inside. For the communication, if you could see it, would be instant, and you would not need the challenge of tonight's channeling. We have said this many times to you and we will say it again as you become used to the voice of my partner speaking to you now, and become used to the power that is before you, represented by the third language being transmitted to you. For we are filling this room not only with love, but with entities of the Kryon group, that they may stand next to you in the aisles, in back of you and in front of you, and encompass you in their arms saying the following thing: "Oh, Dear One, we know your name!"

Your appointment to be here was absolute. For some of you this is so obvious. To some of you it is less obvious. Each of you with an appointment to sit in the chair you are sitting in now are hearing the words of spirit and sampling the energy of the love from the central source. And the reason that you are motivated to be here to receive this energy is because **it is the energy from home**. You resound to it, and you long for it, and you remember it. So it is with great honor that I say this room is being filled tonight with life changing potential. This, of course, is why you are here!

It may seem odd to you that the Magnetic Master comes to you to heal your hearts and give you information about love. But this is what the Kryon energy is for on this planet. Others will come to you with more specific information about lineage and history and future events, but the Kryon is here to enhance your knowledge and invite you to participate in the feeling of what it is like to be a piece of God from the great Central Source. What follows now, Dear Ones, are discussions about the Universe.

Before we continue, we wish to tell you of some things about your area (*being that of Sedona, Arizona*). For there are many in your area who do not live here and may be interested. Now, some of you are totally aware of what is about to be transmitted, for you sit in the middle of a vortex. Make no mistake: a vortex is not a portal. The portals of the new energy and of the New Age are set up and are static. That is to say, they will not move. They are being built and being prepared in the areas that we have told you about, and they will serve as communication portals from you to the rest of the galaxy. They are indeed the libraries of the planet. This area is not one of those, for this is a vortex. It is an area like a whirlwind would be in your weather, or a whirlpool would be in water. That is to say, there is a great amount of energy in motion in a clockwise manner that you sit in tonight.

It may be interesting for you to know that there is a sister vortex in the country you call Peru, over the great high lake there. It corresponds to this vortex and has a counterclockwise motion. Just as if you were to imagine swirling water, the rocks which stick up within your vortex catch energy, as rocks affect the passage of water. And there is a build up of energy around the rocks, just as eddies and currents are created around rocks in a rushing stream. This vortex that you sit in is not new, dear ones, and you should not confuse it as being part of the New Age. For the ones that lived in this area one thousand years ago knew of the same energy anomalies you feel today. And if you look for it in their writings and in their paintings and in their drawings, they tell of it. For the same kinds of interdimensional things happened then as do now. So it is not new, but it is still felt.

As the energy swirls and builds up against the rocks, the rocks are changed. For they become polarized with the energy which sticks to them. This has been well documented through your ages, and you enjoy the specific information for many sources about the specifics of each large rock. For the polarizations of the rocks correspond many times to positive, negative, male and female feelings, different feelings for different areas depending on the size of the rock and the strength of the vortex.

Here is something you may not be aware of. For the different size of the rocks, the edges which receive the energy, and the edges which are on the other side of the receiving, contain different amounts of energy. How you feel will depend upon which side you are on. Now there are many different things that go on within this energy, for it is swirling motion. Let us talk about the effect on human beings first. Those of you who come here for a short period of time will feel invigorated, for the energy is always in motion here. This is not typical of the energy for the rest of the planet.

The energy of this vortex has an eye similar to the eye of a hurricane, a neutral area in the center. Those humans who live here are very aware of the fact that just as it is an invigorating thing to stand in a shower, it is not necessarily appropriate to stand in the shower all of your life. And so it has a telling effect upon humans. It is not a great area for great agreement (laughter)! In fact, many of you already know this; but there are more of you living in the area, living alone than living together! Those who are living in the neutral area of the eye are not affected by this attribute, but this eye is moving with my changes to your grids very slightly to the northwest. It should not affect how you feel, for those of you who live here have become acclimated. You are used to it, as is human nature.

Now let us talk about the effect of the interdimensional plane. For as the drawings of the ancients will indicate to you, this area is filled with travelers, although they may not be of the kind from the New Age that you would expect. The area of the eye is an invitation for visitation, for the magnetic field is weak in the eye, and therefore it promotes a major amount of interdimensional travel, with the interdimensional visitor being able to enter the vortex through the eye. Sometimes you see these entities as ships. You think they are ships because of their size, when actually many of them are just the size they are, visible to you only in the spectrum you are sensitive to. Sometimes you seem to see some of these beings actually disappear into the Earth, into the ground in a magic way! And so some of you have a mistaken belief that ships have landed and buried themselves into the ground. Actually all you are seeing is the coming and going of an interdimensional entity as it visits the internal energy of Earth through one of the few vortex neutral areas that exist. There is much activity here, but so much of it is not understood by you, since you are dealing with appropriate visitors who do not share your time attributes or your lessons. Therefore they will remain very elusive.

You would also be interested to know this. We have told you that in the New Age you will meet new neighbors. Some of you feel that this (Sedona) will be the place where this meeting will take place. Disappointing to many of you, we say that at this time this is not the best place for that meeting. For there are so many comings and goings already that have been happening for eons of time, that it might not be comfortable where the energy is very intense, such as here, for the new activity that we speak of. At the moment the best place for this new activity to happen is in the country you call Mexico. This can change, and may very well change in the next eight years. And so none of this is news to those of you who have lived in this area. For you are well aware of the energies that are swirling around you, also causing visiting humans to feel so invigorated.

We now wish to speak to you about universal things, and we have waited for this energy to do so as we sit in the eye of the vortex (*being on Airport Mesa in Sedona*). For the information which I channel through my partner now is that of science. And we have waited for a number of reasons until this time. We hoped, dear partner, that you would accept the invitation to be here, and since you have, we honor you for being in the "sweet spot," that of being in the right place at the right time. So the admonition now is that you transcribe all of these words for publication. For even as we speak to you in the now, others are reading these words. Now, you may say, "How can they be reading these words? They are being channeled tonight verbally, and the translation and transcription is not even complete... in fact you haven't given the information yet!" And we say to you that in the "now" there is no future and no past. It is universal time, and the way of things. The past and the future is something which is created for you. There are those reading these words right now even as they are spoken. Confusing perhaps, but this will be clearer as time goes on. Those reading this now will actually have a better understanding of the irony of time than you have as you hear it.

The greatest irony of all of your time attributes is how you perceive yourselves. Universal time is far different from yours. When we say, "It is the way of things," it means we represent the "normalcy" of the workings of the Universe. This means, dear ones, that your Earth time attributes are *not the normal*, and are different from all the rest. You, however, tend to look at your Earth attributes as normal, and try to apply your "normalcy" illusion to us within your search for science answers! It would be like birds in a cage trying to understand how their cage applies to the rest of what they see around them... believing that all birds live in a cage as a normal way of bird life for all birds everywhere. You might understand how this would get in the way of finding how things really work.

What is presented next will be done very basically and very simply, so that all may understand. You are pure light. Light is pure science. Therefore you understand everything at the cellular level. Some of these truths will poke at your cellular information, and some of you will say, "I remember that!" Some of you will be uncomfortable, since you are not yet ready to rediscover what you already know.

We speak first of how you view the cosmos, for your cosmology is now becoming your science. Whereas before this time for all of your history of humanism it has been theory, now you are starting to be able to actually observe the workings of it first hand. It is now time to enlighten you as to what you are seeing.

I take you now to a time three hundred years ago, to the country you call Italy, where there sits in a prison a great scientist. Now, three hundred years is not that long ago, and yet this scientist sits there because he had the audacity to say the Earth revolves around the sun. We speak now of Galileo who published the papers wherein he agreed with Copernicus. He agreed that the math did not indicate that the universe revolves around our planet.

Now, in those days, dear ones, there was an interesting triad of energy. This triad was government, religion and science, and in that time they were all combined into one. There was reason why this should be, for it was human intuition that this should take place. It made sense for the time, but as we join this story we see that it was not serving humans well at all.

The reason it was intuitive and rang true was because it was similar to the way it was in Atlantis and Lemuria, one of the most scientific periods you have ever had. Religion, government and science were one, and the governors were also the priests, and the priests were the scientists. And oh how Spirit longs for you to again put that same triad together so that it would serve you in this new age of wisdom. But you were wise to separate them when you did, for the energy did not support the wisdom it takes to combine them effectively.

Now as it goes, the scientist was soon released, for the math told the truth, even though the priests did not wish to admit it. You honor this man, for much of what he had to say is still your science to this day, and the priests eventually had to alter their belief to support the proof of the numbers and observations. They did it oh so slowly, however.

Much the same thing is going on today, and I will tell you of it now. It seems as you sit here in this modern age, your scientists are convinced that all the matter they see in the universe – the Earth, the solar system, the galaxy and all other galaxies as far as they can be seen – were all caused from one expanding event. They have called this event their "big bang." This is indeed a very illogical scientific premise, although metaphorically it makes the same kind of sense that it did to those three hundred years ago, for it promotes the feeling of oneness with God, and the Earth being a central part of everything else you see.

The truth is this, and as I tell you these things, the eyes will roll in the heads of the scientists, just as they did in the heads of the priests who called themselves scientists before. When you look around the universe, Mr. Scientist, what other event do you find that has only happened one time? The answer is that your observations will show you that there is no other attribute that matches such a premise. In fact, you see just the opposite. You see a myriad of wonderful events of vastly varying types happening all around you. As far as you can see, you discover new types of events happening. In fact, as your sharper telescopes look beyond the areas which were hidden before, you discover even more diversity than you had imagined!

So what is it exactly that would bring you to the conclusion that there was only one expanding creative event? Tell me, when you point your instruments to the farthest reaches of what you can see, do your instruments tell you everything is the same age? It should be, to point to one creation. Even when you take into consideration the "paradox of the clock," you shouldn't find objects very far away that are younger than your own planet... and yet you do.

Tell me, as you look around you, is everything in the universe dispersed evenly as it is traveling away from one point of source? It should be, to support the idea of one creative event.

As you already know, this is not the case! The sharper your instruments become, the clearer the lie becomes, if you will admit it. You see large void areas, and areas that have matter (*galaxies*) "clumped" together. There is no even dispersion, and no "trail" that points to the consistent source of one creative event. It's time to start thinking about a new theory, and then to see how it stands up to what you are actually observing with your new scientific eyes.

The truth is that there were many expanding events spaced over a great amount of time. The truth is that your planet sits among one of many overlapping creative events, some of which were earlier than your own. You would be wise to examine what causes them, for when the next one happens you will not be so shocked. It is pure logic and physical mathematics that determines the creative process of matter. This will eventually be a source of great debate, for again it will shake the foundation of the priests who insist on one creation. How can you limit God in such a fashion? Remember, those born with one color receptor will tell you, "There exists only one color in the universe, and (of course) it is the color of God." Limited only by what you think you see, you tend to impose that truth on <u>all</u> things you see.

Now, some of your scientists say they can prove there was only one event, since they feel they can measure (see) the residue of that event all around them in space. How can you be certain that you are not measuring only the residue of your local event? If your galaxy were suspended in a jar of oil, and everywhere you probed you found oil, would you then postulate that all galaxies everywhere were also in oil? Or would you leave open the possibility that far beyond your measuring senses there were jars of other substances? Such is the logic of your conclusions.

Next we wish to give you an admonishment regarding an experiment that is taking place on your planet that integrates with the Kryon specialty. We are now going to explain to you that some of your governments are experimenting with the transmission of energy through the ground of the planet. Let me explain more about this: envision a tube filled with water that is five miles long and one inch in diameter. Now suppose on one end of the tube you quickly push in a measured amount of water. Instantly at the other end, that same amount of water would push out of the tube, since the tube was already full and would overflow. Now, when you did this, you did not suddenly transmit the water five miles. Instead you simply pushed already existing water a small distance, making the same amount spill out the other end.

Through eons of time your planet has been a collector of static energy. (*We define static energy as energy which is stored and ready to become active.*) Through friction with your atmosphere and what you call the solar wind, your planet's matter is filled with static electricity. You see the results of this when your weather "rubs" the earth violently and displaces the electricity, causing giant sparks you call lightning to occur both above and below the weather event. Within your own electronic terminology, this Earth static energy storage system corresponds to what you have called "the capacitor." Therefore, within the scope of this teaching session, you can look at your planet as a giant electronic capacitor filled with stored electricity.

One of your scientists from only one hundred years ago has already shown the viability of the seeming transmission of energy through the ground of the planet. When doing this, he was taking advantage of the energy already stored in the ground (much the same as the tube of water). When he "pushed" energy into one part of the planet, it appeared to come out of a portal somewhere else. The illusion was that energy had been transmitted, when actually it had only been displaced. One of the problems mathematically with this energy transmission is that it is difficult to target where the energy is going to pop out when you push it in.

Today your science is experimenting with this process, and has discovered that SCALAR waves represent the partial solution to helping to target precisely where the energy will appear. SCALAR experimentation also represents high technological advancement in the entire process of energy transmission.

Here is the admonishment: SCALAR waves are extremely dangerous! More so than you know. We ask specifically to those involved with the experiments to SLOW DOWN. Use lower power experiments. If you do not, you will soon discover the relationship between what you are doing and plate tectonics, the movement of the plates of land that carry your continents. Already, even as this channel is being heard and read, there have been movements caused by your experimentation!

The following information will astound you, and will show you the interworkings of past and future. Dear ones, the world map of the future envisioned by the current human you call Scallion, as well as the frightening visions of those past, is a direct result of human experimentation using scalar waves... and is not a result of some kind of end times spiritual scenario. The result of MYRVA, the death rock hitting your planet (see *Kryon Book Two*), would have caused total termination, not just a difference in your water levels. No living creature would have survived such an event. As previously channeled, MYRVA has been disarmed, but much of what the Hopi saw, and Nostradamus saw, and Scallion now sees, is a direct result of your own scientific endeavors. They all had quality, accurate visions of an Earth with the water levels far different than you have now, with much of your population having moved to the center of your continents to escape the encroachment of the sea on the coastlines.

Dear ones, these visions are a direct result of massive Earth crust shift which can happen easily if pushed a specific way – using a large scalar wave. Please take the time to understand the resonance factors of the Earth's mantle before you continue your experiments.

All of these visions are potential futures for the Earth. I am here not only to balance your grids to facilitate the new age, but also to disarm MYRVA, **and to warn you about your scalar work**. My vision for your future shows something quite different than the others, for I continue to tell you that because of your work, the planet will continue far into the future with enlightenment and vibrations as yet unheard of. Your work has invited me to be here. Because of my presence, you are here tonight. Because you are here tonight, I am able to communicate this admonition. Because of this communication, **there will be those who see it and do something about it**. Do you start to see how you have created your own help? My vision for you is one of peace. The news I bring tonight on this matter will indeed be heard by those who need to hear it. By your sitting in your chair tonight, you have actually changed the future of the planet!

We love you dearly! It is only through your actions that this news could have been transmitted to you tonight. We pause during this scientific discourse to say again that "science is Spirit." And that the love we push into your hearts right now is very much like the energy of the planet. We will not give you any more than you can contain, but oh, you can contain so much more! The ones of you who wish to take the gifts of spirit will be different humans, but it is a fearful experience to ask for change, is it not? This is why we honor you so. I speak now to you personally as you hear and read this. We invite you to walk directly into this fear, and watch it dissipate and turn into the higher vibration that you will create by this action. One of you will absolutely do this tonight. You will understand that indeed you have a purpose for being here. Indeed everything that has happened to you up to this point has focused on the energy transmitted to you right now.

The Kryon purpose is love. Look at the information and realize the impact it can have on the rest of your life. Take the action necessary to make it so. Become a human of the New Age!

Now we would like to speak of the patterns in the grass. We have waited until now to speak briefly about this, since there have been no Kryon channelings regarding this. The reason we have waited is twofold. The first is that we needed the energy of this place and those present to enhance the information. The second is that we wished to have those present who have made these patterns their life's work, and they are here tonight. To these we say, "We know who you are! We have honored you in the past with verification, and now we wish to continue the knowledge in a straightforward way."

What you call "crop circles" is what we call the patterns in the fields. Now, the patterns are made by Spirit in an indirect manner, for they are made actually by the ones you will soon meet. It is all part of your coming of age into a new part of the galaxy. The patterns represent a code transmitted with many facets. The patterns are made all at once, quickly, often in your dawn hours. You can tell a real pattern by the fact that the method of "stamping" does not bend the grass; it breaks it. Those who are making these patterns refer to them as "energy stamps." It does not take any kind of ship or traveling vehicle to do this, and it can be (and is) done from a long distance. The entire reason it is being given to you is to allow you to discern information you are going to need in the future regarding COMMUNICATION.

Imagine for a moment the following. Let's say that some of your scientists decided to try an experiment. They set up a transmitter in space, using their finest electronic equipment, and began sending pictures back to Earth for you to intercept. The experiment was to see if you could figure out how to receive the pictures they were sending. If you, in all your wisdom, decided that you would need only electronic clocks to receive their signals, needless to say you would be disappointed. You would receive no pictures on the electronic clocks. You can see that even though you used an electronic device to try to receive the pictures, it was the wrong one. So it would have been far more helpful if the scientists had given you clues so that you could match up the transmission method with the receiving method. Then you would have a far better chance of obtaining the transmitted information.

So it is, dear ones, that these new ones whom you will some day meet send you the messages in the fields of MATHEMATICS, so that you will understand the universal code of geometry to put together the puzzle, to be prepared for communication. Why geometry? Geometry is the common math of all the universe. The math within the shapes is universal to all computation and is absolute. It is the desired method, therefore, of communication of principles of science.

Now there will be additional "eye rolling" when we say that the patterns in the grass are very much like receiving letters from relatives! Some of you will understand totally when we say, "First come the letters; then come the relatives." Those of you with large families will understand this very well. Those who discount the patterns in the grass will have a revelation when the "relatives" arrive.

The patterns, therefore, are messages of symbols and mathematics from the relatives to you personally. Very much like you sent pictures and symbols on the placards of spacecraft sent out of your solar system for any other life form to see and understand. So it is with the patterns in the field.

Now, there are three reactions to these patterns in the fields. The first reaction comes from humans who firmly believe that the patterns could not be created by anything but other humans. They look at the patterns and they simply go on about their business unimpressed. The second reaction is the dangerous one. For these are the ones who are angry. They see the patterns as being a trick, or a fraud on humanity. So they set out to create their own patterns in the grass that somehow will disprove the origin of the original ones. They mimic and successfully copy the original ones, turning to humanity saying, "See, ours are identical. Therefore the originals are fake."

Now the logic of this is unsound. These say, "Because we are able to mimic and copy these patterns, the originals must also have come from humans." Where is the logic in the statement that if you can copy something, therefore the original is not an original? Although this makes no logical sense, humans have grasped it with both arms and agreed that it must be so. Who is actually doing the tricking here?

This trick of logic is not new. Throughout your history there have been many who have tried to discount the existence of God by mimicking the miracles of God. They have said, "We are able to simulate these seeming miracles by illusion; therefore the originals were also illusion, and therefore God does not exist." Look to the scriptures in the book of Exodus for an example.

The third group are the ones who understand they are seeing the beginning of a new paradigm. These are the ones who sit here tonight that we honor, for these are the ones who will make a difference for the entire planet. These are the ones to whom we give the following information: dear ones, all that is being presented is done to give you good information about the workings of the Universe, and the things to come for your planet. One important code that is currently being transmitted in pattern after pattern is an important message about your planetary mathematics. We tell you this again, to the accompaniment of great scientific eye rolling from your established elders.

All your science and your mathematics is surrounded now by what you call a BASE-10 system. It is convenient for you and it is easy, for it allows quick calculation ability. But galactic math and the math of Spirit is all BASE-12. This is information that is critical for you to know and begin to understand for you to communicate correctly with those who are coming.

What follows are interesting examples of how Spirit has given you hints as to the BASE-12 system for eons, that you have essentially ignored. As we notate each one, perhaps a pattern will emerge in your mind that indeed we have been giving you messages all along regarding the importance of the 12.

1. The first and most important clue is the science of Astrology. OH! The scientists are closing the book! They say, "We knew it! Kryon is going to talk about the occult as if it were science. Magic and mysticism have no part in pure science."

We say again, that the reason Astrology is brought up here is because it is scientific! It is not magic. It is the measurement of magnetics at the time of human entry onto the Earth plane to determine the imprint attributes at the cellular level. When you finally understand how magnetics imprint the cells, you will understand why the magnetics of the solar system relate to your life!

We invite you to look at the base-12 system in Astrology. How many signs of the Zodiac? How many houses? Why 24-hour periods? Why are things laid out the way they are? If this represents magnetics of the planet, moon and stars, what is the significance of it all being base-12? The reason is that Astrology has to do primarily with the Earth. This makes it actual geoscience (*Earth related science*), and all geoscience will be base-12.

2. Next we bring to you another important fact, and it shakes hands so well with Astrology. We speak now of geometry. Now, dear ones, we have already told you that the math of the universe is geometric math. It has to do with shapes, and energies around shapes. We cannot give you a more important message than to look at the metaphoric symbolism around the solutions of common geometric mathematical problems. They actually tell of your lineage, and they tell of man and woman and your relationship to God! All this from the shapes within the circles. At each angle and corner there is news for you which is spiritual. In its beauty and its simplicity it is, dear ones, a base-12 system. And those of you who are mathematical and use geometry will understand the beauty of the recurring sixes, threes and nines. We have told you in past channelings of some of the shapes of the New Age. We have shown you what Kryon looks like, and we have given you hints as to the meaning and beauty of your own Merkabahh. Within all of these there are messages determined by the shapes and colors. Geometry is actually the language of the Universe! We have told you to look for the six-pointed three dimensional star. This star is constructed within a sphere, and spherical geometry is the geometry of the Universe. It also represents all dimensionality. It is indeed filled with beauty far in excess of its simple form... and it is all base-12.

3. Do you see it as an accident that the Jewish calendar of twelve months has survived this long? Why twelve months? you might ask. It is because it is geoscience again. It had to be twelve because it corresponds with the Earth and the system of rotation around the Sun. It only made sense, so it remained a twelve-base system. The same is true for your compass, for it is three hundred and sixty degrees, and is geoscience. It had to be that way, for it corresponds to spherical geometry. It is no mystery that all things related to geoscience represent a base-12, for geoscience represents a circle (as in geometry). What a hint this is that everything to do with the Earth works in twelves!

4. Now my partner wants to interject something humorous. All of those who have made great efforts to bring your society into the metric system will be horrified to find out there are twelve inches in a foot, and thirty six inches in a yard. Is it a mistake that your society originally formed a base-12 measuring system? Why twelve? Why thirty six? Why three feet? Indeed! Do you think this was a hint?

5. Again it is Earth geoscience that demands that there be 24 hours in an Earth rotation, and 12 hours in a day. This means that your body resonates to an internal clock in twelves! Think about it.

6. Now let us take this example into the spiritual. It was no accident, dear ones, that Jacob had twelve sons. And that those twelve sons founded the twelve tribes of Israel. For it is a sacred number! It is universal, galactic math. It is intuitive. And when the New Age master arrived on the Earth, do you think it was an accident that He surrounded himself with twelve disciples? No! For it is universal, galactic math, and it makes sense. Do you think this was a hint?

And now we will tell you something else about this sacred galactic math that again will make the eyes roll in the heads of scientists everywhere on the planet. The number which you call "pi" is incorrect! Dear ones, why would Spirit give you such an irrational number within the sacredness of geometry? The number for pi does not go on forever. Also of interest is that your pi is relative only to your own time frame. Universal pi is different from yours. This will only become clear when you understand what time does to spherical shapes (there is a an actual physical relationship change). Therefore pi must be adjusted to correspond to the time frame of the shape! Even within the universe that you can see, there are many values for pi, since there are many areas that have their own specific time/space attributes. Each separate area is therefore relative to its own physics.

7. Those of you familiar with sound healing are already working closely with a musical scale that is common to most Earth musical instruments. Did you ever wonder why we gave you twelve basic musical steps? This is so powerful, it is amazing that you have not immediately plugged it into your mathematics! How do the vibrational attributes of the twelve musical steps correlate to math? It shouts base-12!

8. Let us bring this example list finally to your biology. Dear ones, you have been told by other channels something which has been discussed by Kryon as well: that you have twelve strands of DNA. Why do you think there are twelve? For those who don't believe you have twelve, we ask you then to simply look at the two you do believe in. When you look at the two visible biological strands, what do you see in the organization of them? The answer is that you see the pattern of **four repeated three times**.... over and over and over. So your biology and your DNA structure is base twelve! We also ask those who have studied the ancient science of acupuncture, "How many meridians did the masters teach you were on each side of the human body?" Naturally the answer is twelve!

We ask you to ponder these things. From the biological to the spiritual to the geometric... all the way to astrology. It is accurate and true, and lying there for you to see. And the patterns in the grass tell you these things and encourage you to look at a base-12 mathematical scenario. It says, "Start understanding and using base-12, for you are going to need it when the relatives arrive."

9. Finally we say this for you to ponder the "hints" we have given you regarding using twelve as your base. When you and Spirit planned the important "passing of the torch" for the entire Earth (as channeled in this book), you could have used any date you wished to be symbolic as to the importance of the day. Together we chose 12:12. When you multiply twelve times twelve you get 144. This represents the sacred number of those 144,000 who were asked to take ascension status on this 12:12 date.*

And now, dear ones, we are going to do something that Kryon loves to do. We are going to tell you a story. This will be the story of "Aaron, and the globe of essence." Now, Kryon gives you these

---

* From the writer: Also note, our national USA power grid is 120 volts, 60 cycles! And did you know that all our films are projected at 24 frames per second?

parables and these stories on purpose, for they are metaphoric and usually do not represent an actual person on Earth. These parables and these stories are given to you in love... oh, such great love. For they have to do with self awareness, and they have to do with healing, and they have to do with long, long potential lives of humans.

So Aaron was on the Earth as a wealthy man. And when Aaron was in his fortieth year he was disturbed by what he saw in the mirror. For what he saw there was a man who was beginning to change and age. All around him he saw his friends catching various diseases, and many of them were dying. And he said, "What can I do that would change this? Surely there must be an answer to this."

Now, Aaron was a Godly man with a great lineage, so he said to himself, "I will use my wealth to discover what I can about what some have called the fountain of youth." And so he went to a very wise man and asked him, "Does the fountain of youth exist?" The wise Shaman said to him, "Not exactly, but there is something we know of as the "globe of essence." It is real and it is physical; it will extend your life and will heal your disease. It will also give you great wisdom." Aaron said, "Oh wise man, tell me, where can I find this globe of essence?" And the wise man said, "Well, one of the ways is to find the chalice of Christ." "Oh," Aaron said, "No! that is the holy grail, and I do not believe in that. My religion does not support that Christ was God." And the wise man smiled and said to Aaron, "Aaron, believe it or not, the *globe of essence* and the *chalice* and the *holy grail* were all carried within the Ark of the Covenant." Aaron thought, how can this be? The Ark was considerably before Christ. Aaron ignored this last statement from the Shaman, pursuing only what he heard that interested him.

Aaron said, "Where can I find this?" The wise man said, "It is for you to have if you choose, for we can see your contract clearly, for you to have if you choose, for we can see your contract clearly, and we know that you could be the one to find it. All you have to do is begin your search and trust God to lead the way." Aaron was very excited, for he interpreted this to mean that he was the one scheduled to find the globe of essence for the planet! Once the globe of essence was discovered, Aaron thought, think of those he could help and heal. For he would have a long life, as well as those around him... his friends, his relatives. Oh, this was even better than he had thought. He believed the wise man, for there was no reason not to.

So Aaron began his search saying, "Where shall I go first?" Answering his own question intuitively he said, "I will go first to those spots on the planet which I know have the highest energy." So he came to Sedona (audience laughter). He searched all around, and he spoke to the guardians of the canyons. The guardians said, "It is not here. You must look other places." So his trip took him to some of the most sacred places on the planet. And he said, "Where is the highest religious place?" Again answering he said, "It is my home! I will go there." So Aaron went to the holy land and sat in front of many religious leaders, some of whom had never heard of the globe of essence, and some of whom said, "Yes, we have heard and we know. Continue your search; indeed, you are one who will find it."

So Aaron went into the other areas, the areas of Egypt which were close by. He asked them the same questions and got much the same result. He went to the land of Peru and to the land of India. He sat in front of some who said they personally were the globe of essence; that all he would have to do was to remain with them and give them his attention and his possessions. They repre-sented the globe of essence and he would have a long life as long as he remained with them. Aaron knew better, for he knew that it was an object, something that he could touch, and that it was for all humanity.

Now, this search of Aaron's took him many, many years; he was growing older the entire time, and he was changing. This was frightening him, and so Aaron started to worry. The worry he had interrupted his body's function, and Aaron became sick.

Aaron was on his death bed surrounded by those who loved him. He knew he had not found the globe of essence. He was starting to doubt the wise man that he had seen. "What kind of trick is this?" he said. "What has God done to me?" Aaron was very tired, and longed to sleep.

The next morning he awoke, and this time he stood up. As his guides came closer to him, he realized that he had indeed passed on. Aaron was not happy at this moment, and he said to his guides, "I know who you are, and I know where I am going. What foolish trick is this that I had not found the globe of essence, for I was told by the holy man that I would. Have you deceived me?"

His guides smiled at him, and in perfect love they embraced him with their energy. And they asked him to turn around and look behind him. There in the place where Aaron had lain was the globe of essence! There it was! It was physical, and he could touch it, and it had been in his heart the whole time.

Aaron looked around the table at his relatives and he was shocked! For among those living humans that were sobbing and devastated by his passing... in each one was a globe of essence as well.

Then Aaron understood there was not just one globe of essence. "It was for all humanity," the wise man had said. "You will find it if you search," the wise man had said. But the wise man never said there was only one! And then Aaron knew. And he looked at his guides and he understood. He smiled back and he said, "Thank you. For now I understand my contract, and my lesson." Aaron also understood that all things learned during his lifetime would be passed on to his next incarnation, and he could hardly wait. For he knew of the trip through the tunnel – through the cave where the record is kept of his incarnations. And then on to the hall of honor, and after that the planning sessions and the return to the planet. For when he returned, he knew that he indeed would be the one to find the globe of essence. He would do it as a child, and he would live a very long life. For he would remember this time, and remember the lesson that the globe of essence is the gift of the piece of God within.

Now, dear ones, this parable is not lost on any of you. For there are those of you who sit in this time and in this place by appointment. Some of you who sit in these chairs have growing in you the potential for death. This is not a frightening thing that Kryon talks about, for all of you know that it is simply the way of your biology. But Spirit gives you the ability to reach out and discover the holy grail, for this is the globe of essence which is **Spirit in you**. It is the piece of God that resides in each of you. We have given you channeled information that says, "Reach out and take it and be healthy. Live a long time. Be in your sweet spot. We want you to remain. We don't want you to pass on at all. Live very long lives. Be the warriors of the New Age."

But some of you are saying, "This cannot be, because I look around me and I do not see what you are telling me." And we say to you that when enough of you do this, you indeed will look around you and see the change. But it must start here in this room, and rooms like this all over the planet. You carry with you the seeds of God. We invite you to reach inward and discover the reality of this, and the geometry, and the peace that comes with it.

I come to you and say it is the personal entity Kryon, not the group around the Kryon, that sits at your feet this night. For I come as the master came, to wash your feet. For you are the exalted ones. You are the ones who have chosen to be here and live these lives over and over. You have chosen to have the pain and the suffering of human biology, and the discomfort of human emotion in order to simply raise the planet's vibration. And for that your colors will be known throughout the entire Universe. This is the reason I am here. This is the reason we are here. This is the reason you sit in the chair this night... to hear Spirit say, I love you.

And so it is.   *Kryon*

From the writer...

Some months ago I received a letter from a man named James Watt. Mr. Watt carefully put forward some questions that showed me that although he was fascinated with some of the numerology in the Kryon book, he did not claim to be any kind of metaphysical believer. In fact, the Kryon book was given to him by his mother. He became interested in the Kryon writings because statements made in the first Kryon book meshed exactly with math logic he had discovered, and was showing around the mathematics community. James wrote me, "How can such precise statements be made from a human source if there is no previous logic model upon which to build it? The channelings simply do not suggest a human source. This is a difficult, if not impossible, concept for a 'realist' to fully accept!"

I answered his questions the best I could (not being math based at all), and we started corresponding. Each letter became more fun, since James was getting deeper and deeper into the basic questions of the universe via geometry and mathematics. Each time I would answer, he found something interesting in the correspondence, and so did I. I felt we were developing into the classic "odd couple." He found my logic refreshing in an arena where seemingly it's never used, and I found his ideas astoundingly metaphysical (but I didn't really tell him that, since I was uncertain if it would offend him).

James will tell you that he is not classically trained mathematically. (Thank God!) Otherwise I don't believe he would be so open to consider the spiritual aspects of what it all means. He calls himself an amateur mathematician. I would point out to the readership that this lets Mr. Watt join the ranks of other amateurs such as Francois Viete (father of cryptology and the decimal point use), John Napier (inventor of logarithms), Isaac Asimov, Euclid, Archimedes, and Apollonius... whew! What does he do for a living? He is a visual artist, specializing in illustration, particularly architectural. The architectural part explains his love for geometry.

It became obvious right away that I was dealing with a high-end math guy, with great integrity and a spiritual quest. The quest wasn't necessarily New Age as many think of it, but definitely spiritual and metaphysical (as I define it, anyway). James is using his intellect and intelligence within a very logical science (math and geometry) to tie in the spiritual truths of life. I honor him greatly for this. What a quest!

Watt characterizes himself as a "just the facts, ma'am" kind of person. He is far more at home in mathematics and logic than in the subject of channeling. To him, the object of study is either "true," "false" or "undetermined." I guess that's why I liked him so much – I can really relate to this!

After the Kryon Sedona channeling about math and science that you have just read, I contacted James to tell him what Kryon had said about our math system, and I invited him to write whatever he wanted in rebuttal... or agreement. I have also been intrigued regarding concepts James has found regarding our math system which may very well have been passed over by the mainstream math community... and they have spiritual connotations!

Keeping our correspondence "clean" of trying to convince the other one of any doctrine went unsaid, and gave us both a true feeling of the other's respect for what we really were after... SOLUTIONS! So I am honored to present Mr. Watt's work to you as a mainstream mathematician responding to the Kryon work. We worked together for a few months, and all the while James became more convinced that Kryon was real... from the math hints that Kryon was giving! (Don't miss Kryon's comment to James on page 369, or James' final letter to me on page 370).

I warned you earlier that some math was coming, and this is it. I invite even the most non-numeric of you to scan what James has to say, and just skip over the numbers if you wish. You may be looking at something (even though you might not understand it) that will have great significance in the future of mainstream science. If so, then you will understand the reason why I met James at all, and his work is in this book.

Those of you who are interested in what Mr. Watt had to say about the 9944 can also go to Appendix B, where he presents a short discussion, and some further interesting comment. If some of you wish to have additional numerical and geometric discussions around James work, you can write to the address given in this book, and I will forward your letters to Mr. Watt. Just put "Attention James Watt" on the envelope.

The real fun for me came after James had finished this article. At the last possible moment before the book was to go to press, he believed he found one of the most profound proofs of the base-12 system yet, and it all revolves around prime numbers (look at the boxed paragraph on page 323). James and I both thank Kryon for all the "hints."

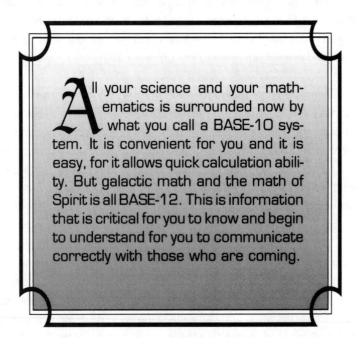

All your science and your mathematics is surrounded now by what you call a BASE-10 system. It is convenient for you and it is easy, for it allows quick calculation ability. But galactic math and the math of Spirit is all BASE-12. This is information that is critical for you to know and begin to understand for you to communicate correctly with those who are coming.

...from page 292

Mathematica
Sole author, James D. Watt, 1995
Portions of this manuscript are under separate
copyright in the Library of Congress

Introduction:

I began an investigation of fundamental mathematics over two years ago as a result of questions raised by the current physics model of creation known as "The Big Bang." It became apparent at an early point that curved form fits the bill for mathematical descriptions and that the core operational assumptions of mathematics from the most ancient days and continuing into our own are biased in terms of the straight line.

If one returns to those founding elements and techniques of mathematics, one sees that there are only two choices in how to express mathematical concepts: straight line math (which we use ubiquitously) and curved, or line-arc mathematics, which is rejected.

26 centuries of tradition and exploration/exploitation of straight-line mathematics have enshrined this format in the mathematically minded, as a sacred agenda to be protected at all costs. This is an important statement, because it contradicts the objectivity that mathematicians claim. It can be clearly demonstrated that modern mathematics is agendistic and should be seriously questioned in its abandonment of "absolutes" and fascination with "self-contained logic systems."

Where a general definition of mathematics may be "a study of universal true possibilities and their description," we now have a conglomeration of Byzantine structures built on the deck of a ship from which the rudder has been removed. The fact that mathematics is the domain of the most thorough and brilliant logicians mankind has ever produced intimidates in a uniquely profound way those who would criticize the current conduct.

Logic is the primary tool of the mathematician. It is an excellent one. Logic demands that something be "true, false or undetermined." It reduces an exercise down to core elements for this determination. The fact that logic is such an intrinsic part of mathematics lulls many into an opiated state that "all is well."

What is forgotten (or minimized) is that there is a weak link in any mathematical exercise. This is the **a priori** (self-evident assumptions) upon which those logic exercises are built. Every true mathematician is aware of the ancient exemplary story of "the commensurate problem." It is an examination of two arbitrary lines whereby a third is found which contains the ratio of the other two in whole units. This seemed to be an easy truth, until it was examined by logic, which in turn led to the finding of **irrational numbers** (numbers which can't be expressed as clean fractions). This finding nearly wrecked, and surely stunted, the growth of Greek "scientific numbers" (arithmetic).

The Greeks maintained that arithmetic was the "mother of all other maths." It was non-numerical geometry which disproved the notions of a universe expressed entirely in whole number concepts. This lesson of the ancients was neither fully understood (with very mitigating circumstances for the ancients) and is ignored in modern mathematics. Today non-numerical geometry is all but snubbed by the mathematics community at large. They have adapted, a la Descartes (the father of **Modernism**), a carte blanche allowance that all logic can be accomplished in algebraic/number theory means. Further, a la Descartes again, they accept and enshrine as sacred that all forms can be expressed using the right angle and a few other straight line geometric formulas (i.e. Pythagoras' Theorem). In short, the entire study of universal phenomena is accomplished strictly in terms of the straight line.

There is reason for this. It is a little arithmetic statement of **N+1** (**N** is any **N**umber) which is the founding arithmetic assumption that, "you can always add one to something." If you start with 1 and add 1 to it in infinite fashion what do you get? You get an arithmetic <u>straight</u> line 1+1+1+1+1... and you have agreement between non–numerical geometry of straight line architecture of form, and linear expansion of number theory. From this are descended all other mathematics disciplines. One should be aware that no matter how exotic the handle stuck in front of some modern mathematical exercise, it is still, at its core, either arithmetic, geometry or some combination of the two. There are no exceptions to this.

Our modern mathematics, with which we have sent men to the moon, is essentially unchanged since the days when men fought each other with weapons of bronze and iron from chariots! The solid and fixated tradition of our math is vigorously defended against questioning the ubiquitous use of straight line terms, in spite of **no** evidence of straight line terms governing natural form. Regarding the assumption of light as naturally traveling in straight lines, for instance, we are simply assuming this, blithely discounting that its natural order may be a currently undetectable arc. Why should light be any different from the rest of nature? The math community defends a traditional and agendistic approach which has devolved into a kind of cult of past personalities being favored over the founding principles of objectivity and unity. They feel that since straight line terms can not find unity, it therefore doesn't exist. Rather than math being countenanced as in error, they say unity and truth don't exist in absolute terms. By this they lay the groundwork in logic to fragment all other human endeavors. It is an astonishing case of collective hubris.

Why should the choice of line character (straight or line-arc) matter? Isn't it a case of "six of one, a half-dozen of the other?" **It is not!** Currently math assumes an easy equality and denies a hierarchical state. This equality allows the qualification of line-arc forms in straight line terms (**pi** is the classic example). Where the Greeks had **hoped** this equality was true, modern math is determined to **force** the universe to comply with egocentric wishes of making a round peg fit snugly into a square hole. When boiled down to essentials, this is the chief aim of calculus.

What determines, in an absolute way, the character of straight and curved lines? A **straight line** is "a series of similar points having **no relation** to points outside the series." A **curved** line is "a series of similar points **having relations** to point(s) outside the series." This is obvious. Draw a curved line and you see an "interior" and "exterior" implied. Further, if one does two bisections of any segment of that curve, the bisectors will intersect at the center point(s) of that line. So at a minimum **2 points** are needed for a straight line, and **3** are intrinsically present in a curved line. The third point (center point, i.e.) is not always overt, but is easily found. It is like a secret the line-arc tries to keep.

Logic extensions inevitably show straight lines as being **always** and indisputably **interior** to a circle (static geometry). This is what Euclid was at pains to keep out of his geometry (which, of course, we still use today, except it is expressed in arithmetic [analytical geometry]). I have found at least 15 verified errors in Euclid's geometry which are either currently obscured and censored from general readership or completely "unknown." They consistently point to an agendistic approach on Euclid's part. Euclid's geometry was an exercise in saving Greek arithmetic as a result of the "commensurability dido." While he is to be commended for his efforts to **save scientific numbers**, the modern mathematician should be challenged for cult worship of **human** mathematics touted as being "objective."

Again, why should the character of line matter? **Since** all straight line structures can be easily demonstrated to be interior only to some circle constant, a two-point element of examination will **never** magically become a **three-point** element. This means no matter how many sides you assign to some "regular polygon in a circle" (this is simply a triangulated figure of equal portions where the center of a circle is the inside corner of each isosceles triangle and the opposite side's endpoints touch the circumference; it's a lot like dividing a pie into equal portions), the sides will never intersect more than two points on the circumference and therefore will never qualify as being a line-arc, falling short of exact measure, being therefore at best an approximation of the circumference's true measure (**2pi**).

The other way to "take the measure of **pi**" is to do so with number theory (the "mother" of all maths). By using sequential series in calculations we have approximated **pi** out to incredible numbers of decimal places. By number theory we have proclaimed **proven** that **pi** is an "irrational and transcendental" number, meaning it goes on "forever in non-repeating series." But we are relying on fundamental number theory **a priori** (assumptions) to be true for that logic to stand. Essentially we say **pi** is "irrational and transcendental" because "you can always add **one** to something."

This then gives you a little introduction into where things stand in modern mathematics. Behind the mostly incomprehensible pronouncements which occasionally come from the ivory tower are some very simple principles which remain unresolved, that many sincerely wish would go away. The weapon of choice for the modern mathematician is to say "there is no absolute truth," or "all that is required for viable math is that it be logically self-consistent," or when these don't work, "math is like a game of chess; you can't change the rules." These are their sacred mantras they chant when confronted by contradictions. Is our mathematics **fundamentally in error**? I believe so. Many mathematicians secretly believe there is error. Most assign the "unknown error" to some portion of set theory. Far fewer opine that the error might be found in Cartesian cavalier disregard for original Euclidean caution regarding magnitude studies (books 6 through 13). I believe I am alone in stating that the error is anciently conceived in Pythagorean mathematics concepts which (though denied) are still with us today: in particular the **assumption**, "you can always add one to something."

You Can Always Add One to Something

The Pythagoreans were an astonishing group of devotees to a master named Pythagoras. They were the first group of people to look to "scientifically derived number theory." By this they meant to divorce all human prejudice out of number theory and plumb the depths of the Universe, on the Universe's own terms. They almost did it too. Had they had the concept of zero and the ability to add numbers in columns (this was missing in Western mathematics also up to about 600 years ago), they would have derived number theory the way the Universe does, indeed, do numbers.

They decided numbers were relative increments of measuring and that these could be applied to the Universe. Since the Universe was the sum of "everything to be studied," it was the "grand **One**," or "**Unity**." The obvious diversity of nature (and the fact that you and I both exist independently of each other) they called this "**ability** of **unity** to diversify-" the **Dyad**. These two concepts are still with us today. Their "Dyadic operation" is our "**squaring**" (now you know where squaring comes from). On the above, ancient records are very clear. It gets fuzzy after that, however. The Pythagoreans made a logic jump and added the assumption "you can always add one to some number." Why? Because they couldn't get the **Unity/Dyad generator** to work. They "jumped" to a self-evidency that $1+1 = 2$, $2+1 = 3$, etc. based on common observation. This in turn is the sole justification for infinity.

Since unity is the sum of its parts, our measuring device (numbers) must, in its least parts, calibrate to the total. It doesn't matter **how many** units one settles on, only that they "calibrate the unity." This is where the idea of **number base** comes from. It is completely arbitrary. Since we are trying to measure something, it is handy to make the units "uniform." Why should we needlessly complicate things? Our fingers are "handy numerators," so why not use them?

It is important to note that the fact that our base is arbitrary indicates that the study of magnitudes is an **arbitrary science**. It was an error, continued to this day, on the part of the Pythagoreans to insist that numbers "are the mother of all other maths." How can the arbitrary (arithmetic) be the "mother of geometry" when geometry is a universal **constant** (a compass does what a compass does, oblivious to what numbers are used to describe it). Is it not paradoxical then, that non-numerical geometry is all but snubbed by modern mathematics?

"Scientific numbers" must then be derived from geometric constants, not the other way around, as is currently practiced. This was the chief art of Euclid. He made it seem as though there was an equality between line-arc and straight line, where one could be used to interpret the other. He suppressed vital information about the line-arc, broke up geometrically unified phenomena (side/angle bisectors in all triangles, i.e.), attached false riders to postulates, common notions and definitions and failed to complete theorems to their logical conclusion – all of which I can prove to be the true case. He did this with consistency of forethought. He did it for admirable reasons, too: to save Greek math after the "commensurability dido." His efforts were extraordinary and not yet fully understood by the modern mathematics community, because they continue to wallow in scholastic arcanery concerning his work.

Back to numbers. These "units" (fingers) are the "least irreducible reflections of the unity." That is, each unit is a whole entity in itself, possessing all the qualities of the original unity's integrity. Since these units are "reflections of the unity," one could say, "well, I can further reduce, by the same operation to unity, the units themselves... so where does the "irreducible" hold sway? This is a "universal yardstick" if one wants to make a "unit yardstick" go ahead. If I have a yardstick, I only have 36 inches to that yard stick. I can further subdivide, by the same logic, those inches if I want. This is why units are a "reflection of the unity."

What we **do** have now is a grand "one" (**unity**) and a local "one" (**unit**). How does one calibrate the two so that they are in agreement within the system? This is what stumped the Pythagoreans, and is still unresolved today. We have failed to **calibrate unit to unity** (so we ignore it). And this is where the Dyadic operation (squaring) comes to play.

If I decided to use the number of my fingers for the base (base 10), I write a mark for each finger like this:

$$11111 \quad 11111$$

By applying the Dyadic operation (squaring) to it I get:

$$1111111111^2 = 12345\underline{67900}987654321$$

Note that the **8** is missing in the **ascending** sequence. How can this be? Is it a fluke? Through any number of calculations one can do, this missing 8 in the ascending series won't materialize as an intrinsic member of the series! Further, an amazing amount of high symmetry immediately arises bearing out that this is exactly "what the universe intends." The reciprocal of **8** is **125** (integers for **unity**, **Dyad**, and **middle integer**, **base 10**).

Some quick snapshots of symmetry resultant are as follow:

- $123456790 \times 8 = 98765432$
- $^1/_{.1111111111} = 9$
- $^1/_{.1111111111}{}^2 = 9^2 = 81$
- $^{\sqrt{9.87654321}}/_{2.2222222222} = \sqrt{2}$
- $^1/_{.987654321} = 1.0125$
- $^{987654321}/_8 = 12345\underline{67}901234... = ^1/_{9}{}^2$

Again, **nowhere** in the <u>integrated</u> mathematics (which even we can't avoid) will you ever find the missing **8** in the ascending series. It simply does not occur! **If** you add the figure in, you are imposing "non-native" conditions in the series and you immediately get **asymmetry**, as in:

$$\sqrt{1234567\underline{8}9} = 11111.111\underline{06} \ !$$

The "authority" of unity math is that <u>nothing</u> ascends except that it has first descended. There is a number hierarchy extending **down** from that unity. You cannot go up and down the sequences as if there were no difference between them. This phenomenon is born out in geometry as well as in the nature of triangles, which I can show by proof to exist as a fundamental condition of mathematics (this is one of Euclid's artful obscurings with circumscription and inscription of triangles).

This brings us to the Pythagorean logic jump of "you can always add one to some number." **No, you can't** – for two reasons: The first is, unless you have demonstrated calibration of the **ones**, by forfeit of logic you are saying, where **N=1**, that **1** is unity and **N+1** is in reality **unity + 1**. You have just abrogated your condition of **unity**!

The second reason is <u>since</u> (not if) the **8** is always missing in the ascending series, every time you do some "universal number calculation," i.e. **pi**, you will hit a "glitch" at the **8th** operation and wing off into error! IF you assume **N+1** is a universal concept, all your calculations for universal phenomena are in error. **N+1** is a local and uncalibrated statement, invalid for universal calculations. What we have, by ubiquitous use of **N+1**, are some very good **approximations**. These approximations have lulled us to assume that the math techniques are correct and the asymmetry is a phenomenon of the universe, not our erroneous math. But if you think you're going to discover the "theory of everything" with this math, you are deluding yourself.

This format is not the place to go into the detail required to demonstrate the veracity of what I say. There is consistent, ample evidence already completed in both geometry and number theory, parts of which have already been seconded independently.

The reason this section is included in book three of the Kryon Writings is something of an extraordinarily set of events. I have not been overly concerned with things like numerology and channeling, rather the opposite. My mother gave me a copy of the first book to look at for my opinion. I zeroed in on the **666** section and applied unity number theory to it. At first I was very skeptical, but the more I looked at it, the more I saw something very unique running through the commentary that is not quite apparent at first.

It was quite easy to "break the code" of **666**. I have become quite used to the **unity mathematics** answering what are riddles using standard mathematics. I should say, on the other hand, I haven't figured any symmetry to **9944** mentioned, but I think it **is** mathematical.*

See Appendix B "Watt's solution to 9944."

Since I am not a numerologist, once I broke the code, it seemed to me that it was too simple and I must not have 'gotten it.' After all, scholars have been trying for 20 centuries to break it. I checked out a couple of numerology books at the town library to see what these books said about it. There was next to nothing, beyond "we don't know."

What I did was to break the number down into its primes, which are $666 = 37 \times 3^2 \times 2$. I also found in the numerology books that for centuries numerologists assigned the **888** as "the divinity of Christ." Breaking that number into primes you get $888 = 37 \times 3 \times 2^3$! Look at the **3**s and **2**s in the two numbers; their "character" is the reverse of each other! It seems obvious to me, in some arcane book somewhere, someone else must have broken **666** into primes also and then invented the **888** "antidote." So I wrote to Lee Carroll and asked him "if he knew the significance of **37** (37 is the sum of 1+2+3+4+5+6+<u>7+9</u> the **unity mathematics ascending series**). According to his sources, **37** has not received much attention from numerologists and was considered rather unremarkable.**

What happens is that there is a verifiable numerological symmetry intrinsic in regular mathematics and physics constants involving 37 in a major way! And it also seems to occur with previously unknown frequency in what little I know of numerology.

** *From Lee: Oops! Subsequently I have found out that although the numerologists don't analyze 37 as significant, the Sacred Scholars do! The gematria of 37 means "God," "only Son," "only begotten," "power," "glory," "Holy Master," and "The head of the corner."*

Kryon says that **27** is a significant number to him. check the following sequences out:

- $^{27}/_{999} = ^1/_{37}$, $^{37}/_{999} = ^1/_{27}$ and of course 37 x 27 = 999

- 9+9+9 = 27, $^1/_{27} = .037037037...$, $^1/_{37} = .027027027...$

- 27+37 = 64 = 8^2 = 2^6 = $(^1/_{125})^2$

- $\sqrt{27} + \sqrt{37} = 10[^1/_{(\sqrt{37} - \sqrt{27})}]$

The whole of "triple numbers" is as follows:

111 = 37 x 3	444 = 37 x 3 x 2^2	777 = 37 x 3 x 7
222 = 37 x 3 x 2	555 = 37 x 3 x 5	888 = 37 x 3 x 2^3
333 = 37 x 3^2	666 = 37 x 3^2 x 2	999 = 37 x 3^3

If you sum up any of the triple digit numbers, i.e. **4+4+4 = 12, 12 x 37 = 444**. In other words, the numbers are cyclical! The only common element of all the triple numbers is **37**! Is **37** the abomination referred to in the apocalypse of St. John? Or is it referring to the fact that our standard understanding of mathematics is the "abomination?" To wit, "by assuming to **ascend without authority** to the knowledge of the universe, we seek to shape the universe according to our own egocentric and erroneous designs. For certainly any assignment of particular meaning to the number 37 is missing in **both** standard mathematics and numerology. And what is the Bible story "The Tower of Babel" about, if not unauthorized ascension? Again, how does Jesus cite his authority to teach? It is "descended from God!" And Christ only ascends after having descended!*

*Also see Revelations 17:10-11. "And the beast that was, and is not, even he is the **eighth**..." The seven "Kings" may be interpreted as geometrical divisions. First King – point. Second King – line. Third King – triangle... etc. Seventh King (not yet come) is a heptagon (seven-sided regular polygon). This is a "mathematically impossible construction." The fit of the interpretation is even tighter than space here permits.

What is fascinating about this is that these instances indicate a unity math logic and make little or less sense under the standard mathematical philosophy. Nor could they have been "invented" by their authors, since their modeling logic was the same as we still use in mathematics! They are strong indications of the reality of "divine revelation," writing something down without knowing the reasoning except that "one must do it." Other consistencies attest to some form of "knowledge different from the standard." Check First Corinthians 1:22–24.

Some other numerological items occur in conjunction with the "triple numbers." All of them times some multiple or divisor of 18 equal **1998.*** While this is not mathematically exceptional, considering the numerological facet which seems rather potent, and **Kryon's** dates of operation, Lee thought I should provide it as part of this inclusion.

$$111 \times 18 = 1998 \qquad 222 \times 9 = 1998 \qquad 333 \times 6 = 1998$$
$$444 \times 4.5 = 1998 \qquad 555 \times 3.6 = 1998 \qquad 666 \times 3 = 1998$$

777 (is a standard 7 division sequence, long admired in mathematics as an elegant curiosity)

$$888 \times 2.25 = 1998 \qquad 999 \times 2 = 1998$$

Lee's note: remember that 1998 is a numerology 27 (Kryon's "important number" or 9. 18 is also a 9.

Further, I found that $888 \times 2 = $ **1776**. Lee beat me to the punch and found that $^{1998}/_{1776} = $ **1.125**, (which is a unity mathematics symmetry of **Unity**, **Dyad** and **middle integer base–10**). This **125 symmetry** abounds in significant ways throughout standard math.*

So, is the mystery of **666** deciphered? I think so. The mystery is that our mathematics system is uncalibrated and we can expect dire consequences by refusing to adjust it. On the other hand, if we simply calibrate the ones, we will enter into that "new golden age" where

*An amusing note – 50 states minus the 13 original colonies = 37!

theology and science are in perfect agreement because both are finally dealing with the truth (the truth is **ONE**).

Which brings me to the next point. I was privileged in that Lee Carroll sent me, prior to publication, a **Kryon** channeling that the universe actually uses a "**base-12**" system. He asked me if there was any mathematical credence to such a statement.

This question goes a long way to showing how thick-skulled we humans can be. For two years I had been looking at circle constant geometry wondering, "why does the circle divide naturally into **6** parts (hexagon)? I had the unity math of the "missing integer" and all the ingredients to say, "Ahaa! A universal system must be **base-12** (six is the middle integer, and the base-12 equivalent of our 10 is the system's missing integer). The evidence is much more insistent than these points alone. The pentagon yields a fascinating ratio discovered and proved by Euclid and called the "**golden ratio**." This is a **geometric constant**. A constant is a mathematics statement which is unalterable and holds for all situations. The golden ratio holds for a condition native to the circle's divisions regardless of what base it might be described in arithmetically, or what part of the universe you are running the compass through its paces in. It describes the relation of the pentagon (five sided regular polygon) sides and angles to each other and is considered the most perfect of geometric symmetries possible.

In its geometric function it is acting in exactly the same capacity as the missing **8** of the ascending order in base-10. Further, the fact that the circle divides naturally on the secondary level (the primary division is that the compass "walks around the circle" exactly **6** times) into triangles (three sides) and squares, etc. (four sided figures) shows that the circle is a **base-12 phenomenon**.

Some interesting things occur arithmetically with the golden ratio as well. Some are well known and others may be presented here for the first time. I am currently having them checked for "prior knowledge" by those more knowledgeable in the history of mathematics.

In Arithmetic the golden ratio is expressed as $\sqrt{5}+1/2$! Note that it is in terms of **Unity (1)**, **Dyad (2)** and **middle integer**, **base (5)**! This is no accident, nor is it an isolated symmetry. One finds the **1**, **2** and **5** presence to be an overwhelming rule of arithmetic. One of the best known symmetries is 'the ratio of all numbers in Fibonacci series is the golden ratio.' Fibonacci was a medieval mathematician who discovered that symmetrical patterns of growth are found in simple conditions applied to numbers. You can find out more about him through any number of math books in your local library. The classic Fibonacci sequence story is of a farmer buying a mating pair of rabbits and figuring out how many he will have if the rabbits give birth to bunnies on a monthly basis. He can know how many rabbits he will have at any given month (assuming the rabbits live forever)! Another way of stating the "ultimate" relation of Fibonacci series is, "**all** numbers, by addition of **1** to the reciprocal of that number, in sequential operation will proceed to **become** the golden ratio. In short, no matter how random or long the number you can concoct, it is **intrinsically** related to the golden ratio.

I am going to write out some mathematics notations for some figures. I know that the vast majority of readers will get a dull headache and look to put this material down. This is a result of misery incurred in school days in poorly taught math classes. I promise you, you can understand these notations, as I will walk you through them and you will see they are not "mystifying," only a commonly agreed shorthand. A little later I will include a couple of less commented on equations which are meant for those more comfortable with math shorthand. I could just as easily explain them too, but this book is not about mathematics and I don't want to take up an inordinate amount of space. I am simply deferring to why you bought this book in the first place.

In mathematics, the common symbol for the golden ratio is **Ø**. We can write out a referral definition so you can check back on it to remind yourself what is going on.

Golden Ratio $= \emptyset = {}^{\sqrt{5}+1}/_2 = 1.618033989...$

So, when I write the symbol $\emptyset$, you know what it looks like as a straightout number and as a "unity math" figure (1, 2, and 5). The arithmetic representation of $\emptyset$ does some neat things symmetrically which are unique to the golden ratio:

$^1/_\emptyset = \emptyset - 1$ ...... $^1/_{1.618033989} = .0618033989$

$\emptyset^2 = \emptyset + 1$ ...... $1.618033989^2 = 2.618033989$

$^1/_\emptyset + 2 = \emptyset^2$ ...... $0.618033989 + 2 = 2.618033989$

This particular type of symmetry is found nowhere else in arithmetic or number theory. There is a "close cousin" in the relation of $\sqrt{2}$ and $\sqrt{.5}$, which is to be expected in unity math, but the marvelous symmetry of $\emptyset$ is as if the number is saying, "I am the **fulcrum** upon which all of number theory is balanced."

The question germane to this format is, "Is there some arithmetic evidence to support the claim of the **Kryon Writings** of a universal system of number theory working in **base-12**? The answer is "Yes, there is some very good arithmetic evidence," and I will show it to you. If you have a good hand calculator which does the squaring and (square) root functions, get it out and follow along.

Before we go on to the golden ratio evidence, I want to show you some more general facets of what happens in base-10 regarding the relation of 12.

Using your hand calculator, punch in some number (not too big so you don't push the numbers off the screen, and avoid "perfect squares i.e., $\sqrt{9} = 3$ or $\sqrt{25} = 5$"). Good examples are 6, 7, 2, 53, etc. Next find the square root of your number and add 5 to it. Now you push the "square" button and see what happens! The irrational portions of the two numbers are identical! This extends into "infinity." It works for **all numbers.**

For those of you who don't have a hand calculator handy, I will work out an example for you here:

- Pick some random number (we choose 43).
- Find the square root. $\sqrt{43} = 6.557438524...$
- Add five to it. $6.557438524 + 5 = 11.557438524...$
- Square the number. $11.\textbf{557438524}^2 = 133.\textbf{57438524}$

Do you see that the bolded "irrational portion" of the two numbers are identical? What is going on here? There is a general algebraic identity which shows the mechanism. This is:

$$2x(\sqrt{n} + x) - (\sqrt{n} + x)^2 = x^2 - n$$

Where **n** = any number, and **x** = any number.
(In our case we use $x = 5$).

To work this out, simply pick some value for **n** and some value for **x**, then run it through the operation, making sure you add the figures **inside** the parenthesis first. If $x = 5$, then $2x = 10$. $2x$ is acting like the "base-10 modifier" to the equation, so it automatically "converts the irrational portions of the two numbers $(\sqrt{n} + x)$ and $(\sqrt{n} + x)^2$" to the same series. When we subtract one from the other, we "wipe them out" and are left with $x^2 - n$.

Some interesting things arise concerning notions of irrational numbers, but of more interest to the question of **base-12** is the summation of the equation "$x^2 - n$." For **base-10** (where $x = 5$), $x^2 = 25$. We can use this $x^2 - n$ to see what various number series will do in the field of "possibilities." $x^2 - n$ is the difference between the two numbers $2x(\sqrt{n} + x) - (\sqrt{n} + x)^2$. It looks like this:

$$x^2 - n \text{ (where } x = 5)$$

*25 − 0 = 25	25 − 9 = 16	25 − 18 = 7
25 − 1 = 24	25 − 10 = 15	25 − 19 = 6
25 − 2 = 23	25 − 11 = 14	25 − 20 = 5
25 − 3 = 22	25 − **12** = **13**	25 − 21 = 4
25 − 4 = 21	25 − **13** = **12**	25 − 22 = 3
25 − 5 = 20	25 − 14 = 11	25 − 23 = 2
25 − 6 = 19	25 − 15 = 10	25 − 24 = 1
25 − 7 = 18	25 − 16 = 9	*25 − 25 = 0
25 − 8 = 17	25 − 17 = 8	

* 0 (zero) is not a number, so one can see the only **positive** possibilities for **n** are the numbers 1 through 24, **which is a cycle of 12**! Since x = 5 and we have seen that it "converts the fraction portion of the two numbers $(\sqrt{n}+x)$ and $(\sqrt{n}+x)^2$" and is doing this specifically in a base-10 format, we see that the base-10 format is working within the parameters of positive field possibilities of **12**. That is not a coincidence! You can also see that the 12 and 13 are the "changeover" points in the progression (underlined).

This reinforces the "missing integer of the ascending order" function of 10 in a base-12. In short, it is doing exactly what it should be doing **if** there is a **unity mathematics system**. It is a predictable outcome.

Having played around with the above, I thought I would check out what happened when I introduced the **golden ratio** into this situation. Again, if there is credibility to the contention of unity mathematics and a universal base-12 system, it would stand to reason that it would show high symmetry. It should be predictably so.**

Since I was looking for symmetry with the number 12, I also had to check other numbers to ensure I wasn't simply finding a general

** Ø itself follows this elementary algebraic identity: $(\sqrt{1.25} + .5) = Ø$. Note again 1, 2+5, generating Ø.

principle which worked for all numbers. It had to be specific for 12. A search of relations found this one:

$$12 - (\sqrt{5} + \emptyset) = 8.145898034...$$
$$11 - (\sqrt{5} + \emptyset) = 7.145898034...$$
$$10 - (\sqrt{5} + \emptyset) = 6.145898034...$$
$$\text{Etc.}$$

As you can see, each number is one less than the one prior and all have the .145898034... in common. A check of the square roots of the numbers revealed nothing special or related between the numbers, **except for the 12**. In short, the .145898034... does not carry over any significance to any other integer except for the 12, where symmetry plays out in spades!*

Here are four of the relations;

- $(\sqrt{5} + \emptyset) - [\sqrt{12 - (\sqrt{5}+\emptyset)}] = 1$

- $\emptyset [\sqrt{12 - (\sqrt{5}+\emptyset)} - \sqrt{5}] = 1$

- $1/\emptyset + \sqrt{5} = \sqrt{12 - (\sqrt{5}+\emptyset)}$

- $(\sqrt{5} + \emptyset)^2 - 12 = \sqrt{12 - (\sqrt{5}+\emptyset)}$

or
- $(\sqrt{5} + \emptyset)^2 - \sqrt{12 - (\sqrt{5}+\emptyset)} = 12$

Also,
- $12 - (\sqrt{5} + \emptyset) = 8 + (1 - 1/\emptyset)^2$

- $(\sqrt{5} + \emptyset)^2 - (\sqrt{5} + \emptyset) = 11$

- $\emptyset/\sqrt{5} - (\emptyset/\sqrt{5})^2 = .2$

*.145898034... = $(1 - 1/\emptyset)^2$

When one considers, in base-10, that 9 is the last integer before a repetition of the series and is bound up intrinsically in the symmetries of base-10, it should also be found for 11 in base-12, as occurs on the previous page.

Summary

In summing up, remember what we have done: We found there is a **unity/Dyadic** generation of numbers. We found, intrinsic to standard math operations, that there is a missing integer in the ascending order of any base system of numbers. This tallies exactly with the unity/ Dyadic generation of numbers. The unity (1) Dyad (2) and middle integer, base (5) play a significant role in all mathematical operations. The **golden ratio** is a geometric constant. Regardless of what base it is described in, it remains the same wherever one goes in the universe. The geometric constant ($\emptyset$) is expressed in base-10 in terms of 1, 2 and 5, and all numbers proceed to it.

In specific regards to the **base-12** validity question, we found a general algebraic identity which, when working in base-10, where X=5, irrational portions of all square roots are "wiped out" and that the positive limits of the base-10 series is a **12 cycle**. We found that the introduction of the golden ratio into a similar type of equation gave rise to a series of highest possible symmetry working only for the integer **12** and ancillary symmetries to those integers which are critical parts of base-12 system. The same formulas revealed nothing of interest for other integers, showing that the **golden ratio is specific to base-12 type of operations only**, by two separate methods of number/algebraic calculations and the standardly accepted conditions of circle division in non-numerical Euclidean type geometry.

> When the fact is introduced that **ALL PRIMES** greater **than 3 are of the form 6n ±1**, it seems inconceivable to this author that anyone may logically maintain a position against base-12 as the universal and non-arbitrary choice of number theory expression.

The question of universal validity for base-12 should be positioned for competent rebuttal in the general forum. The author's own opinion is that the evidence presented is extraordinarily high that base-12 should be accepted as "a universal base" and that our entire system of number theory, based on the assumption of (N+1) that one can always be added to any number, is in serious error at a fundamental level. To continue practicing mathematics in the historical method of straight line terms is to willingly abrogate the authority of "objective reasoning" in favor of agenda.

Those wishing to know more about these and other math proofs should write to Lee Carroll (address on title page). Should there be a large response, we may be able to bring out what would be a "new age math primer." It is certain that mankind cannot look to a "paradigm shift" until the mathematics is corrected. Mathematics is the base of every other logical exercise. Unless the math changes, there is no new age, only the new window dressing in the same shop. The effect of these math discoveries has been that it can be shown for the first time in the history of mankind that what have heretofore been regarded as "articles of faith" actually have the imperative of logic backing them. Enormous questions of theology, philosophy and ethics which have been unresolved for centuries may now be resolved. The answers by logic are extraordinary. Personally I have come to an astonishing, and I believe inevitable conclusion, about the nature of the physical universe itself. All that remains to say at this point is welcome to the **real** New Age.

Sincerely,

James D. Watt

James also contributes some brief 9944 solutions
and other surprising revelations in Appendix B
of this book (page 365).

Chapter Eleven

My Book Is Falling Apart!
There are no accidents.

My Book Is Falling Apart!
Chapter Ten

There are no accidents...

Are any of your Kryon books falling apart? This is the story of why that happened. Perhaps you will feel differently about your loose book after you read this:

Okay, come on... how can there be no accidents? I walk out of my house Monday morning to go to the recording studio. I accidently step on the sleeping cat, who screeches and leaps eight feet into the air and knocks the porch plant off its hanging hook. I lean down to comfort the cat (whom Jan named Jasmine) and the plant falls on my head (freshly watered of course). The plant (that Jan named Augusta), not content with only clubbing me, also drains itself all over my fresh clothing. Hearing the commotion Jan rushes out onto the porch to see how Jasmine and Augusta are doing (she knows I'm indestructible... at least that's what I tell her).

So I start to go back into the house, late for work now, whispering things like "hecky darn" and "poopie!" Naturally I can't walk back into the front door because now I'm soiled. I have to go to the back door (we have a rule that says soiled channels have to go to the back door – which Jan named "back door"). On the way to the back yard (through an overgrown path that I swear I never saw before), I slip in the mud and ruin my shoes. More "hecky darns."

Metaphysical equipment needed for certain Kryon Books.

Now It's obvious I have to take a shower again, find fresh clothing, and try the "go to work" thing again (sigh). I'm really starting to get overwhelmed, rushing to get out the door, when the phone rings. "It's for you." Jan says. A giant "hecky darn."

The phone turns out to be someone at work. "Boy, are we glad we caught you!" the voice says. "The client needs you to stop on the way in to pick up the music he forgot. The musicians are starting to arrive, and you are the closest one to his office! Leave right now and the timing will be perfect."

This is one tiny episode in a very large and complex scenario of how Spirit honors our everyday lives, and our lifetime contract with "accidents." These accidents can be as minor as what I have described here, or as heavy as the death of a child. Even then, Spirit says there are no accidents. When you read the Kryon story in the Karma chapter about "David The Loved" (page 209) you got to see how David's contract with his parents provided for his passing. Not an accident, but a fulfillment of contract – on schedule for all concerned.

On the "everyday" front, Spirit honors our intent to be in the right place at the right time (see the parable on page 230). Sometimes we are blocked by seeming accidental things in order to have the correct situations present themselves to us, especially when we are co-creating our own reality (as Kryon tells us we have the power to do). Sometimes we find ourselves in a strange place that seems to be "the wrong place at the wrong time." Again this has nothing to do with predestination. When we give the intent to co-create our reality, we place ourselves in the hands of Spirit and our guides to show us the path to implement **what we ask for**. Sometimes we are nudged left or right (or stopped) to allow for the window of opportunity we asked for to present itself. How many times have you said, "If this or that hadn't happened to me, then I would never have met so and so, or got that job, or moved to such and such a place"? This is a great example of Spirit honoring your intent. We always have the choice to ignore what we are given, and miss various windows. It's really sad when this happens, since there is so much planning that goes into getting the windows ready for us.

I printed several thousand Kryon Book One and Two last year that were part of a reprint scenario that seemed very normal. I had done it before, and had prepared the funds for it, and ordered the books in plenty of time to meet the distributor's requests for more books. I was pleased and honored that again Spirit had given me good direction on the reprints, and again I celebrated the fact that Kryon's words were going out to so many people. I do this at every reprint.

It wasn't until the books were in the stores that we began to get an indication that something was wrong. Somehow the binding glue used to hold the books together was starting to fail. It seemed okay when it was fresh, and it seemed okay when it got to the distributor, but like a tiny time capsule, it had a surprise for us all. Slowly many of the books in the entire reprint scenario began to fall apart as the books were read (only after being purchased, of course).

I reacted first with action, then with reaction (as is my style). I did a full recall of all the books in the distributor's warehouses (thousands of books). I ordered new ones with the correct glue, knowing that they would be late for the demand and therefore would cause a back order situation and a loss of sales. Then I hit a wall of self pity and anger. "Why?" I asked Kryon. "Where is the appropriateness in the Kryon books being defective, when they are helping so many people? Where is the appropriateness in the financial sting to my pocketbook that goes with all this?" Okay, I got mad. I couldn't see any reason for the bad books. I knew how co-creation worked, and believe me I didn't remember co-creating this!

In the Sedona workshop I was telling the crowd about this episode. I got to the same point in this story asking "Why?" when a man stood up and offered an answer: "Because you went to the lowest bidder!" he shouted. After I tweaked his nose (and offered to introduce him to my plant and my cat) I told him that this was not the case (but it was a very funny moment and I laughed a lot about his witty retort... perfectly timed. I hate it when workshop attendees are funnier than I am).

I try to make every part of the Kryon work top quality, and the same was true in the printing of the books. It just seemed that this whole thing was wrong! So I asked Kryon, "Did I create this?" He answered, "Yes." "When and How?" I asked, incredulously. "When you asked for the Kryon work to go to everyone who should have it," he replied.

I didn't understand.

A week later I was speaking to the buyer at one of my largest distributors. I had called to give her the latest update as to when the replacement books would arrive. Casually in conversation I also asked, "So do you just throw away all those books that are defective?" "No," she replied, "WE HAVE A PRISONS PROGRAM."

I about swallowed my tongue! "What do you mean, a prisons program?" I asked. She told me that the books will get sent to correction facilities all over the nation. She went on to tell me that as the Kryon publisher, it would be difficult for me to get the books into the prisons due to governmental red tape. **The books had to be defective to qualify for the program**.

It wasn't much after that before we started getting letters like the one on page 331. The "accidental" bad glue on the Kryon books had brought them to humans in the darkest corners of the country, humans who needed to hear about the new energy and make decisions... just like you and I did. Kryon was right. I had indeed created it with my intent. I'm very glad I did. My anger turned to understanding, and to this day I stand in awe of how spirit honored my request with an "accident."

If you have a book like this, I will replace it if you wish. It might take a while, since the mail is great and the requests are numerous. Many have chosen to keep the books, and participate in this miracle of Spirit... smiling with the tape and glue in their hands as the pages continue to pop out.

Some have found that the local instant printing shop can cut off about 1/4 inch of the spine, and **plastic spiral bind** the book like a cook book. This allows it to open flat and no pages fall out – all for under $5. I recommend this for those who have marked their book in a personal way, and wish to keep it together.

I just wanted you to know how it all came to be, and the real energy behind it all.

Lee Carroll

...ritings
...Del Mar #422
...92014

...roll

When I picked up your <u>Kryon Book I</u>, I was moved severely. I must tell you right now that I am incarcerated 4¹/₂ – 9 years. It seems these books are drawn to me. When the library cart comes around, books leap out and actually demand my attention.

I recognize what Kryon is saying, but I am locked up. I have no one to teach me about implants or imprints thoroughly. I am not a master, but a new pupil. I feel my incarceration will hinder any progress, for I don't know what to do, or how to tap into this wonderful love power source ripe for the taking.

I also have syphilis. I have so many questions, it's unreal. I feel I don't have much time, so I would like to work with the remaining time I have. Is it possible for Kryon to talk to my higher entity to find out what I must do to enjoy the happiness like other enlightened entities? I am very sincere in my requests.

Thanking you in advance,

Ronald Fludd
Southport Correctional Facility
Pine City, New York

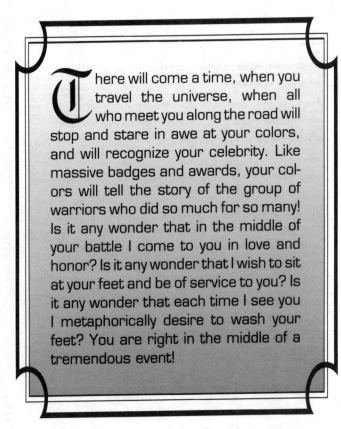

There will come a time, when you travel the universe, when all who meet you along the road will stop and stare in awe at your colors, and will recognize your celebrity. Like massive badges and awards, your colors will tell the story of the group of warriors who did so much for so many! Is it any wonder that in the middle of your battle I come to you in love and honor? Is it any wonder that I wish to sit at your feet and be of service to you? Is it any wonder that each time I see you I metaphorically desire to wash your feet? You are right in the middle of a tremendous event!

...from page 18

Chapter Twelve

Kryon News

On The Internet
[www.kryon.com]

The Kryon website features lots of goodies! See the daily updated Kryon seminar schedule, and some of the latest channels (including all the United Nations transcriptions). See what Kryon products are available, learn about the foreign translations and Kryon web sites in other languages, and read the latest Kryon book reviews.

Receive "marshmallow messages," personally chosen and sent to your e-mail each day. Join in a chat room with others of like mind. Spend time on the message board. Find others in your area of the same consciousness. From the products to the chat rooms, our web site is a "family" area - warm and toasty - filled with love and joy!

*Webmaster - **Gary Liljegren***

The Parables of Kryon

Kryon Book Four

Color-illustrated Hardback

...and soft cover (New this year!)

A fully color-illustrated book of 20 of Kryon's parables. Some have asked, "Are these parables also in the other Kryon books?" The answer is, only half of them. Ten are only found in this book. Complete with the channeller's interpretations, this book is a wonderful quality hardback gift!

"For anyone who is ready for the next evolutionary step, this information from Kryon is invaluable. It is both self-healing and planetary healing...Kryon really lets us know that all is well and we have work to do"

Louise L. Hay - **Best-Selling Author**

Published by Hay House • ISBN 1-56170-364-8 • $17 (hard cover)
ISBN 1-56170-663-9 • $10.95 (soft cover)

Books and tapes can be purchased in retail stores, or by phone
~ Credit cards welcome ~

1-800-352-6657 - <kryonbooks@aol.com>

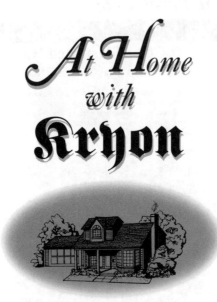

At Home with Kryon

Get together for a personal afternoon or evening with Kryon and Lee Carroll...in the comfort of a cozy living room or community center with a small group of dedicated lightworkers. It's called *"At Home with Kryon,"* the latest venue for joining in the Kryon energy. The special meeting starts with an introduction and discussion by Lee Carroll regarding timely New Age topics, then it continues with individual questions and answers from the group. Next comes a live Kryon channelling! Group size is limited to 50 or 60 people. Often lasting up to five hours, it's an event you won't forget!

To sponsor an *"At Home with Kryon"* event in your home, please contact the Kryon office at 760/489-6400 - fax 858/759-2499, or e-mail <kryonmeet@aol.com>. For a list of upcoming *"At Home with Kryon"* locations, please see our web site at [www.kryon.com].

Timely. Informative. Provocative.

MAGAZINE

The *Kryon* Magazine brings you timely information about our transformation
into the New Age with several information-packed issues per year. It's filled
with the latest Kryon channels and parables, science and medical news,
reader questions, inner child features, how-to information about working
with your New Age tools, upcoming seminar schedules and much more.
Stay tuned to the latest news about these changing times by subscribing
to the *Kryon Magazine*. Just $24 for four issues; $40 for eight issues.
(*Australia and New Zealand - see below*)

TO ORDER THE *KRYON MAGAZINE:*

- PHONE (credit card orders only): Call 1-800-945-1286 or 1-303-642-1678
- FAX (credit card orders only): Complete this order and fax to: (303) 642-1696
- EMAIL (credit card orders only): e-mail all information contained in form below to: <Kryonqtly@aol.com>
- MAIL Complete coupon below, include check, money order or credit card
  information to: *Kryon Magazine*, PO Box 7392, Golden, CO 80403 - Make
  checks payable to *Kryon Magazine*.

Name _____

Address _____

City _____ State _____ Zip _____

Computer e-mail address (optional):_____

❏ Four issues $24* ❏ Eight issues $40.00* CO residents add 4.2%

*US dollars. Orders outside US, please add $10 *per year* for shipping.

Payment: ❏ Check/M.O.   ❏ MasterCard   ❏ VISA

Credit Card Number: _____

Expiration Date: _____

Signature: _____ Phone: _____

---

* For Australia and New Zealand, call direct: 1-800-44-3200 <crystals@senet.com.au>

NOVO DOBA

Kryon - superiorna inteligencija s one strane našeg uma:

"DOŠAO SAM SPASITI OVAJ SVIJET"

Scenarij naših života samo je ono na što smo pristali još prije ovozemaljskog rođenja, kako bi odigrali vlastitu ulogu na putu do kvalitetnije razine postojanja koja je pred nama. Međutim, i u okviru te unaprijed zadane uloge možemo pronaći - sreću.

Piše: Drago PLEČKO

Od svih "onostranih" inteligencija koje "kanaliziraju" svoje poruke kroz ljudske medije možda je najzanimljiviji već u prošlom broju spominjani Kryon. Podatjelimo se: radi se o porukama koje je u razdoblju od posljednje tri godine iz racionalnom umu teško shvatljivih sfera "primio" jedan kalifornijski businessman, a bave se putevima izlaza iz krize modernog svijeta. Za razliku od niza drugih koje nam nude poplavu katastrofičnih poruka, ova, kako se i sam naziva, "grupa svjetlosnih impulsa", govori o ljubavi kao osnovnoj pokretačkoj i iscjeliteljskoj sili u Svemiru, a ovo naše vrijeme označava razdobljem koje Čovjeku pruža jedinstvenu priliku da aktivira svoje najdublje i najsnažnije potencijale i tako utječe na cijelu planetu pomažući joj izaći iz krize koja postaje sve očitija iz dana u dan. Prirodno je da netko tko se ovim stvarima bavi dugi niz godina posumnja u autentičnost fenomena koje možemo, uvjetno rečeno, dokazivati isključivo intuicijom ili još bolje, nekom vrstom unutrašnjeg uksutva koje je nemoguće priopćiti okolini. Međutim, Kryonova učenja toliko su originalna, svježa i uvjerljiva da ih teško možemo svrstati uz rame bilo koje druge takove inteligencije s izuzetkom jedne, možda dvije koje su se javljale u ranijim godinama.

Kryon tvrdi da "nikada nije hodao u ljudskim cipelama", drugim riječima nikada nije bio ljudsko biće, ali savršeno poznaje način na koji ljudi funkcioniraju, jer je sudjelovao u krojenju povijesti ljudskog roda, koja, prema njemu, počinje još prije 500 tisuća godina. O sebi govori kao "magnetskom servisu" koji postupno mijenja magnetsku mrežu Zemlje djelujući tako na čitavu vrstu, koja treba kroz te promjene evolurati u viša stanja ili će, ukoliko se ne prilagodi, odumrijeti kao što su zbog istih razloga na ovoj planeti ranije odumrle već dvije civilizacije. Radi se o

zahvatima viših bića koji su dio za nas nesagledivog instrumenta preživljavanja cijelih kozmičkih regija. Dakle, s vremena na vrijeme, kada postanemo, na ovaj ili onaj način opasni za ravnotežu, moraju nas prilagoditi globalnom konceptu superiornog bića kojeg Kryon naziva Duhom, kakada dajaći do znanja da govori o onome što mi nazivamo Bogom.

Kryon treba svoj posao obaviti u vremenu od 1.siječnja 1992. do 31. prosinca 2002. godine. U svojim se porukama zna čuditi što manatvenici još nisu shvatili promjene koje izaziva. Razdoblje svog djelovanja na Zemlji definira kao "prozor mogućnosti", kratko vrijeme u kojem se stvaraju jedinstveni uvjeti za ljudska bića da u vrlo kratkom vremenu dožive izuzetno brz i značajni napredak.

Kako nas vidi Kryon?

Svatko je od nas svjestan dijela sebe koji je angažiran u životu na ovoj planeti. Taj je dio nas okrenut prema van, ali postoji i onaj drugi dio duše koji je "stalno s Duhom", odnosno stalno je svjestan svoje stvarne, božanske prirode. Kada se rodimo na Zemlji, dolazi do rascjepa i mi u određenom smislu gubimo vezu i sjećanje na taj drugi, skriveni dio nas. Kryon govori o reinkarnaciji, ali ne na onaj standardni način "kako sijat, tako ćeš i žeti", već ukazuje na činjenicu da je svaki naš život na ovoj planeti za koji se upotrebljava riječ "izražaj" (expression), prije svega u službi šireg plana. Onaj tko je u svom

14

Kryon in Croatia

Piramid
Magazine

Kryon in Israel

New Age The Light Era
Magazine

Jan Tober

The phone crackled one early morning in Jan's life: "This is Benny Goodman," the voice said. "You come very highly recommended and I want to hire you, but I've never heard you sing. Can you hum something for me?"

Such is the stuff that fairy tales are made of – at least for a girl jazz singer! But this call was simply one of many that had already marked an amazing career for Jan. While still a teenager she replaced Ann Richards as vocalist for the Stan Kenton Band, and went on to be featured on the bandstand and on Stan's regular TV show from the Rendezvous Ball Room at Balboa Island. From there she went on the road for two years with the Les Elgart orchestra, then two tours with Si Zentner and the Four Freshmen. Along the way she also did shows with Rowan & Martin, Jimmy Rogers, Corbett Monica... then Fred Astaire called her to represent his new label!

When she got tired of the road, Jan settled down in Del Mar, California and proceeded to do a local 90 minute daily TV show for over two years. It was at this time she was contacted by Goodman's agent – and turned him down! When Benny called personally, however, she accepted and was back on the road again. This time with the King of Swing.

You would think that for the vocalist selected in 1980 to represent the United States in The French International Music Festival in Cannes France, Jan would have no time for anything but her music. In fact she is also an extraordinary design artist, with paintings, clothing and jewelry for sale in galleries and boutiques in several states.

Jan has been an active Metaphysician all of her life and actually foresaw the Kryon work long before Lee did. It was due to her efforts that Lee was guided to the right place and the right time, and the result is the Kryon work!

Jan also has created three cassettes: *The Crystal Singer* (1995) is a 17-minute channeled meditation tape. This tape works well for peace and healing (we get letters)! In 1997 she also released *Guided Meditations*. This tape is two great half-hour guided meditations with channeled Celtic harp accompaniment. In 1998 she finally recorded *Sound & Color Meditation*, a CD of the exercise that opens every Kryon seminar. She remains dedicated to using her voice and other talents in changing the planet.

In 1999 she co-authored the best-selling book *The Indigo Children* (page 88), along with Lee.

Lee Carroll

After graduating with a business and economics degree from California Western University in California, Lee started his community's first recording studio and quickly attracted national commercial work. Twenty seven years later Lee finds himself with 39 Clio nominations (three first place statues), and numerous other distinctions including a studio Grammy nomination.

Where does Kryon fit into all this? As Lee tells it, Spirit had to hit him "between the eyes" to prove the Kryon experience was real. But 1989 was the turning point when the first psychic told him about Kryon, and then three years later when the second unrelated psychic told him the same thing (spelling the name KRYON in session)!

Timidly the first Kryon writings were presented to the Metaphysical community in Del Mar, and the rest is history with Kryon Book One being released in 1993. Kryon Book Two followed in 1994, and Kryon Book Three in 1995. The full color illustrated hard cover *Kryon Parable* book came in 96 (Hay House), Kryon Book six, *Partnering with God* in 97, and another Kryon Hay House Book *The Journey Home*, also in 1997. Kryon Book Seven, *Letters from Home*, in 1999, and Kryon book 8, *Passing the Marker*, was released in 2000.

Lee and Jan started the Kryon light groups in Del Mar in 1991, and quickly moved from a living room setting to a Del Mar church (holding up to 300 people). Now they are hosting meetings all over the globe with audiences up to 3,000. Kryon has a very active and complete web site (page 334) with a constant stream of literally thousands of visitors who come to chat on-line and find others of like mind. In 1995 the national *Kryon Quarterly Magazine* was started. This beautiful full color 40 page periodical, without any advertising, now has over 3,500 subscribers in over 12 countries.

In 1995 Lee & Jan were asked to present Kryon at the United Nations before a UN chartered group known as the Society for Enlightenment and Transformation (S.E.A.T.). The meeting was so well accepted that Kryon was brought back for a second visit in 1996, and a third in 1998

In 1999, along with Jan, Lee wrote the bestselling book, *The Indigo Children* (page 88). This book has topped the metaphysical sales charts, and broached mainstream publishing. You can find it in the parenting sections of major stores world-wide.

Lee continues the Kryon work even as you read this.

Help With Magnetics

All around the planet are wonderful magnetic facilitators and knowledgeable people who are having their work greatly enhanced by the new energy. Perhaps you are considering healing with magnets? Some of you are also very interested in magnetic shielding, as Kryon has suggested. If you are looking for resources and don't know who to ask, we recommend the very best thing is to go to your local metaphysical book store and ask them. Often on their bulletin boards will be business cards and flyers from qualified individuals in your area. Each time Jan and I visit a bookstore anywhere on the planet, it seems that this is the place where the networking is.

But some of you live in remote areas. You have written to us that you do most of your work by mail, and need help. For you we give the two resources below. On the left is a wonderful book on magnetic healing. If you are interested in healing with magnets, it is best to see a facilitator, or at least read up on it if you can't see someone personally. Please don't obtain mail order magnets and go at it blindly. Kryon tells us that this can be dangerous! The book *Magnetic Field Therapy* by Robert Allen Walls is a great manual for the use of small magnets in healing. See the information at below left to order it.

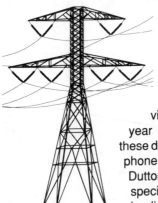

Many of you have also heard about the New Age magnetic shielding inventions. Jan and I have experimented with some, and actually have an active device plugged in at our home. After over a year of trial and error, we can recommend these devices and can also give an address and phone numbers for information. Marv and Linda Dutton-Steindler in the Los Angeles area are specialists in this field, as well as in magnetic healing. See below right to order information.

Magnetic Field Therapy
Inner Search Foundation, Inc.
PO Box 10382
McLean, Virginia 22102
(703) 448-3362 Phone
(703) 448-0814 Fax

Energy Integrity Associates
Marv & Linda Dutton-Steindler
1800 S. Robertson Blvd.
Los Angeles, CA 90035
(310) 859-0270 Phone
(310) 859-0270 Fax

Appendix A

Mystery of the 9944
Unraveled

Appendix A

Mystery of the 9944 unraveled

From the writer...

On page 15 of *Kryon Book One,* the number 9944 is given by Kryon. He tells us that it is an important formula that relates to the transmutation of energy. As in much of the Kryon information, I got a great big "wink," as much as to say "go figure it out." Typically Kryon will drop something like that and never come back to it, expecting us to pick up the ball, so to speak, and run with it.

Since 1992, many fine metaphysicians have speculated what that number could signify. I, in my own way, just figured it was the purity of Ivory soap (9944/100 percent pure). Now you have great insight into my simple mind.

Not until I opened the gateway of invitation to the country regarding this book did I get information that gave me chills. It didn't come from me, or Kryon. It came from mathematicians and metaphysicians... exactly where Kryon wanted it to come from.

This appendix and the next one are new reference materials for those mathematically inclined, and interested in the Earth science of the 9944. Basically, this Kryon formula is everywhere! It points to our math, our chemistry, our planetary attributes, our solar system, our atomic structure, our lineage, and our biology. (Did I leave out anything?) It's actually getting to be the great mystery that hides at every junction. No wonder it's also the purity of Ivory soap (ha ha)!

Randy Masters calls himself "Artist in Resonance." Besides being a musician (a good one), he holds a degree in Interrelations of Film and Music from the University of California at Santa Cruz. He is currently teaching music and arts, and private workshops in California.

Randy composes, records, teaches... and is an expert in the Sacred Sciences of Geometry and Unified Field Harmonics. He has written an extensive work on the relations of music and sacred geometry for Drunvalo Melchizedek, and has done harmonic geometry work for the Templar project.

He and his partner, Wesley H. Bateman, are together collaborating on a project that will extend the outstanding twenty year work that Wesley has already done called *The Rods of Amon Ra*. The new work will be called *Drums of Ice, Harps of Fire*. Randy and Wesley say this new work will be the decoding of the Egyptian and Mayan pyramids and the "Cydonia" monuments of Mars.

When I asked Randy to give me some comments on Kryon's 9944, and the channeling regarding the base-12 information and pi, I never thought I would get an exhaustive writing such as what follows! I contemplated if it should be in *Kryon Book Three* or not. Then I realized that this material is extremely valuable. It will be the precursor to other books on the subject, and after all... it is about a Kryon mystery.

Even if you don't understand any of what is to follow, please consider the importance to those that will. Sometimes math can seem boring, but Kryon tells us that the elegance of the shapes and formulas around us are sacred and joyful. This, therefore, is a reference appendix section, to be used over and over as you would an encyclopedia. Some will devour this section and consider it the most valuable part of this book. Some won't bother to read it at all. I fully understand the human nature of this, and only ask you to honor the place of this NEW technical information for our New Age. I am honored to have it presented in this book.

Don't miss Kryon's message to Randy on page 369!

Harmonic 9944
by Randy Masters

*Grateful acknowledgment to Andy Tran
for his fine transcription work.*

"Harmonic 9944 is the harmonic of the 5th dimension, just below the 6th dimension" according to musician/sacred scientist Sammy Figueroa (As told to him by his alchemy teacher).

The number 9-9-4-4 may be operated on using math processes such as addition, subtraction, multiplying, dividing and various cubing, squaring and rooting (cube root, square root, etc.) functions producing numbers with many meanings.

Keys to music, math, archetypal or sacred geometry, astronomy and all branches of science, as well as the numerical translations of sacred texts and words, called "gematria" are easily revealed with these number processes.

These numbers are not cold static or seemingly "left brain" stuff, but living breathing vibrations and pulsations of our oscillating, dynamic, multidimensional reality. In the ancient Greek mystery schools where the "secrets" of creations laws were taught; music, mathematics, geometry and astronomy were called the "Quadrivium" and the four essentials of basic education.

Part One
Earth - Sun - Moon

In this article I will explore each of these areas as well as some specific areas of the sciences of chemistry, physics, biology, and Earth electromagnetic grid engineering.

The diameter of our sun is reported to be 864,000 miles and can be derrived from the formula of 2 sets of 9944 :

$$(9 \times \sqrt{9}) \times (9 - 4)^{\sqrt{9}} \times (4 + 4)^{\sqrt{4}} = (9 \times \sqrt{9}) \times (9 - 4)^{\sqrt{9}} \times (4 + 4)^{\sqrt{4}} .$$

This formula of 9's and 4's conversing also reduces to this simple formula of factored prime numbers (prime numbers are numbers that can only be divided by themselves and number one).

$864,000 = [2^8 \times 3^3 \times 5^3]$ shows prime 2, 3, and 5 only are needed. $864,000$ = musical note G## (+1). (+1) means x 81 = 80, the musical comma interval.

$8 + 6 + 4$ reduces to a 9 ($8 + 6 + 4 = 18$ and $1 + 8 = 9$). Numeral reduction is also a key to the energy and character of numbers, especially the number 9, as in 9 months of pregnancy and our main 9 planets and the 9 Gods of the ancient Egyptian pantheon (TMU, SHU, TEFNUT, SEB, NUT, OSIRIS, ISIS, SET, NEPHTHYS), which are nine expressions of one creator, not 9 Gods, as in polytheism!

The mean (average) diameter of our moon

is 2,160 miles = (135 x 16) = [9 x (4 x 4) – 9 x ($^9/_9$) x (4 x 4)]. The ancient Mayan unit of measurement called the Hunab was (135:128) = (1.0546875) which is an important value in Wesley Bateman's Amon Ra System. 2,160 = musical note C# (+1).

This Hunab can be found by dividing the diameter of the moon by 2 to the 11th power = 2048. In other words, it is a lower octave (Multiple of 2) of the moon's diameter. Our study of the Mayan and ancient Egyptian sacred temples shows that the Hunab was a common unit of measurement.

The sun's diameter is therefore 400 times that of the moon.

Formula: (9 x 9) x (4 x 4) divided by [(81:25)=(3.24)] = 400 [Ratio 81:50 =1.62] is a value of Phi (Greek letter) used in the Great Pyramid of Giza Egypt and 3.24 represents 2 times this value of Phi.

This 1.62 is one of the Golden Mean Values expressed throughout creation in nature and art and it is one of the most beautiful of proportion.

Also 9 x 9 x 4 x 4 equals 1296, the number "most Holy" in the temple of Solomon. The Templar Project that Kryon referred to is to be a modern day reconstruction of the Temple of Solomon and the major Pyramid of the new age on Earth.

The Templar is also very important to the Earth's electromagnetic grid structure. A grid much like our body's energy meridian system. 400 is also 20 squared and the number 20 is called Holy of Holies in the Temple of Solomon. The temple dimensions were 20 x 20 x 20 cubits based on a cubit measurement of one of the following: 1.728 feet = 20.736 inches, or 1.65 feet = 19.8 inches.

One quarter of the sun diameter is 216,000 miles . Now, the number 216 is very important in sacred texts as it is the Hebrew gematria for Palmoni, "the numberer of secrets" and "the wonderful numberer."

Palmoni was the being who spoke to Daniel in 547 B.C. The 216 Palmoni number can be rearranged to 1-6-2 creating a numerical anagram and a value of 100 times the 1-6-2 Phi value. 2-1-6 also resolves to a 9 in (2 + 1 + 6). (6 x 6 x 6) = 216 also.

Formula [9 x $\sqrt{9}$ x (4 + 4)] = 216, showing 9-9-4-4 as a "number of secret."

The earth's mean equatorial radius is most often rounded down from 3963.5303 miles to 3960 miles. 3960 is 11 times 360, the 11 is from the reduced numerology of Kryon from 83 to 8 + 3 = 11 and the K in Kryon has the English alphabet value of 11 also. 3960 = musical note B(11).

In the mystery school, the letter "K" is often meant "towards God," Especially with the "K" in the "Knight" relating to King Arthur's Round Table.

The 360 represents the degrees of a circle as well as the symbolic round table. The Earth symbolic equatorial diameter of 7,920 is a ratio of (11:3) = 3.666666 times the moon's mean diameter. Notice the 11 again suggesting Kryon's English gematria. (11:3) = musical note B^{b11} (-1) = [$\sqrt{256:81}$ x (33:32) x 2].

The "Palmoni Ratio" for (11:3) would be (792:216) = (7920:2160) and again 9 emerges from (7+ 9 + 2 + 0) = 18 and (1 + 8) = 9. 79.2 is the atomic mass of selenium.

The sun/Earth ratio is (1200:11) = 109.$\overline{0909}$ or (21600:198) to show the Palmoni num-

Note: 9600 = D# based on middle C = 256. 9900 = D#(11) based on middle C = 264. 9944 = D#(11)(113). Each one of these three notes is the 75th harmonic of its respective C. 9600 x (33:32) = 9900. 9900 x (226:225) = 9944.

ber again. The combined diameter equals 874080 miles, and this number also resolves to a 9.

The Encyclopedia Brittanica lists the mean distances in miles of our 9 main "established" planets from our sun as: Mercury 36 million, Venus 67 million, Earth 93 million, Mars 142 million, Jupiter 483 million, Saturn 886 million, Uranus 1782 million, Neptune 2793 million, and Pluto as 3672 million. The total is 9954 million miles, which is 9944 plus 10 . The number 10 represents our base 10 numerical system (10 fingers). The value would read 9 billion, 9 hundred 54 million miles.

In the mystery school 10 represents reproduction. The phallus is represented by one, representing unity, joined "with" the zero of the void; the womb and the cosmic mother, Nut. 10 = musical note E.

10 is also the 1 joined with the 9 months of pregnancy. The nine also represents completion and death. Finally, the 9 + 9 + 5 + 4 becomes 27 and reduces to 9.   9 = musical note D.

The current ratio of the Earth equatorial radius (3963.5303 miles) to its polar radius (3950.1833 miles) is (297.000133843:296) which can be reduced to $(297:296) = [(3^3 \times 11) / (2^3 \times 37)]$. Using (297:296) and a 3960 equatorial radius produces a polar radius of $3946.\overline{666666} = (11840:3) = $ musicl note $B^{(37)}$.

When we divide 3946.666 by $(2880 = 360 \times 8)$ we get $1.\overline{370370}$. 37:27 = $1.\overline{370370}$. It is called the physical constant of hydrogen. Peter Tompkins says in his book Mysteries of the Mexico pyramids:

"When a physicist tries to calculate the optical properties of a material or the way an object will behave in the presence of light, the 'Hydrogen Constant' enables him to make experimental results fit theories which may be largely based on assumption." (37:27) = musical note $F^{(37)} = [(4:3)(F) \times (37:36)]$. 486 feet is the height of the Great Pyramid x (37:27) = 666 = $E^{(37)}(+1)$. In the Grand Gallery of the Great Pyramid are 7 ceilings composed of 37 slabs and there are 27 pairs of slots in the Grand Gallery ramps. This actually gives us 37 over 27 or $^{37}/_{27}$, the Hydrogen Constant. $(^{37}/_{27}) \times 100 = C\#^{(37)}$.

In the King's chamber, the north wall has 27 blocks and the south wall has 37 blocks. Also note that 37 times 27 equals 999. (9-9-5-4 can be expressed as 9-9-9) .(5 + 4 = 9). Furthermore 37 + 27 equals 64 or 4 to the 4th power from "4-4" in "9-9-4-4." The East and West walls have 18 blocks each.

There are 64 hexagrams in the I-Ching relating to the 64 condons of the genetic code. 37 – 27 = 10... our number of reproduction, also suggesting one as diameter and zero as the circumference of a circle. [See Pi section]. 64 = musical note C.

Tompkins further states "The Hydrogen Constant should be particularly useful when we will have to cope with very large amounts of energy. In other words, the fraction $^{37}/_{27}$ or $1.\overline{370370}$ is the physical constant which forms a connection to the level of the atom multiplied by 100. This number is the average fine constant for hydrogen and **deuterium** (an isotope of hydrogen)." This information was published in 1972 by the Bureau of Standards in Washington D.C.

Lee note: Kryon has indicated that Deuterium is part of the formula for the eventual discovery of true cold fusion!

Note: Randy Masters gives musical names to physical data regardless of units. Example: 12 units = note "G." This does not mean that 12 inches is truly a note "G" frequency in cycles per second.

I personally suggest that the Earth ratio (297:296) represents some type of shape shifting or pulling of the Earth like a macrocosmic "Atom." This ratio suggests a spheroid or a "minimal" oval rather than a circle, possibly creating dynamic rather than "static" behavior – a type of genesis effect propelling the life force of the planet.

Ratios where the numerator is one unit larger or smaller than the denominator are called "superparticular" (296 + 1 = 297) (Expressed as N + 1:N).

The most listed atomic weight of the element hydrogen is 1.008, which equals $(126:125) = (2 \times 3^2 \times 7 : 5^3)$.

Again, "superparticular" both for the Earth and hydrogen, our physical reality steps down into the material realm from the etheric realm and does it through hydrogen (which is the fundamental building block of all matter). The 1.008 number can also be realized through the formula (using two sets of 9-9-4-4):

$$[(9 - \sqrt{4}) \times (\sqrt{9}) \times (4 + \sqrt{4}) : (9 - 4)^{\sqrt{9}}].$$
1.008 = musical note D^{bb} [7].

Now it is very interesting to note that playing with the two above ratios (297:296) and (126:125), that ratio (297:126) is equal to Archimedean pi = (22:7), divided by the musical ratio (4:3) = the perfect fourth interval, or the distance from note C or (Do) up to the note F or (Fa), if tuned properly.

Now when 4:3 is divided by 2 to become (2:3), it equals 0.**666666**, suggesting the "triple 6" (666) for "time, the magnetic compass system and gravity" (see Kryon Book One, P. 25) expressed in base six, 3600 seconds in a minute divided by 60 = 60, and 360 degrees divided by 60 equals 6. The

ancient Babylonian civilization used a Sexagesimal System and divided the circle by the six sided hexagon to produce 60.

The frequency of the Earth's 24-hour solar day reveals some interesting insights into the DNA.

The formula:
$$[(9 \times \sqrt{9}) \times (4 + 4) \times (9 + 9 + \sqrt{4})^{\sqrt{4}}] = 86,400.$$

There are 86,400 seconds in a 24 hour day and [1/86,400 seconds x (2N = 2 to any whole number power)] gives the frequency or cycles or pulsations per second (called Hertz) of the solar day. This turns out to be simple (1024:675) times 2 to any power and is musically named A^{bb} (-1) relative to (Do) or C = 2 or any multiple of 2 Hertz or 2 cps (cycles per second). 86,400 = musical note $E^{\#}$ (+1).

Swiss scientist Hans Cousto in his book *The Cosmic Octave* reports that Fritz Popp did a study at the University of Marburg in Germany that determined the maximum resonance of the DNA to be 854 trillion Hertz or 8.54E14 Hertz.

Now, 854 trillion Hertz divided by 2 to the power of 42 = 194.172118829 Hertz, and our 24-hour day. Note (1024:675) x (2^7) = 194.**18074074** Hertz (or cycles per second), or x 2^{42} = (8.54015929339E14 Hertz).

[(Brackett M8 = 19440 angstroms): (Paschen M5 = 12814.453125 angstroms)] = (1024:675) = solar day A^{bb} (–1). This shows hydrogen spectral lines ratios producing an octave of the Earth day.

The 24-hour day is only 1.00001865262 times higher than the Fritz Popp value! (See Suppliment A, item 13).

1.62 in base-10 becomes $1.513\overline{888}$ = (109:72) in base-12. Ratio (1024:675) in base-10 = $1.51\overline{703703}$. Fibonacci ratio (13:8) = 1.625 becomes $1.516782\overline{407407}$ = (2621:1728) in base-12, symbolic π = 3 divided by 2 = 1.5.

Another important Earth related frequency is the quartz electro-stimulation frequency. When electricity is applied to quartz crystal, it gives off a frequency of 786,432 cycles per second, which is a note G = 3Hz. (Remember 3 as the "power number" Kryon mentions) times 4 to the 9th power or 262144.

Our simple Kryon key formula is:
$[(\sqrt{9}) \times (\sqrt{4})$ to $(\sqrt{4} \times 9)$ power$)]$ = 786,432.

A large amount of the Earth is composed of silicon dioxide, which is quartz crystal. This assists Earth like a grant crystal radio, to be programmed with all sorts of frequency stimulation and thought programming. I'm suggesting that the high quantity of quartz in the Earth is acting as a super quartz computer.

During a full moon, the moon emits a frequency of 12 hertz (according to a Stanford University study), producing much erratic human and other creature behavior.

The 12 hertz is a lower octave (Multiple of 2) of the quartz electric-stimulation frequency 786,432 divided by (2^{16} = 65536) = 12. **It appears that base-12 is being suggested in both cases**.

When one wants to compute the circumference of a circle, area of a circle, volume of a sphere, a value of pi must be used (e.g., the diameter of a circle times pi equals its circumference).

When you multiply, the ratio (2048:2025) called the "diaschisma" in music terms times any multiple of 3, or 12, or 786,432, you get the earth's 24 hour solar day frequency in some particular octave. This diaschisma is found in the ratio of old Egyptian pi = (256:81) = (3 $^{13}/_{81}$) and old Babylonian pi (25:8) = (3 $^1/_8$).

(256:81) / (25:8) = (2048:2025)

In the special lines of hydrogen expressing color frequency in angstrom units, the Brackett M5 line (40500 angstroms) divided by the Paschen M5 line = (12814.453125 angstroms) = (256:81) or Egyptian pi exactly = (3.**160493827**), and Paschen M5 divided by Balmer M6 = [4100.625 angstroms] equals (25:8) = (3.125) = Babylonian pi exactly! (See note 14).

I'm not suggesting that these are the true values of pi as Kryon suggests the study of 9-9-4-4 will reveal, but these values are maintained in the ratio of hydrogen spectral lines or in the "hydrogen rainbow" and their ratio to each other expresses the ratio of the 24-hour day, and quartz electro stimulation, and possibly hints at the relationship of our DNA resonance (resonance = to resound) and quartz crystal! The high silicon content in lettuce may also be of importance nutritionally to increase human frequency.

Part Two
The Many Faces
of "Pi"

The quest for the true value of pi has been in the forefront of research by civilizations and individuals for centuries, or perhaps eons of time. Kryon mentioned the key 9-9-4-4 to help us find the value for pi as he said that our scientists were not using the correct value.

Furthermore, he stated that we needed to know the correct value if we wanted to travel beyond this galaxy. In addition, he stated that pi was not a constant (contrary to most current applications) and that it varied with mass *(mass varies with time attributes)*.

Basically, pi is the value that when multiplied by the diameter of a circle produces the circle's circumference. The formula "$4/3$ pi times the radius cubed" produces the volume of a sphere.

The area of a circle uses the formula "pi times the radius squared," and the surface area of a sphere is determined by "pi times the diameter squared." The torus shape, which is basically a donut shape and is the single known shape that can maintain itself in a vacuum, is also known as the "hypersphere."

The rings dolphins blow to play with are toroids as is our universe. The surface area of a torus uses the formula "4 pi squared times the radius squared" and the volume of a torus is calculated by "2 pi squared times the radius cubed." The math of cones and cylinders all involve pi.

So what is the value of pi? The current scientific value is 3.141592653589793 (16 places value), but it is a transcendental number. That means that its formula cannot be solved by whole number ratios or even the square root of whole numbers, so it is beyond irrational and is termed *transcendental*.

Scientists feed formulas for dividing a polygon (a many sided figure approaching a circle) into greater and greater divisions producing a pi value of over 500,000 decimal places without a repeating number sequence.

Note: Many engineers today use 3.1416 value for pi for tolerances of 1/10,000th of an inch = $(2^3 \times 3 \times 7 \times 11 \times 17 : 1000)$ = 3.1416.

Readers could consult Petr Bechman's book *A history of pi* (St. Martin's Press 1971) for more historical continuities. I will focus on some interesting known formulas that can be related or derived from 9-9-4-4, as well as some 9-9-4-4 formulas that I found in preparing this chapter.

KRYON mentioned that pi was a whole number. When 9944 is converted from base-12 it becomes 16900 in base-10. (16900 / 3:2) produces 12675 and (12675 / 4096) octavizes 12675 down to 3.094482421875. (My formula #1). Musical note G [169]. See page 363. 4096 = 2^{12}, making 12675 as a whole number and an overtone. **Notice the "944" after the decimal.** Also (12675 / 30) equals 422.5 and that is the precise pitch of composer G.F. Handel's tuning fork (An "A" note in his day and an "A^b" note by today's pitch references). 12675 = $(3 \times 5^2 \times 13^2)$ = musical note G (13^2). The fraction or ratio for 12675:4096 = 3 and $387/4096$.

Formula 2a $(3379022163 : 2^{30})$ = $(3.146959620527923107147216796875)$ = E### (+3)(1243^2). 3379022163 = [$9944^2 \times (2187:64)$].

Formula 2b $(208581615 : 2^{26})$ = $(3.108108267188072204589843750)$ = E### (+2)(1243^2). 208581615 = [$9944^2 \times (135:64)$].

Note: Formula 2a divided by (81:80) = Formula 2b.

Formula 3a $(6215 : 2^{11})$ = $(3.034\ 66796875)$ = F## (+1)(1243). 6215 x (Fibonacci 8:5) = 9944. Pythagorean 3:4:5 triangle) = (7458:9944:12430). (6215 x 2) = 12430. 7458 = A# (+1)(1243).

Formula 3b $(100683:2^{15}) = (3.07260$ $1318359375) = F^{\#\#} (+2)(1243).$ $100683 =$ $[9944 \times (81:8)]$.

Note: Formula 3a x (81:80) = Formula 3b.
Formula 4a $(104878125:2^{25}) = (3.12561$ $16926670074462890625) = E^{\#\#\#\#} (+2)$ $(1243).$ $104878125 = [(9944:8) \times 84375]$.
Formula 4b $(1699025625:2^{29}) = (3.164681$ $83882534503936767578125) = E^{\#\#\#\#}$ $(+3)(1243)$.

Note: Formula 4a x (81:80) = Formula 4b.
All ratios may be multiplied by $(32805:32768 = \text{Schisma})$ or $(531441 :524288 = \text{Pythagorean comma})$.

A musical whole number pi = $(405:128) = 3.1640625 = (3.125$ G$^{\#}$ equals Babylonian pi) x $(^{81}/_{80}$ comma$) = $ G$^{\#}(+1)$ note. This value is also found in the hydrogen lines.

I found that this ratio times the ancient Archimedian pi value (see Note 1) $(^{22}/_{7} = 3^{1}/_{7}) = 9.944196\overline{428571} = (4455:448)$, and this is the exact difference between two spectral lives of hydrogen (Lyman M3= 102.515625 millimicrons minus Lyman M8= 92.$\overline{571428}$ millimicrons 9.944196$\overline{428571}$ exactly). $(405:128)$ is a just tuned G$^{\#}$ $(+1)$ note and 102.515625 is $[64 \times (6561:4096)]$ which = 1.601806640625 and is the Pythagorean cycle of fifths G$^{\#}$ $(+2)$ note, and $(102.515625 \times 64) = 6561.9$. $9.44196\overline{428571} = $ G$^{\#\,(11)}$ L (-1).

$$9.944 = E^{\flat} (1243)$$

Notes:
- A millimicron = one billionth of a meter.
- 1 millimicron x 10 equals 1 angstrom.
- Lyman M8 = 92.571428 = (648:7) is the musical note F$^{\#}$ L $(+1)$.
- (L) means prime 7 in the denominator of the whole number ratio.

The Balmer M3 spectral line of hydrogen equals 6561 angstroms exactly. Much musical and spectral line data is encoded in

the Great Pyramid of Giza (See Wesley Bateman's *The Rods of Amon Ra,* 3-Volume Set).

$(405:128)$ divided by the musical ratio $(81:80 = 1.0125)$, called the **comma**, equals $(25:8) = 3.125 = 3^{1}/_{8} = $ Babylonian pi. 3.125 is also found in the ratio of hydrogen spectral lines and in the Great Pyramid.

3.125 is the note G$^{\#}$ $(25:8)$ in just tuning using prime 2, 3 and 5 only. The $(+1)$ and (-1) in the musical ratios refer to multiples or divisions of the $(81:80)$ comma.

The Babylonians used the sexagesimal system based on 60, and their formula for 3.125 was $(3/\text{pi} = 57/60 + 36/60^2)$ which becomes $3/0.96 = 3.125$. 3.125 is the omega major value of pi in Wesley Bateman's Amon Ra system (see note 16).

Bateman's omega minor value is the old Egyptian value mentioned in the Rhind Papyrus or the Ahmes Papyrus ~ 1650 B.C., found at Thebes.

That value is $(256:81) = 3.\overline{160493827}$. That was noted as $(16/9)^2$ in the Rhind Papyrus and $[4 \times (8/9)^2]$. 0.160493827 is a repeating sequence.

$(256:81 / 2) = (128:81)$, which is the Pythagorean musical ratio of the minor 6th (cycle of 5ths) called A$^{\flat}$ (-1) relative to C = Do = $(1:1)$.

This ratio is also found in the spectral lines of hydrogen (Brackett M5 = 40500 angstroms divided by Paschen M5 = 128 14.453125 angstroms equals $(256:81)$ exactly). 256:81 can be expressed as "4 to the power of 4, divided by 9 squared." $[4^4 / 9^2]$.

When 3.125 is considered a base-12 value, then the base-10 equivalent is 3.16 decimally, and 3.16 can be expressed as (79:25). Notice that the Ahmes Papyrus value 256:81 = **3.160**493827 contains **3.16** as the first three digits followed by a zero! Interestingly, the 8th root of 9944 is the irrational value 3.16005862344.

When the musician Les Brown did experiments dropping an object into various liquids, he found that the rings were formed at the ratio of the 4th root of pi. The 4th root of (256:81) = (4:3) x (4:3) x (4:3) x (4:3), and (4:3) is the musical interval of the perfect 4th that will create the Pythagorean cycle of fifths (3:2), or cycle of fourths (4:3).

The ratio (3:2), or perfect fifth, is the octave complement of (4:3). (3:2) x (4:3) = 2 = the octave. No other $\sqrt[4]{}$pi value will create the perfect 4th musically. Many of the hydrogen lines are in (4:3) or (3:2) ratio, or octave multiples of (3:2).

Some interesting inversions happen with (405:128) = G#(+1) and (256:81) = Ab (−1). [(128:405) = (256:81) x (10)] and [(81:256) = (405:128) divided by 10]. [(405:1280) x (256:81) = 10].

Now, the Hindu mathematician Brahmagupta (b-598 A.D.) used the square root of 10 ($\sqrt{10}$) = 3.16227766017 for pi and in China, Hou Han Shu (130 A.D.) used 3.1622, the first five digits of the square root of 10. The Covelle and Nelson book *Life Force In The Great Pyramid*, concludes that the square root of 10 was the key value in the overall layout of the Giza Pyramid.

The square root of 10 is an irrational number and I believe the quote that "*whole numbers rule at the atomic level*" (as evidenced by the hydrogen spectral ratios which are all whole number ratios) rules out "the square root 10" as pi. *(Geometric forms generate frequencies and can influence the be-*

havior of forms, energies, objects and our own DNA and brain waves.)

(405:128) in base-10 = 3.1640625 becomes (3.12733973681) in base-12, or ratio (112058237:35831808) in base-12.

(25:8) = **3**.125 in base-10 becomes 3.10011$\overline{5740740}$ = ratio (5357:1728).

The ratio of the above two values of Babylonian pi is [(25:8) / (5357:1728)] = 1.00878160635, suggests a value close to the atomic weight of hydrogen of 1.008 =(126:125).

Some tables list the atomic weight or atomic mass of hydrogen as 1.00797, rather than 1.008. My value is [(245:243) / (3888:3887)] = 1.00797113413. The number 3888 angstroms is Balmer M8 spectral line of hydrogen.

The number 3887 = 13 x 13 x 23 is the 23rd harmonic of 169, which is an Fb relative to pi = (12675 / 4096), which equals note G (13 x 13 x 75).

(243:2) = 121.5, which is Lyman M2 in millimicrons (see note 9). And Lyman [(M7 = 93.0234374995) x 64] / 243 equals 24.5. This accounts for all the numbers in my formula except 3887, and that is one overtone below 3888. My point is that my formula demonstrates whole number ruling. Note also the superparticular ratio (3888:3887).

Very interesting next discovery: Let's return for a moment to the difference between Lyman M3 and Lyman M8 equalling 9.9441964$\overline{28571}$ millimicrons. When I back engineered the formula to produce an exact 9.944 millimicron value, then Lyman M3 becomes 102.5136 and Lyman M8 9.944 millimicrons lower becomes 92.5696. The original ratio of Lyman M3/Lyman M8 = (567:512) is still maintained, and which turns out to be a superparticular ratio (N + 1:N) of (50625:50624) below the original ratio.

Therefore, [(Babylonian pi = 3.125) / (506 25:50624)] creates a new pi value of 3.1249382716 = (6328:2025) factored as (2^3 x 7 x 113:3^4 x 5^2) for a new G# note.

This also generates the equivalent for [G# (+1) = (405:128) = 3.1640625] or 3.164 = (791:250) = (7 x 113/2 x 5^3). It further generates for Egyptian pi = (256:81) = 3.160 493827 = A^b (−1) musically, a new A^b (−1) of 3.16043139764 = (12959744:4100625).

The reciprocal of the Rydberg constant used to calculate the Amon Ra value (omega major) is 91.125 = (729:8) and 9.1125 grams is the ancient measure called the Heavy Quedet, used to weight gold and silver. Also 91.125 is used for millimicron values of the hydrogen lines.

The Sargent/Welsh book, The Key To The Periodic Chart of The Atoms, lists the mass of the electron as (9.1091 x 10 $^{-28}$) grams.

A new Rydberg reciprocal emerges from the (50625:50624) ratio division of 91.1232 = (56952:625) = [2^3 x 3^2 x 7 x (113:5^4)] for the generation of new spectral line values and pi = 3.164 and 3.12493827160.

(91.1232 / 3.164) = 9.16363 = (1008:110) = (504:55).

Remember 1.008 as a value for the atomic weight of hydrogen. 110 Hz is A = $^{440}/_4$.

Notice that a Fibonacci Spiral based on 240 produces 1008. [240 x (8:5) = 384]. [384 x (13:8)] = 624; [624 x (21:13)] = 1008. These ratios are from the Fibonacci series 1, 1, 2,

3, 5, 8, 13, 21, 34, 55, 89, 144 etc. See Bonnie Gount's book Beginnings of the Sacred Design for some excellent insights here.

[The Vela Pulsar modulating frequency 11.2 divided by (11:9)] − (6) = 3.16363 = (174:55) = 2 x Fibonacci ratio 89:55. 3.164 in base-10 converts to 3.12731481482 = (540 4:1728) = (1351:432) and 1351 = (7 x 193) and (16 x 27) = 432 = 216 Palmani 2 = "numberer of secrets." There are 432,000 miles in the Sun's radius.

Notice that (624 / 200) = 3.12, another pi likeness. 240 degrees = 0.666666 or $^2/_3$ of 360 degree circle and 1008 = (360 x 2.8) (See note 11) and Vela Pulsar "11.2" divided by 4 = 2.8.

Bonnie Gaunt points out that the 595 million mile elliptical orbit of the Earth around the Sun times the 5,280 feet in a mile (see note 12) equals 3.1416 $E^{(12)}$. ($E^{(12)}$ means 10^{12}). 5 x 7 x 17 = 595. (note: 595,000,000 = $B^{####}$ $^{(17)}$(L)(+1). 595,000,000 divided by 2^{21} divided by [(51:50) x (36:35)] = (1171875:4096) = 286.102294921875 = Great Pyramid rectification value.

The value 3.1416 can be expressed as (3927:1250) or 3(177/1250ths), or 3 degrees, 8 minutes and 29.76 seconds of arc. 3927 factored to (3 x 7 x 11 x 17).

This value of pi was noted by the famous Egyptian Ptolemy who also founded the Library at Alexandria. [Ptolemy, 2nd century A.D. pi = (377 / 120) = 3.141666 and 377 factored = (13 x 29).

The Hindu Aryabhata published the value 3.1416 expressed as (62,832 / 20,000) in 499A.D. Bashkara (1114 A.D.) another Hindu used the same value. The ancient Hindu astronomical documents, the

Siddhantas (pub. 380 A.D.), used the same value as do many scientists and engineers, since it represents transcendental pi rounded up to 4 decimal places.

I found further that when 29.76 seconds of arc is expressed as 93 / 3.125, we see 93 representing the 93,000,000 miles it takes light to travel from the Sun to Earth. 29.76 also equals 744 / 25. (744 gematria = "two great lights")

When I converted this value to base-12, I got 3.11193094136 = (64529:20736). The numerator 64529 factored as (173 x 373) and the denominator 20736 can be expressed as $(9 \times 9) \times (4^4) = (144)^2$. More base-12.

20736 is also 12^4 and 20736 which is an E (+1) note relative to C = 2N, or a Pythagorean ditone third = [(81:64) x 2N]. Also 20736 is called the "Harmonic of Universal Consciousness" by William B. Corner in *Harmonic Mathematics* (Tesla Book Company). (Pyramid phi 1.62 x 12800 = 20736). 207.36 = [(1.62 = 81:50) x 128)] = A^b (+1) note. 1.62 is a key pyramid phi value. The frequency of the 39th octave of the planet Uranus's rotation around the Sun is 207.356091622 Hz. This easily rounded up to 207.36.

Since 144^2 equals 20736, Conner expresses 20736 as (89 phi x 144) where phi = (144:89), a Fibonacci Series 1, 1, 2, 3, 5, 8, 13, 21, 34, 55, 89, 144. Also Egyptian pi = (256:81) generates 20736 as a product of (256 x 81).

Our mean Lunar diameter is found by multiplying each number of the number "64529," thus 6 x 4 x 5 x 2 x 9 equals 2,160. This includes "216" as "Palmoni," "the numberer of secrets," times the reproductive number 10.

Another very important value is sacred texts, sacred structures and temples and in the measurements of the Earth is the number 3,168 (see note 12).

The combined feet of the lithosphere = 10 miles thick, and the atmosphere which is 50 miles thick is 60 miles or 60 x 5,280 feet = 316,800 feet. (B. Gaunt, *Beginnings*) and the 9,954 (9944 + 10 = 9954) million mile distance total of the nine planets from the Sun, divided by transcendental pi equals 3168.45660707 million miles (B. Gaunt).

Also a circle whose diameter is the sum of the mean diameter of Earth = 7,920 miles and the mean diameter of the Moon 2,160 miles, times a pi value of (22:7) = 3.$\overline{142857}$, equals 31,680 miles (Another Gaunt observation, thank you!).

In Greek gematria, Lord = 800, Jesus = 888 and Christ = 1480. The sum of 800 + 888 + 1480 = 3,168 exactly.

The diameter of Sarsen circle at Stonehenge equals 105.6 feet (see note 8). (105.6 =A^b when C = 66). Symbolic pi which equals 3 times 105.6 = 316.8. A "symbolic" pi of 3 is used in the Bible frequently. A square based on the diameter of Bluestone Circle at Stonehenge of 79.2 feet equals (4 x 79.2) = 316.8. 79.2 is an E^b note or C = [66 x (6:5)] = 79.2, so 316.8 equals E^b also. Recall the atomic mass of selenium = 79.2.

The diameter of these two circles is (105.8 / 79.2) = (4:3) = 1.$\overline{333333}$ or a perfect 4th interval, and the 4th root of Egyptian pi 256:81.

A pi value of 3.168 = (396:125) is an A^{bb} [11] based on C = 264. The long scale of Station Stone Rectangle of Stonehenge equals 264 feet.

The gematria of 264 = "truth," x 10 = 2640 = "the light." (264 x 2) = 528. 528 = "key."

[396 = (9 + √4) x (9 x 4)] and 125 equals 9 x (9 + 44).

If 3.168 is in base-10, then the base-12 equivalent is 3.$\overline{1296296}$ expressed as (169:54) is an A^{bb} (–1) harmonically, when my first formula 12675:4096 = 3.0944 82421875 is a G note, and middle C = 264.0625 or (4225 / 16). [(169 / 54) x (81:80)] = 3.16875, A^{bb} = (4563:1440).

This new C = 264.0625 in ratio (4225:4224) times Station Stone Rectangle C = 264 (see note 7). Perhaps 264.0625 is the intended Stonehenge value.

The Bethlehem 31.68 degree north latitude divided by the arc sine of $^1/_3$ = (19.471 2206345 degree key angle in the prime platonic solid, the tetrahedron), is 1.627 01664136 (a close phi ratio).

One phi ratio in the Great Pyramid is 1.62 = (81:50) = A^b (+1) and Fibonacci ratio (13:8) = 1.625 = $A^{b\,(13)}$. Most of the vortexian and volcanic activity in Earth and other planets of our solar system is at 19.47 degrees north and south latitude, above and below the equator. There is a very important angle in Sacred Geometry (natural law of Geometry) and in life force of the planets. (It is the angle of the ratio of face/height of an equilateral Tetrahedron.) D# (+3) = 19.4619506835.

I found an interesting pi value considering the (arc sine of $^1/_3$) plus (20:3) = 6.$\overline{666666}$ to equal the (√ pi) / 4.

(19.4712206345 + 6.$\overline{666}$) = 26.1378873012 degrees creating a sine of 0.440532901682 [4 x (0.440532901682)^2] equals 3.1051 0779944. Notice the last two decimal places of "9-9-4-4." And (7 x 11 = 77); (9 x 11 = 99);

(4 x 11 = 44). 3 + 1 + 1 = 5 with the next 5 = 55 = 5 x 11.

(20:3) = 6.$\overline{666}$ is the omega minor value of Planck's constant in the Amon Ra system, or (5:3) major 6th interval times 4, or two Hunabs = [2 x (135:128)] times omega minor pi or Egyptian pi (256:81).

Planck's constant is known as the "Universal Unit of Action," called h, with a normal scientific value of (6.625 x 10^{-27} erg sec.) This equals to (13:8) = 1.625, + 5 = 6.625; all Fibonacci numbers.

Pyramid phi (1.62 + 5) = 6.62 which is ratio (331:50). 17 into (331 prime) equals 19.4705882353 close to the 19.47122 06345 tetrahedral angle.

A tetrahedron is a pyramid of 4 triangular sides, or a 3-sided pyramid around a triangular base. The Platonic solid equilateral tetrahedral, is composed of 4 equilateral triangles with 3 equal edges each and three 60 degree angles per face.

The acute angle of the tetrahedron face (slope) with respect to the central axis (from the center of the base to the top vertex), is 19.4712206345 degrees = arc sine of $^1/_3$.

Going back to our 9-9-4-4 cue, (99 + 44) = 143. 1-4-3 might imply the anagram 314 or a pi of 3.14. The number 314 is a number associated with Metatron, the Being emanating from the Great Central Sun of our Universe who is in charge of our Universe (see J. J. Hurtak's *The Keys Of Enoch*). Metatron is said to be the creator of the electron. Fibonacci series sum (1 + 1 + 2 + 3 + 5 + 8 + 13 + 21 + 34 + 55) = 143. I found several examples where subtracting hydrogen spectral lines from 9944 left a remainder of 143 = (11 x 13) = (144 – 1). 81 + 50 + 12 = 143. (81:50) = 1.62. (99^2 + 143) = 9944.

3.14 = (157:50) and uses prime 157. 3.14 in base-10. It converts to 3.$\overline{111111}$ in base-12 expressed as (28:9), an A^{b7} note. Neither values are whole numbers without decimals when multiplied by 2N. The standard ratio of the height to the base of the Pyramid of the Sun in Teotihuacan, Mexico = (2932.8:233.5 feet) = 3.14004282655 x 4. (a (4:pi) ratio. We could also consider 3.143 = (3143:1000) = (7 x 449:2^3 x 5^3) and (3143 – 768) = 2375. (2375:768) =3.0924479166$\overline{6}$. The first "2" + 7 = 9 and the immediate two "4's" reveal a "9-9-4-4" clue.

The base-12 version of 3.143 is 3.1128 47$\overline{222222}$ or (1793:576) and 1793 factored to (11 x 163). The denominator 768 = (3 x 256), a key value in the base of the Great Pyramid of Giza expressed in feet. 9944 / 8 = 1243 and (1243:768) = 1.6184895833$\overline{3}$, a very close golden section phi ratio. One side of base = 768 omega minor feet. Phi ratio = [(1 + √5) / 2] = 1.61803398875. (1243:768) = G#$^{(11)(113)}$.

We could use an anagram of 1-2-3-4 and create a pi of 3.124, which would be a superparticular value below Babylonian pi of (3.125:3.124) = (781:250) = [(11 x 71):(2 x 5^3)]. [(3.124:9944) x 10] = 3.14159292035.

Returning again to my formula number one = (12675:4096); we can multiply this octavized whole number by (65:64) = [5 x 13):2^6] another prime 13 overtone, to get 3.14283370972 = (823875:262144) = [(3 x 5^3 x 13^3) : 2^{18})]. This value is even closer to standard pi, and it is an octavized "whole number."

A musical formula that is very close to a note in the Chinese cycle of 5ths expressed as ratio (3^{49} : 2^{76}) is 3.16710025178, a cyclic diminished sixth interval.

This is also close to Egyptian pi (256:81)

which is a Pythagorean minor sixth = A^b (– 1) = 3.$\overline{160493827}$. Egyptian pi (256:81) is an undertone, since the numerator 256 is a multiple of 2. [12^4 / (6561 Balmer M3)] = (256:81).

For any value of pi to qualify as a whole number, it must be an overtone and thus capable of being expressed as a whole number ratio with a denominator being a multiple of 2 to some octavized power, as in (405:128) or (25:8).

Finally, when the decimal value is multiplied by the correct value of 2 to the Nth power, a whole number is produced; eg. (25:8) = 3.125 and (3.125 x 8) = 25 and 25 is our whole number.

In the 38th power of 2 which is 2748 77906944, there are 68,719,476,736 whole number possibilities for pi between symbolic pi = 3 and an upper limit of 3.25 which is Fibonacci ratio [(13:8) x 2] or (2 phi) when phi equals 1.625.

I choose 2 to the 38th power as my upper limit overtone octave denominator because all the ratios could be expressed with 12 digits in the numerator and 12 in the denominator, and no ratios would require scientific notation of 10 or E to some power.

In this octave pi of 3.14159265359 equals (863554413089 : 274877906944). In the 2^{37} octave this value of pi equals (431777206545 : 137438953472). The best octave ratio for this standard value of pi is [(107$\mathbf{944}$301637) : (34359738368)] = 2^{35}. Note the "$\mathbf{944}$" in the 4, 5 and 6th numbers in the numerator.

This numerator (107944301637) contains no multiples of 2, and is the lowest numerator (whole number) and overtone that will produce pi (equals 3.14159265359) on my calculator, which handles 12 digits with 11 decimal places.

$107944301637 = (3^2 \times 127 \times 94439549)$. Notice "9-4-4." 94439459 adds up horizontally to 47, and $(4 + 7) = 11$. The value $(107944301637 : 2^{35})$ is a rational number.

Interestingly, the 16th root of $94439549 = 3.15099049527$, which is an irrational number. Notice the 9-9-4.

Returning to the number 3168 once again, but considering it as base-12, creates 5408 as its base-10 equivalent. $3168 =$ musical note $G^{(11)}$ when $C^{(11)} = 264 \times 2^N$. $(113:36) = (9944:3168) = 3.13\mathbf{888}$. 5408 factors down to $(2^5 \times 13^2)$. This is an F^b note (ratio 32:25) in a musical system based on formula no 1 = $[(12675:4096) =$ pi = note G]. The G note divided by (75:64) becomes an $F^b = 2.640625$, and (2.640625×2048) becomes 5408. So the famous 3168 number (which is contained in a very famous Egyptian cannon of harmonic proportions) feeds directly into formula no. 1 harmonically!

The F^b is important as the product of pi times phi. For example, Egyptian pi = $(256:81)$ $A^b(-1)$ times pyramid phi = $(81:50)$ = A^b $(+1)$ equals $5.12 = (128:25) = F^b$ or $(36:25) \times 4$.

Our 5408 value becomes 5.28125 or $(5408:1024) = (169:32)$, which is an overtone. Wesley Bateman calls 5.12 the omega minor value of (pi x phi) and he names (pi x phi) as "ankh." His value for omega major ankh is $5.0625 = (81:16) =$ Babylonian pi = [3.125 x (pyramid phi) = 1.62].

The number $(5.0625 \times 16) =$ whole number 81 based on a lower octave of 81. Musically, it is a note E $(+1)$ or $[(C = 4) \times (81:64)]$

and a Pythagorean ditone (large major third) interval. One important aspect of 81 is that it is the sum of the atomic numbers of the three magnetic elements Iron (Fe) = 26, Cobalt (Co) = 27, and Nickel (Ni) = 28. $[(26 + 27 + 28) = 81]$.

Some researchers say the base of the Great Pyramid measures as 288 reeds (see note 1), or 72 reeds per side at the rock level. $(904:288) = (9944:768)$.

One important Egyptian cannon includes five multiples of 81: (1296, 2592, 5184, 10368 and 20736). No other number is repeated as many times. (As published in *The Dimensions of Paradise* by John Michell.)

Remember: $[(9 \times 9 \times 4 \times 4) = 1296] = (800 \times 1.62 \varnothing)$. $(9 \times 9 \times 4^4) = 20736 = 12^4 = (1.62 \times 12800)$. The two terms of Egyptian pi = $(256:81)$ multiplied as $(256 \times 81) = 20736$.

Now, let's consider pi as an undertone ratio (like Egyptian pi 256:81) when the numerator must be a multiple of 2, and the denominator an appropriate whole number.

Likely candidates would be:

1. $(256:82) = (3.\overline{\mathbf{12195}})$. $[82 = (2 \times 41)]$.
2. $(256:83) = 3.0843373494$. 83 is a prime number. Also 83 is Kryon's English gematria total.
   In example 2 the last 3 digits are "494" and the sum of all the digits is 48 or (4×12), **implying base-12**.
3. $(256:80) = (16:5) = (3.2) = [2 \times (8:5)]$ and $(8:5)$ is a Fibonacci series ratio and a low value for phi $[(8:5) = 1.6]$.
   Phi = $[(1 + \sqrt{5}) / 2] = 1.61803398875$ and is an irrational number.
   The kings's chamber in the Great Pyramid has a length to width ratio of $(2:1)$ and a floor diagonal of square root of 5.

The square root of $[(\sqrt{3}.2)/4] = 0.4472$ 135955, and is the sine value for the acute angle of the floor's diagonal = 26.5650511771 degrees.

Twice this sine is 0.**894**427191 which is $(2/\sqrt{5})$ and contains a "944" and is the cosine of this angle.

4. (512:163) = 3.14110429448 using prime 163. Notice the "9-4-4" in the decimal portion.

5. (2048:659 prime) = 3.10773899848 (Prime 659). The 998 contains 9-9-4 + 4.

6. (4096:1317) = 3.11009870919 = (32768:10536)
10536 = $(2^3 \times 3 \times 439)$ to the base-10 value of 6120.
6120 is in the Egyptian cannon and is $F^{\#\#\,(17)}$ (+1) musically. **612 implies base-12.** 1317 = (3 × 439) and 439 is one overtone below the common tuning standard of A = 440 Hz.

7. The ratio (2048:666) = 3.**075075**. The 666 is (37 × 18), and (256:81) Egyptian pi divided by (37:36) = (2048:666), or the subharmonic prime 37 value for A^b (–1). 666 = $E^{(37)}$ (+1) musically. 666 = 486 x (37:27).

The Egyptian cannon contains 2664 which is Brackett M8 = 1944 millimicron (see note 2) spectral line of hydrogen times (37:27) = the physical constant of hydrogen = 1.**370370**.

Our ratio could also be expressed as (8192:2664). 2664 is $E^{(37)}$ (+1) or E (+1) = 2592 = [(81 x 32) x (37:36)]. (666 x 4) = 2664.

In Wes Bateman's Amon Ra system, Green Ankh [Green pi x 1.62 = Green Ankh = $(\sqrt{648}/5) = 5.09116882454$] when squared equals 25.92. Also Green ankh is the diagonal of a square with sides of 3.6.

The square root of 648 is found in the Great Pyramid, and is common in Bruce Cathie's world grid analysis. The square root of 648 is the Amon Ra Green A^b note.

8. (16384:5185) = 3.15988428158 and (1037 x 5) = 5185 = [5 x 17 x 61].

The simplest decimal value for the base angles of the Great Pyramid is 51.85 degrees for 51 degrees 51 minutes. 5184 is in the Egyptian cannon and (16384:5184) = (256:81) = Egyptian pi.

One of my favorite pi values is Wes Bateman's Red pi = (84823:27000) = 3.141 $\overline{592592592}$, and 84823 is a product of prime (271 x 313). [(Red pi / 4) x (27:2 =13.5)] = 10.602875 Hz, the most common alpha wave generated in meditation.

The diameter of the hydrogen atom is most often listed as 10.6 crystal angstroms. 10.6 generates a pi of 3.1407 = (424:135). Egyptian pi = (256:81) generates (10.$\overline{666}$) as an alpha wave which equals a note F when C equal 8 Hz.

Angstrom/1.0020 = crystal angstrom = KX.

The 13.5 Hz is called the alpha ceiling frequency and is $^1/_{16}$ of 216, the Palmoni number. All of the above values except the simplest 10.6 are found in the Great Pyramid.

[(Babylonian pi 3.125 / 4) x 13.5] = 10.546875 Hz or the Moon diameter 2160 divided by 204.8. [The Mayan Hunab (135:128) = 1.0546875].

The Earth's Schumann Resonance hovered around 7.83+ Hz and (2.5 x Red pi) = 7.85398$\overline{148}$ = (84823:10800) which is a Red Ra C (–1) note.

I calculated a 7.8310546875 Hz based on [(33:8) x (243:128)] creating a Pythagorean $B^{(11)}$ (+1) or (8019:1024). Notice the last 8 digits (1-0-5-4-6-8-7-5) after the 7.83.

The (8019:1024) generates a pi of (8019:2560) = 3.132421875 or $G^{(11)}$ (+1). The Egyptian cannon contains number 114048 which is $A^{(11)}$ (+1) or 891 when octavized. Notice both numbers contain 8-1-9. (9944 / 8) = 1243. The first (4) decimal places = 1324, an anagram of 1243.

$[G^{(11)}$ (+1) x (10:9)] = $A^{(11)}$ (+1).

8019 is a comma of (81:80) times the mean Earth equatorial diameter of 7,920 miles. (8019:2560) is also (33:16) = [C x (1215:800)], and 1215 angstroms is the Lyman M2. Most intense visible spectral line of hydrogen. Of special interest, (800:81) is the Amon Ra value for Green pi squared, and is the sequence 9.87654320987 654320 or 8 times the sequence (100:81) = 1.234567901 = an E (– 1) note.

Green pi is the geometric mean of Babylonian pi and Egyptian pi. Green pi = 3.125 x$\sqrt{256:81/25:8}$ = $\sqrt{2048:2025}$. Green pi is an irrational number = $\sqrt{2}$ x (20:9) = ($\sqrt{1.62}$) x (200:81) = ($\sqrt{800}$:81) = ($\sqrt{800}$/9) = (4/$\sqrt{1.62}$) = [($\sqrt{9:8}$) x (80:27)] = 3.14269680527. A square of side = 0.9 has a diagonal of ($\sqrt{1.62}$).

Also of special interest is 3.0944 = ($\sqrt{9}$ + 0.0944) = (1934:625) or (9670:3125). The number 1934 is the base-10 equivalent of 1152 = 9 x 128 = D.

1152 is the Amon Ra omega minor circumference of the Balmer circle relative to hydrogen or [(256:81) x 364.5] = The omega major Balmer Constant = (729 / 2) = 364.5.

1152 = (12^2 x 8) **implying base-12**. 1934

= (2 x 967). 1934 can be rearranged into 3.149 and 3149 = (47 x 67). (47 + 67) = 114 = (2 x 3 x 19).

114 is called the "Number of Harmony" in the book *Two Thirds* by Percy and Myers. (800:7) = 114.$\overline{285714}$ = $A^\#$ (L). B^b (–1) = $\sqrt{256:81}$ x 64 = 113.$\overline{777777}$. (L) = subharmonic 7.
(96 + 5 + 6 + 7) = 114.

The Balmer circumference (Amon Ra) divided by 10 = 115.2, and 115.2 divided by (96:95) = 114 or a $B^{b(19)}$, when 115.2 = B^b = (64 x 9:5). $C^{(19)}$ = 63.$\overline{333}$ = (190:3).

The Egyptians used grids of 19 x 19 and 19 x 18 squares behind their art to guide the harmonic proportions. The ratio (19:6) = 3.1$\overline{666}$ can be implied from this grid = $A^{b(19)}$. (1140:360) = 19.6. *Note: The "Flower of Life" has 19 circles around 12 circles around 6 circles around 1. The "Flower of Life" or Metatron's key, contains all of the geometry of our universe, once you know how to decode it.* (19 x 6) = 114, the number of harmony. (19 + 12 + 6 + 1) = 38. (3 + 8) = Kryon 11.

Several other pi values are found in the hydrogen spectral lines (in angstroms):

1. [(Balmer M9, 3834.35064934 angstroms) / (Lyman M2, 1215)] = (243:154). This ratio x 2 = (243:77) = 3.155844 = [3^5: (7 x 11)].

2. [(Lyman M3, (6561:64) millimicrons) – (Lyman M8, (648:7))] = **9.944**1964286 = [(405:128) x (22:7, Archimedean pi)].

3. [(Balmer M11, (49005:13)) / (Lyman M2, (121: 39))] = (11^2 : 3 x 13) = 3.102564.

4. (a). [(Balmer M8, 3888) / (1296 number Most Holy)] = (3, symbolic pi).
    (b). [(Balmer M8, 3888) / (Lyman M2, 1215)] = 3.2 = (16:5).
    (c). [(Balmer M8, 3888) / 1200] = 3.24 = 1.62 (Pyramid phi x 2).

5. [(Lyman M6, 937.$\overline{285714}$) / (Lyman M2, 1215)] x 4 = 3.$\overline{0857142}$ = (108:35) = [3 x (36:35)] = GL. GL musical note.

6. [(Lyman M6, (6561:7)) / 300] = 3.12$\overline{4285714}$ = (6561:2100).

7. [(Lyman M7, 930.234375) / (Lyman M2, 1215 / 4)] = 3.0625 = (49:16) = a whole number overtone.

8. [(Lyman M7, (59535:64)) / 300] = 3.10078125 = (3969:1280). [3969 = Balmer M7]

9. [(Lyman M8, 925.$\overline{714285}$) / (Lyman M2 / 4)] = 3.$\overline{047619}$ = (64:21) = 21st undertone.

10. [(Balmer M11, (49005:13)) / 1200] = 3.1413$\overline{461538}$ = (9801:3120).

11. [(The Moon diameter, 2160) x 16] = 34560 when divided by (256:81) = Brackett M6, 10935.

12. [(Earth mean radius, 3,960) / (Balmer M10, 3796.875)] x 3 = 3.12$\overline{888}$ = (704:225)

13. [(9 x 9 x 4⁴) = 20736 = 12⁴] / (256:81) = (Balmer M3, 6561) and [(6561:2048) octavized] = 3.20361328125 = G#(+2) = [3.125 x (81:80²)]].

14. [(Lyman M5, 949.21875 angstroms) / 300] = (405:128) = 3.1640625 = G#(+1) = [3.125 x (81:80)]].

15. [(Brackett M5, 40500 angstroms) / (Paschen M5, 12814.453125 angstroms)] = (256:81) = 3.$\overline{160493827}$ (Egyptian pi).

16. (Lyman M2, 1215 angstroms) x (3.125 = 25:8 = Babylonian pi) = (Balmer M10, 3796.875). **9944 in base-10 converts to 5908 in base-12. 5908 = (2² x 7 x 211).**

17. 21.1cm wavelength of hydrogen is broadcast by radio telescopes for SETI research. 20 Hunabs = 21.09375 = E#(+1).

The famous rectification factor of the Great Pyramid listed by most researchers as 286.1 can be derived from 5908, which is the base-12 value when 9944 is the base-10 value.

[(7 x 211 x 3¹³ x 5) : 10 billion] = 286.110031127. This shows the possibility that it was built on base-12 mathematics. The number 5908 is the musical note F##(+2)(7)(211), and C(7)(211) = (11816:6075). Since 5908 contains prime 211, this suggests 21.1 cm wave length of hydrogen. (See #17 on this page.)

Here is one of my favorite formulas:
5908² = 34904464

(34904464 / 16) = 2181529 and (2181529 : 694400) = (311647:99200) = 3.1416028 **2 258 06451612903.**

2181529 = (1477 x 1477). 1477 = (7 x 211). 694400 represents ¹/₁₄₄ = .0069$\overline{444444}$. (694400 / 400) = 1736, and 1736 in base-10 equals 1008 in base-12.
1008 is 1000 times the atomic weight of hydrogen = 1.008 (on many charts).

The quartz electrical stimulation frequency 786,432 cycle per second, when multiplied by 4 becomes 3145728. This number can be converted to 3.145728 = (49152:15625) = Bᵇᵇᵇᵇ(−1) musically.

786,432 is a G note relative to C = 2¹⁸ and is a higher octave of the power number 3. The number 3 is called symbolic pi as it is used in many Holy texts and remains 3 in both base-10 and base-12.

[786,432 / 486, (486 Red Ra feet in height of Great Pyramid)] = 1618.$\overline{172839506}$ = (131072:81) = 512 or 2⁹ times Egyptian pi of (256:81) and is musical note Aᵇ(−1).

This is very close to the irrational value for Ø x 1,000 where Ø = ¹/₂ (1 + [√5]) = 1.61803398875. When expressed as (16384:10125) = 1.618$\overline{172839506}$ or the 10125 undertone and the note Bᵇᵇᵇ(−2).

The actual value of Ø = ¹/₂ (1 + √5) when multiplied by 1000 and then divided by 512 becomes 3.16022263428, an irrational pi value.

$$\sqrt{10} = 3.162227766017.$$

Here are some other irrational pi's based on geometrical (and irrational) and "exceptional" Ø.

1. (Ø²) x [(6:5) or 1.2] = 3.1416407865 (close). *Note: The octave complement of (6:5) is (5:3), a Fibonacci ratio. There are (20) hexagons and (12) pentagons (a ratio of 5:3) on the surface of a soccer ball, grouped (6) hexagons around (1) pentagon.*
2. (4 / √Ø) = 3.14460551104 (higher).
3. [(1 / Ø) x 5] = [(Ø − 1) x 5] = 3.09016994375 (low).
4. [(1 / Ø x 5)² / 3] = 3.18305009375 (high value).

I will conclude this part by shedding another "angle" on pi: the angle at which sunlight is reflected in a prism is 26 degrees 5 minutes = 26.08333333 (see note 3) = (313:12) ratio containing prime 313. This easily suggests 3.13, 3.12, (3.13 − 0.12) = 3.11, and (3.13 + 0.12) = 3.25 = (13:8) Fibonacci ratio x 2.

The sine of 26.08333 degrees times 4 and then squared = 3.09306685233, which is irrational and just below my formula number 1 (12675:4096) = 3.094482421875, which generates a prism angle of 26.089751043 degrees. √26 is close to (phi x pi).

Notice in 26.08333, "26" is the Kryon Hebrew gematria total and "83" is the Kryon English gematria total. There is a lot to a name!

Notes

1. This reed measurement is not the RA system value for the base. One reed = 10.56 ft. = Fᵇ ⁽¹¹⁾.
2. 1944 is the base-10 value for 2160, when 2160 is considered in base-12. Remember the Moon's mean diameter = 2,160 miles. 2160 is in the Egyptian cannon.
3. (30° − 26.08333°) = 3.91666° = (47:12). 47 is the atomic number of silver, the greatest electrical conductor of the elements. 12 = mg. = magnesium atomic number.
4. (26.08333 / 8.3) = 3.14257628112 = (1565:498).
5. (26.08333 / 8.333) = 3.13 = (313:100). In the Amon Ra system, Red pi = (84823:27000), and 84823 = (prime 271 x prime 313). (313 − 271) = 42 the Rainbow Angle.
6. (a). The Queen's chamber shaft inclination angle = 39.5° = (79:2) measured by Rudolf Gantenbrink's "upuaut" robot camera. Note the 79:2 relates to 7,920 miles, Earth mean diameter. [(100:81) x 32] = 39.5061728394 = E (-1). (1/1.62 x 2) = 100:81. [3950:(9944 / 4)] = 1243 = 3.1777 9566567.
6. (b). 39.5 = 39° 30' (3930:1243) = 3.16170555109. (3 x 131) = 393. (81 + 50) = 131.
7. Pythagoras also used the 22 / 7 value of pi.
8. (Balmer M10, 3796.875 angstroms) divided by (Lyman M2, 1215 angstroms) = the most intense visible spectral line of hydrogen, equals 3.125 Babylonian pi exactly. (Paschen M5) divided by (Balmer M6, 4100.625) = 3.125 also.
9. Angstrom value divided by 10 equals millimicron value.

10. Also, "2.8" is a perfect number, where the sum of the parts equals the number. [(Vela pulsar 11.2) divided by 4] = 2.8.

11. 7,920 mean Earth diameter divided by (3:2) = fifth = 5,280.

12. Bethlehem is located 31.68 degrees N. Latitude (B. Gaunt). 864,000 mile diameter of the Sun divided by 11:3 = 3,168, 000 megalithic miles. (Mean diameter 2,160) x 4 x (11:3) = 31,680 megalithic miles.

12. If so, then [3.168 x (4225:4224)] = 3.16875 = A^{bb} or [3.1296 x (81:80 comma)] = 3.16875 = (4563:1440).

13. Sacred Hebrew word for God (YHWH) = (IHVH) = 10.565. The 3 letter version YHW = IHV. YHVH = IHVH = Tetragrammaton = YOD HEH VAV HEH.

14. The 4 hydrogen spectral line series discoverers are: (1) American physicist Fredrick S. Brackett (Infrared hydrogen lines). (2) American physicist Theodore Lyman (1906 Lyman series). (3) German physicist Fredrich Paschen (1908 observations). (4) German mathematician Johann Jakob Balmer (1885 discovery).

Formula 1
G "13 x 13" musical note = $G^{(169)}$

- (12675:4096) = $3^{387}/_{4096}$ = 3.09448 2421875 (base-10).
- 12675 = (3 x 5^2 x 13^2) = (4096=2^{12}).

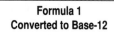

**Formula 1
Converted to Base-12**

This value of pi equals (63259746151 /20639121408) = 3.06504065267427 87984475816694609561550576639739877051262510796118477874307 77828583041203068637910887.

The next 6 formulas are musical **whole number pi values**, and overtones.

Formula 1a.
(12675:4096) = 3.094482421875. Musical note $G^{(169)}$.

Formula 1b.
[Formula 1a x (81:80) called "The comma of Didymus"] = 205335 / 2^{16} = 3.1331634521484375. Musical note $G^{(169)}(+1)$.

Formula 1c.
[Formula 1a x (32805:32768) called "schisma ratio"] = 415803375 / 2^{27} = 3.0979765579104423522949 21875. Musical note $F^{\#\#(169)}(+3)$.

Formula 1d.
[Formula 1a x (531441:524288) called "Pythagorean comma"] = 6736014675 / 2^{31} = 3.13670126 4884322881698608398 4375. Musical note $F^{\#\#(169)}(+4)$.
Note: (Formula 1c) x (81:80) = Formula 1d.

Formula 1e.
[(Formula 1a) x (Schisma ratio) x (Pythagorean comma)] = [(3^{21} x 5^3 x 13^2) : 2^{46}] = 3.1402430723428409464759170077 741146087646484375. Musical note $E^{\#\#\#(169)}(+7)$. *Note: Formula 1e = (formula 1c x formula 1d) / (formula 1a).*

Formula 1f.
[(Formula 1a) x (65:64) called "The prime 13 adjusting ratio)] = (823875 / 2^{18}) = 3.142833709716796875. Musical note $G^{(13\text{ cubed})}$.

Note: The three most important microtonal ratios of *5-limit just intonation* are "The comma of Didymus," "The Schisma ratio," and "The Pythagorean comma." These are the ratios that are used in formula 1b through 1e. **All these ratios can be extracted from the spectral lines of hydrogen.** The (comma of Didymus) x (Schisma ratio) = Pythagorean comma.

Supplement A

1. (9944 in base-12) becomes (16900 in base-10). $9944 = (2^3 \times 11 \times 113$ factored). $16900 = (2^2 \times 5^2 \times 13^2)$.
2. Kryon clue "pi is a whole number."
3. 16900 is too high and too low to be an overtone whose ratio is close to pi.
4. The following is the key base-10 solution: [16900 / (3:2) perfect 5th] = 12675 = $(3 \times 5^2 \times 13^2)$. (12675:4096) = 3.094482421875 (base-10). The 12,675th overtone is a whole number! $4096 = 2^{12}$; the 12th power is a clue!
5. (12675:4096) converted to base-12 = (7403:2454) = 3.01670741646. 12675 = (65 x 65 x 3). [(9 x 9) – (4 x 4)] = 65. *(I converted the whole numbers in the ratio to base 12, then I derived the decimal value from my new whole number ratio).*
6. Notice in 2454, $2^2 = 4$ and $3^2 = 9$ plus 4-0-9 reveals 4-9-4-9. 7403 contains Kryon "11" = (11 x 673); (7 + 4 = 11); (11 x 3 = 33).
7. (12675 – 4096) = 8579 and (7403 + 2454) = 9857. These are numerical anagrams of 9-8-5-7. (9 + 8 + 5 + 7) = 29, (2 + 9) = 11 —> "Kryon 11." (7403 – 2454) = 4949 —> "9-9-4-4."
8. (12675:4096) = 3(387/4096ths) as a fraction. (7403:2454) = 3(4 /2454ths)

9. (12675:4096) / (7403:2454) = (15552225:15161344) = 1.02578142149.
10. Hebrew gematria (12675/1200) = 10.5625 = (10Y) – (5H) – (6V) – (2B) – (5H).
11. G.F Handel's Tuning Fork = 422.5 Hz. Handel's trumpet player, John Shore "invented" the tuning fork. (30 x 422.5) = 12675 = note G (13 x 13) by today's standard. 422.5 in Handel's day was note A which is an A^b by today's standard (8:5) x C = 1:1 making middle C 264.0625 as 1:1.
12. When A = 440, then 440/(5:3 major 6th) = 264 (middle C). C = 264 x (4225:4224) = 264.0625 = C x 16 = 4225 (Superparticular). pi = G relative to C = 264 = (12672:4096) = (99:32) = 3.09375 = 3 ^{3}/$_{32}$.
13. (3.09375 + 18) = 21.09375 = (675:32) = E$^\#$ (+1); a possible hydrogen wavelength in centimeters (rounds up to "21.1"). The reciprocal (32:675) is a low octave of the Earth's 24-hour day (DNA note) = A^{bb} (–1).
14. The hydrogen resonance frequency = 1,420,405,752.7 Hz. This value divided by 2^{30} and then taken to the 4th power = 3.06231745977. A close value is ratio (49:16) = (7^2:2^4) = 3.0625 = an overtone. (Balmer M7 = 3969 angstroms) divided by (49:16) = 1296 = 81 x 16 = "9 x 9 x 4 x 4."
15. (32768:9944) = (4096:1243) = 3.29525341915 undertone = B^{bb} (-1) (11↓)(113↓).

Don't miss Kryon's message to Randy Masters on page 369.

Appendix B

Watt's Solution to 9944

Appendix B

Watt's Solution to 9944
Sole author, James D. Watt, 1995
Portions of this manuscript are under
separate copyright in the Library of Congress

In the first book, *Kryon - The End Times*, pages 14-15 mentioned **9944** as "an important power formula." Those familiar with the Kryon Writings also know similar importance is attached to the numbers **11** (Kryon's character, and the 11:11 window) and **33** ("... will give you insight as to my service"), says Kryon.

The solution here is formated to get in under the publishing wire (days before this book was printed). I am sure the figure is in no way complete. Some other reader(s) will undoubtedly find more, using my findings as a starting point. Those of you who attempted to "decode" it should take heart from the fact that one needs to know that the base-12 system is critical to the solution. This information was missing from the initial statement. As of this writing, I have no way of knowing if this is the "Kryon solution" or not. I simply know that what is offered here is a highly probably solution and that one would be hard pressed to surpass it because of the elegance and dovetailing of detail within it.

Discovery Sequence

This is included because the random playing around with numbers is what brought the sequence to light and sheds some intelligence on how the process works.

In one of many permutations I have performed, I reversed the numbers 9 and 4 and subtracted them from 9944.

$$9944 - 4499 = 5445$$

I divided 5445 by 5 and found 1089 or 33^2. Kryon quoted "... 33 gives insight as to my service." 33^2 can be subtracted cleanly 9 times from 9944, leaving a remainder of **143**. Also of interest is:

$$33^2 \times 9 = 99^2$$

By adding increments of 33^2 to 143, the following sequence of identities is found:

$143 + (33^2 \times 1)$	=	1232	*Each number in this portion adds numerologically to 8.*
$143 + (33^2 \times 2)$	=	2321	
$143 + (33^2 \times 3)$	=	3410	

$143 + (33^2 \times 4)$	=	4499	
$143 + (33^2 \times 5)$	=	5588	
$143 + (33^2 \times 6)$	=	6677	*Each number in this portion adds numerologically to 26.*
$143 + (33^2 \times 7)$	=	7766	
$143 + (33^2 \times 8)$	=	8855	
$143 + (33^2 \times 9)$	=	9944	

The addition of 33^2 increments can be continued of course, and an interesting thing happens at the 13th addition:

$$143 + (33^2 \times 13) = \mathbf{14300}$$

In the "Mathematica" section of this book (see page 305), I mentioned the need of arithmetic systems to be calibrated. Part of the calibration process is a "field of numbers" produced in each base. For **base-10** this field is 100, of which **99** is the **penultimate** (next to last) number. In base-12 the field is 144 and 143 is the penultimate number. On the top of the next page is a comparison of number lines for base-10 and base-12. Look at the relation of 11_{12} and 13_{10}.*

The subscripts (12 and 10) simply denote which math base the number is in.

Base-12	1	2	3	4	5	6	7	8	9	a	b	10	<u>11</u> ..
Base-10	1	2	3	4	5	6	7	8	9	10	11	12	<u>13</u> ..

The penultimate number is a composite of the highest **single** integer and **11**, that base. So $9 \times 11_{10} = 99$ (base-10). And $b \times 11_{12} = bb$. bb is **143** in base-10. Looking at the comparison table, you see that $11_{12} = 13_{10}$. One can "substitute" 11_{12} for 13.

- $11_{10} \times 11_{12} = 143$
- $143 + (33^2 \times 11_{12}) = 14300$

In short you have Kryon's "11:11 window" as in "$11_{12}:11_{10}$" !! Further, $33_{10} = 29_{12}$ and $2 + 9 = 11$. If you subtract 143 from 9944 you get 99^2.

- $143 + 99 = 242$
- $^{242}/_2 = 11^2$!

(and... $143 + 37 = 180$!)

If you add $4499 + 5588 + 6677 + 7766 + 8855 + 9944 = \underline{43329}$

- $^{43329}/_{33} = 1313 = 13(101)$
- $^{43329}/_{13} = 3333 = 3(1111)$

Also, $33^2 = $ **1089** and is the reverse order of $99^2 = $ **9801**!

As to what all this means, I don't have any opinion yet. It is too new. However, it seems to be some form of "base bridging" – an instrument of translation perhaps. It certainly is a very elegant number puzzle.

James D. Watt

Kryon's Messages To James and Randy

To James:

So, James, you think the power transmutation formula of 9944 could possibly be the transmutation tool for 10 to 12? You are very correct, my friend. It is an important tool, and is also hiding at many junctions in seemingly unrelated areas. It must be! Since everywhere you look, you are actually observing base-12. Therefore, solutions in base-10 will always point to a base-12 series, and the 9944 and 143 will show itself in numerous places... as pointers to the sacred geometry. Your alchemy of 10 to 12 will reap you much if you continue to examine it!

To Randy:

You already know your contract. You have come here this time to integrate numbers with tones! We have been giving information that all vibrations are languages – color, tone, shape and numbers. You are putting them together properly, and are honored greatly for your intuition and science. Of all those on the planet, you are the one who would not be surprised to know that when Universal entities meet each other, they often "sing" their "pi" to let others know where they are from! There will come a day when humanity wonders why they didn't put this together sooner.

Kryon

From Lee: When this page was finished being laid out, Kryon gave each of you 11 lines of type! No accidents. This is your own personal 11:11 – a code change in your life to allow the new information to flow in! Thanks to both of You!

The Final Math Letter

Dear Lee:

I left a message on your answering machine to call me, but I am faxing this letter anyway. It might by too late to include in the book, since I know you have to draw the cutoff line somewhere.

I wanted to show you what I found in regard to 143 (base of the number 9944). It has to do with increasing your confidence in addressing skeptics in regard to the base-12 issue.

A lot of what I have already given you is material that skeptics have never seen. This item seems tailor-made for you because it is drawn directly from hints that **Kryon** gave. I believe no one has seen this before and put "two and two" together.

If you look in my "Mathematica" section, you will see reference to "... *a standard 7 division sequence, long admired in mathematics as an elegant curiosity.*" (page 316). You also have my letter answering a question you had concerning what that sequence was. So you know this question has come up before.

The reciprocal of 7 is a repeating series of 142857... . It has been known that the integers can be "stacked" to cancel them out like this:

$$
\begin{array}{lll}
1/.007 = & 142.8571428... \\
+\ 1/7 \qquad + & \quad .1428571... \\
\hline
& 142.9999999... & \text{or } 143!
\end{array}
$$

By diddling around and simplifying the statement, you come up with:

$$\frac{1001}{7} = 143$$

It turns out (surprise, surprise) that 1001 is 91 x 11 and **91 is the base-10 equivalent of base-12's <u>77</u> !!** This is **Kryon's** 11:11 window, yet again. This means that the very nature of 7's makeup also points undeniably to a base-12 symmetry! It **does not** indicate base-10.

There is more to be revealed, but I am not sure how much significance is attached. Careful study is needed; however, based on the above. I think mathematically one has to accept the phenomenon that a Channeled Spirit entity named Kryon is in fact occurring, barring prior knowledge of this 7 pattern turning up in a library somewhere.

In my limited experience, and from talking about this in the past to more qualified mathematicians, this relation has not been noticed in many studies done on the peculiar symmetries of 7. **This could be the first documented case of an off-planet source of knowledge**. If there is no "prior knowledge," then this is an extraordinary event!

I hope this brightens your day. Sincerely,

James D. Watt

Index

Index

Index

Kryon Live Channelled Audio Tapes

▶ **Ascension in The New Age** - ISBN 1-888053-01-1 • $10.00
Carlsbad, California - "Kryon describes what ascension really is in the new age.
It might surprise you!"

▶ **Nine Ways to Raise the Planet's Vibration** - ISBN 1-888053-00-3 • $10.00
Seattle, Washington - "Raising the planet's vibration is the goal of humanity!
Find out what Kryon has to say about it."

▶ **Gifts and Tools of The New Age** - ISBN 1-888053-03-0 • $10.00
Casper, Wyoming - "A very powerful channel. Better put on your sword, shield
and armor for this one."

▶ **Co-Creation in The New Age** - ISBN 1-888053-04-6 • $10.00
Portland, Oregon - "Tired of being swept around in life? Find out about
co-creating your own reality. It is our right in this new age!"

▶ **Seven Responsibilities of The New Age** - ISBN 1-888053-02-X • $10.00
Indianapolis, Indiana - "Responsibility? For what? Find out what Spirit tells us
we are now in charge of...and what to do with it."

Music and Meditation

▶ **Crystal Singer Music Meditation Tape** - ISBN 0-96363-4-1-5 • $10.00
Enjoy two soaring 17 minute musical meditations featuring the beautiful singing
voice of Jan Tober.

▶ **Guided Meditations Tape** - ISBN 1-388053-05-4 • $10.00
Jan presents two guided meditations similar to those delivered at each Kryon seminar
throughout the United States and Canada, with beautiful Celtic harp accompaniment
by Mark Geisler.   Side One: "Finding Your Sweet Spot"   Side Two: "Divine Love"

▶ **Color & Sound Meditation CD** - ISBN 1-888053-06-2 • $15.00
A complete color/sound workshop — an exercise to balance and harmonize the Chakras.
Jan guides us through the seven Chakra system using the enhancement of the ancient
Tibetan signing bowls.   Side One: 30-min meditation   Side Two: 12-min meditation

Kryon Books On Tape

Published by **AUDIO LITERATURE** *Read by Lee Carroll*

▶ **The End Times** - ISBN 1-57453-168-9
▶ **Don't Think Like A Human** - ISBN 1-57453-169-7
▶ **Alchemy Of The Human Spirit** - ISBN 1-57453-170-0
Each audio book contains two cassettes, 3 hours, abridged - $17.95

▶ **"The Parables of Kryon"** - *Read by Lee Carroll*
Published by **Hay House** *and scored with music!* ISBN 1-56170-454-7 - $16.95

▶ **"The Journey Home"** ***Unabridged!*** - *Read by Lee Carroll*
Published by **Hay House** - *a six tape set!* ISBN 1-56170-453-9 - $30.00
(seven hour listening experience)

Books and tapes can be purchased in retail stores, or by phone
~ Credit cards welcome ~ 1-800-352-6657

 Kryon Book One: "The End Times"

Published by **The Kryon Writings, Inc.** ISBN 0-9636304-2-3 (White Cover) $12.00

 Kryon Book Two: "Don't Think Like A Human"

Published by **The Kryon Writings, Inc.** ISBN 0-9636304-0-7 (Blue Cover) $12.00

 Kryon Book Three: "Alchemy of The Human Spirit"

Published by **The Kryon Writings, Inc.** ISBN 0-9636304-8-2 (Fuchsia Cover) $14.00

 Kryon Book Four: "The Parables of Kryon"

Published by **Hay House** ISBN 1-56170-364-8 $17.00 (hard cover - with illustrations)

 Kryon Book Five: "The Journey Home"

Published by **Hay House** ISBN 1-56170-552-7 $11.95 (soft cover)

 Kryon Book Six: "Partnering with God"

Published by **The Kryon Writings, Inc.** ISBN 1-888053-10-0 (Green Cover) $14.00

 Kryon Book Seven: "Letters From Home"

Published by **The Kryon Writings, Inc.** ISBN 1-888053-12-7 (Purple Cover) $14.00

 Kryon Book Eight: "Passing The Marker"

Published by **The Kryon Writings, Inc.** ISBN 1-888053-11-97 (Cream Cover) $14.00

 "The Indigo Children"

Published by **Hay House** ISBN 1-56170-608-6 $13.95
